The Transforming Power of the Nuns

The
CRANSFORMING POWER
of the NUNS

Women, Religion, and Cultural Change
in Ireland, 1750–1900

MARY PECKHAM MAGRAY

New York • Oxford
Oxford University Press
1998

Oxford University Press

Oxford   New York
Athens   Auckland   Bangkok   Bogota   Bombay
Buenos Aires   Calcutta   Cape Town   Dar es Salaam
Delhi   Florence   Hong Kong   Istanbul   Karachi
Kuala Lumpur   Madras   Madrid   Melbourne
Mexico City   Nairobi   Paris   Singapore
Taipei   Tokyo   Toronto   Warsaw

and associated companies in
Berlin   Ibadan

Published by Oxford University Press, Inc.
198 Madison Avenue, New York, New York 10016

Oxford is a registered trademark of Oxford University Press

Library of Congress Cataloging-in-Publication Data
Magray, Mary Peckham.
The transforming power of the nuns : women, religion, and cultural
change in Ireland, 1750–1900 / Mary Peckham Magray.
p.   cm.
Includes bibliographical references and index.
ISBN 0-19-511299-7
1. Monasticism and religious orders for women—Ireland—
History—18th century.   2. Monasticism and religious orders for
women—Ireland—History—19th century   3. Ireland—Church
history—18th century.   4. Ireland—Church history—19th century.
I. Title.
BX4220.I7M34   1998
271'.900415—DC21   97-8446

9 8 7 6 5 4 3 2 1

Printed in the United States of America
on acid-free paper

For
Scott and
David

PREFACE

The reemergence and phenomenal growth of women's religious orders in Ireland occurred during a period of profound social, cultural, and religious transformation. That transformation resulted in the destruction of traditional, Gaelic Catholic culture and the construction of the orthodox, bourgeois Catholic culture that exists to the present day. The main argument of this book is that, rather than being the product of the so-called "devotional revolution" as is commonly assumed, women's orders were in fact at the center of the creation of this devout, bourgeois Catholic culture.

This claim that women religious were central to the religious and cultural change of the nineteenth century rests on a number of arguments, each of which will be developed in the following chapters. First among them is that women religious were in the vanguard of religious reform in Ireland. They were forming new orders and new convents throughout the country long before the 1840s and 1850s, when popular religious change was becoming obvious. In fact, beginning in the late eighteenth century, they encouraged the very policy that promoted that change, creating the very institutions that became so intertwined with nineteenth-century Catholicism. Together with reform-minded friends and relatives—among them priests, bishops, and laypeople alike—they developed a new form of women's religious activism that proved to be a very effective method of bringing post-Tridentine Catholicism to Ireland.

Second, the women's orders were able to have the impact that they did because of the social and cultural significance of the women themselves, especially the early leaders. By any measure, the women who were responsible for the reemergence and development of the women's congregations were influential members of their society. They were typically members of wealthy and prominent Catholic business and professional families from the towns of the south and east. They were also frequently descended from the former Catholic landowning class. More than a few were raised as Protestants. Because of these factors, they tended to be self-assured, assertive, and ambitious women. They may have cloaked their goals in religious selflessness, but they had ambitions for their orders and for the people of Ireland.

Third, women's orders were extremely popular, and they spread quickly throughout the length and breadth of the island. Convents flourished in the nineteenth century because Irish women were drawn in large numbers to the new apostolic orders, which were an integral part of the broader nineteenth-century female culture of charitable and evangelical organization. In joining, women expected to be able to do what they called meaningful labor. They also expected to know a spiritual and personal life that was rich in intimate, loving relationships with other religious women. Because they provided a spiritually and socially engaged life, convents offered a style of living found highly desirable by the many Irish women who flocked to their doors.

Fourth, those who joined used their wealth and that of other members of the Catholic elite to build one of the most impressive institutional networks in the country. Palatial convents were constructed throughout the island. Related institutional buildings such as schools, hospitals, orphanages, refuges, factories, workshops, and reformatories proliferated, attesting to the cultural prominence of these women and their work. Moreover, within ten or fifteen years of commencement, most of these institutions were further expanded and their buildings enlarged. In fact, the century witnessed an almost constant increase not only in the number of these establishments but also in their size. Women's orders in the west of Ireland consciously continued their building projects through periods of famine or distress because so many people depended on the regularity of the wages provided by convent expansion.

Finally, the extensive religious and charitable work that these women undertook had great effects on the process of religious change in Ireland. No sooner was a convent established than word spread about what a "help to religion" the new congregations were, as some among the Catholic hierarchy were quick to realize. In the early years, priests and bishops made special trips to visit the new convents to see for themselves the effects of the women's work. Many others came into contact with individuals who had been educated or cared for by the new sisterhoods. All were impressed and enthusiastic about what they saw. As a result, many bishops and priests in the late eighteenth and early nineteenth centuries began to lobby religious orders to make foundations in their dioceses and provided ready episcopal approval and enthusiastic encouragement to laypeople prepared to fund the enterprises. The growing authority and impact of the women's orders eventually brought them into serious conflict with the reforming Catholic hierarchy, however. By 1870, when their attempt to exert unchallenged control over the Irish church was all but complete, Irish bishops had also gained control over the women's religious movement.

ACKNOWLEDGMENTS

There are many people I wish to thank for helping me to complete this work. Without their encouragement, support, and friendship it would not have been the very gratifying task that it was. My first thanks go to my former graduate student community at the University of Wisconsin, especially Lisa Hendrickson, Marybeth Carlson, Carolyn Pittis, Sue Hartwick, Martin Dowling, Nancy Curtin, Maribeth Kazmierczak, Joyce Follet, Maureen Fitzgerald, Leisa Meyer, and all of the other members of the British history seminar and the women's history dissertators' group. Suzanne Desan and Jeanne Boydston read this work in its various stages; their comments and criticisms have been enormously valuable. It is hard to express how grateful I feel to all of them for helping me to sharpen my thinking and my analysis; they helped me make this work very much better than it would otherwise have been. For their support and encouragement during the process of revising the manuscript, I owe much to my wonderful colleagues at Wesleyan College, most especially Robin Starbuck and Petra Schweitzer, friends extraordinaire. Friend and colleague Kayanna Pace of the Art Institute of Atlanta produced the fine maps for this book. Chris Swafford helped me with the index. The Sisters of Mercy, the Sisters of Charity, the Presentation Sisters, the Holy Faith Sisters, and the St. Louis Sisters kindly and generously provided me with the photographs and illustrations, and on very short notice, I must confess. I would also like to thank Marie and Dermot O'Brien not only for providing me and my children with a home while we were in Ireland but also for convincing me, one terrible Friday afternoon, not to give it up and go home.

My archival work was made pleasant by the many religious women who provided both research material and warm hospitality. It goes without saying that this work would have been impossible without their support. My heartfelt thanks go to Sister M. Anthony and Sister Rosario at the South Presentation

Convent in Cork; Sister Laurentia at the Mercy Convent in Athlone; Sister Angela, Sister Aloysius, Sister James, and Sister Jerrod at the Charity of Refuge Convent at High Park; Sister Miriam Commins at the St. Louis Sisters Generalate in Monaghan; Sister Ursula at the Ursuline Convent in Blackrock; and Sister Magdalena at the Mercy Convent in Baggot Street, Dublin. I owe a special debt of gratitude to two religious women for their help and their friendship: the late Sister Francis Brigid Flannery at the Sisters of Charity Generalate in Milltown, Dublin, and Sister M. Assisi at the Holy Faith Convent, Glasnevin. I also wish to thank David Sheehy, archivist at the Dublin Diocesan Archives, for his help and pleasant company during the many hours I worked in his office. The University of Wisconsin, the Woodrow Wilson Fellowship Foundation, and the Charlotte W. Newcombe Fellowship Foundation supported my research and writing, support for which I am very grateful.

I wish to thank most especially Jim Donnelly, colleague and friend, for watching over this project with such interest and care from the very beginning to the very end. Mary Fisher came into my life toward the end of the endeavor, but her love and support have sustained me to the finish. Scott and David Peckham, to whom I dedicate this book, have been there always, and that has meant everything to me.

CONTENTS

Map 1.   Ireland.

The labels on the map:

Raphoe, Derry, Down & Connor, Dromore, Armagh, Clogher, Kilmore, Killala, Achonry, Ardagh & Clonmacnois, Elphin, Meath, Tuam, Killmacdungh, Galway, Clonfert, Ardagh Clonmacnois, Kildare & Leighlin, Dublin, Tuam, Kilfenora, Killaloe, Ossory, Ferns, Cashel & Emly, Limerick, Waterford & Lismore, Kerry, Cloyne, Cork, Ross

Legend:
- Archdiocese of Tuam
- Archdiocese of Armagh
- Archdiocese of Dublin
- Archdiocese of Cashel

noncontiguous diocesan areas not represented

Map 2.   Ecclesiastical provinces and dioceses of Ireland.

The Transforming Power of the Nuns

ONE

Women Religious and the
Devotional Revolution

THE CATHOLIC CHURCH in Ireland enjoys a relationship with the Irish population that is unique in the Western world. The high level of religious practice and the historically controversial nature of Catholic influence on Irish society both reflect that unique relationship. Yet a high level of religious practice
was not always characteristic of Irish society. Contrary to the popular view that
Catholicism embraced the Irish of all classes at all times and was virtually syn-
onymous with being Irish, recent scholars have shown that Catholicism had to
be taught aggressively to the majority of the population.[1]

Political and religious instability during the seventeenth century, which had
resulted from England's long campaign to subdue the island, meant that reformed
Catholicism, formulated at the sixteenth-century Council of Trent, had never
taken hold in Ireland. The religious situation was worsened by the Williamite
victory of the 1690s and the harsh anti-Catholic penal legislation that followed,
resulting in the final political defeat of Catholic Ireland, as well as the attempted
eradication of the Irish Catholic church. Although the period during which the
intent to actually destroy the church was short-lived and by the 1750s the anti-
Catholic legislation was no longer enforced, the policy was very destructive,
creating severe problems for the church and a great sense of insecurity among
the group of men who were charged with trying to hold the outlawed institution together.[2]

The problems were many. First, the long period of instability and suppression disrupted the hierarchical organization of the church. Legislation passed in
1697 that banished bishops from the country caused severe disorder. Although
the authorities never succeeded in totally eliminating the bishops, within ten
years only two were left in the country, one of whom was in jail. For fifty years
after the penal legislation went into effect, Rome struggled to fill Irish sees, some
of which were vacant for decades at a time.[3] Lack of a complete, well-organized

episcopal structure exacerbated the problems of the rank-and-file clergy. Priests in Ireland during the eighteenth century were generally undisciplined and un-ruly. Church leaders, troubled by problems of clerical discipline, found them-selves faced with a multitude of transgressions, such as drunkenness, factional-ism, ignorance, laxity in performing pastoral duties, and the occasional sexual scandal. Priestly improprieties were believed to have impaired the church's ability to influence the religious and social behavior of the prefamine population, and reformers thought this behavior required considerable modification.[4] Finally, general lack of religious zeal that characterized organized religion in general during the eighteenth century hampered the church's work. Not only priests but also their bishops lacked religious enthusiasm at this time. In this atmosphere, it was very difficult for the church to combat the thriving popular culture of folk belief and practice so prevalent among the Irish masses.

After 1800, the institutions of Irish Catholicism moved rapidly to counter-act this decay and to combat Protestant proselytism, which was widespread in the country. Though effects of the reform movement were at first restricted to the urban areas of Munster and Leinster, a conscious process of evangelization gradually spread this revitalized Catholicism to the Catholic population (both urban and rural) throughout the island during the nineteenth century, a process that one historian has called a devotional revolution.[5]

In his influential article, "The Devotional Revolution in Ireland, 1850–1875," Emmet Larkin suggested that a revolution in Catholic practice occurred during the decades immediately following the famine of 1845–1850. According to Larkin, in this crucial period the majority of Irish Catholics, who had formerly had mini-mal and sometimes unorthodox contact with a disorganized and disreputable in-stitutional church, became devout and faithful practicing Catholics. Spearheaded by Paul Cardinal Cullen, the devotional revolution was underwritten by the in-creasingly prominent large tenant farming class, which was to become the foun-dation of both the Catholic nationalist movement of the late nineteenth century and the new Irish state of the twentieth. Larkin argues that this class gave its money, as well as its sons and daughters, to rebuild and reform what quickly became a well-disciplined, well-organized, highly centralized, and powerful institutional church.[6]

A number of historians have challenged Larkin's concept of a revolution dur-ing the latter half of the nineteenth century, favoring instead the notion of gradual change beginning as early as the late eighteenth century.[7] They have suggested, among other things, that church infrastructure was already being rebuilt in the decades before the famine and that prefamine church attendance was higher in some places than Larkin estimated. They have also suggested that Larkin placed too great an emphasis on the role of Paul Cullen while ignoring the crucial part played by earlier reforming bishops, for example, Daniel Murray, Archbishop of Dublin from 1823 until 1852. Still, despite the modifications that have been made to the devotional revolution thesis (which have in general been accepted), all agree that a transformation of Catholic institutional structures and practices did occur during the course of the nineteenth century. By 1900 the result was, first of all, an outwardly more devout population that practiced its religion in impressive new churches and educated its children in an entrenched Catholic school system and, second, the proliferation of a network of Catholic social-welfare institutions such as hospitals, orphanages, refuges, and reformatories.

In their analyses of nineteenth-century religious change in Ireland, Sean Connolly and Kevin Whelan have suggested that changes in devotional attitudes and practices were part of a more complex cultural transformation that was taking place at this time.[8] In doing so they have broadened the terms of discussion beyond a determination of whether the devotional revolution began in the prefamine or the postfamine period or which of the Irish bishops ought to be credited with leading the church reform movement. Rather, as their work has shown, religious change was long-term (beginning in the eighteenth century), its origins as well as its progress were regionally based, and among its motivating forces was a particular group of the Irish Catholic laity. Perhaps most important of all, religious change was part of a larger cultural transformation that resulted in the victory of one indigenous Catholic culture over another rather than the victory of reforming churchmen over the Irish people. It is within this more comprehensive context that the profound impact of the work of the women's religious orders will be most apparent.

Over the course of a hundred years, the very nature of Catholic society and culture was transformed and a new Irish identity forged. During the eighteenth century a distinctive Irish Catholic middle class came into prominence in the south and east of Ireland as a result of surplus wealth produced by the widespread agricultural boom of the 1740s to the 1810s.[9] This influential segment of Catholic society, which included both strong farmers and affluent commercial and professional Catholics, especially in the provinces of Munster and Leinster, began to challenge the political, social, and religious dominance of the Protestant ascendancy.[10] From the foundation of the Catholic Committee in 1759 to the political and religious emancipation of Catholics and the regeneration of the Catholic church, the Catholic merchant and professional classes proved to be the driving force.

The increasing prominence of this group of Catholics was part of a complex, nineteenth-century process of social, economic, and demographic change referred to as the "modernization" or "embourgeoisement" of Ireland. During this century there occurred a significant alteration in the underlying social and economic structures of society that was made more pronounced by the effects of the great famine of the 1840s. In the seven-year period from 1845 to 1851, one million people died of starvation and disease, most of them from the ranks of landless laborers and cottiers (holding small pieces of land). In addition, more than one million people emigrated during these cataclysmic years. The social and economic effects of famine death and emigration were striking. Before the famine, the poorer, landless rural classes had outnumbered the tenant farming classes (which emerged from the famine years relatively unscathed) by a ratio of more than two to one. By 1881 the two rural classes were roughly equal in number.[11] For the rest of the century the number of laborers and cottiers continued to decrease, increasing the relative importance of the farming classes.[12] Furthermore, the Irish who died or emigrated during the famine were largely from the western regions of the country, an area where traditional Irish culture—characterized by a high marriage rate and a very young age at first marriage, decidedly unorthodox Christian customs and attitudes, and the almost exclusive use of the Irish language—was still firmly entrenched. The farming classes, which became much more prominent (and more prosperous as well) in the postfamine period, as well as the urban commercial and professional classes of the south and east, were part of a very different culture that was much less insular and much more exposed to a broad range of influences. The dynamic culture of this segment of Irish society gradually replaced the traditional, rural, Irish culture of the prefamine period and became the dominant culture of the country by the late nineteenth century.

"Modernization" was, in effect, a cultural revolution, the imposition of one indigenous Catholic culture over another. The ethos of the wealthier Catholic classes of the south and east, which was shaped by a distinctive Norman-Gaelic tradition and by a more anglicized, modernizing worldview, gradually replaced the prefamine, Gaelic Catholic culture of the north and west, which was, according to one scholar, "embedded in a complex web of archaic beliefs and practices of a magical or naturalistic kind dismissed as 'superstitious' by the official Church."[13] It was the destruction of this traditional Gaelic culture and the construction of a new, bourgeois Irish Catholic culture (characterized by a much lower marriage rate, a higher average age at first marriage, greater and even exclusive use of the English language, and greater conformity with post-Tridentine Catholic belief and practice) that occupied so much of the time, energy, and money of the wealthy Catholic classes.

Crucial to both the religious and the cultural transformations of the late eighteenth and nineteenth centuries were female religious orders, which reappeared in Ireland after two hundred years of legal proscription.[14] Although neither the Reformation of the sixteenth century nor the anti-Catholic penal laws of the late seventeenth and early eighteenth centuries destroyed the Catholic faith in Ireland, they did come close to obliterating Catholic religious orders. Women were prohibited by law from living together openly as religious communities; those communities who did were liable to summary and sometimes brutal dissolution.[15] Nonetheless, in 1750, despite two hundred years of persecution, there were twelve houses of women religious in Ireland belonging to four old, established orders.[16] Few of the women living in those convents envisioned that religious life in their native land would ever be any different. By the late eighteenth century, however, great changes were under way. At this time a new style of religious life began to emerge as the Catholic world witnessed the appearance and rapid expansion of the uncloistered, socially active, modern sisterhoods.

During the high and late Middle Ages, female monasticism, renowned for its spiritual and intellectual vigor and for the distinguished status and authority it enjoyed within the church and feudal society, was besieged by male leaders of the church. Religious women in the twelfth century found their former religious autonomy seriously challenged during a period of monastic transformation. The old contemplative, other-worldly emphasis of the Benedictine era gradually gave way to a "this-worldly," socially involved monastic ideal exemplified by the new Franciscan and Dominican orders. Monastic organization was also transformed: the single, isolated, and autonomous abbey was replaced by centralized and highly bureaucratic orders with houses all over Europe.[17]

This monastic reform excluded women from its effects. In fact, as the physical freedom and worldly involvement of monks were enlarged, a nun's freedom to interact with society was increasingly circumscribed, for then the idea of permanently enclosing women within their convents evolved. The policy was formally established with the papal bull of 1299, *Periculoso*, which called for the total and permanent cloister of religious women and their subjection to the local bishop. As a result, the great religious orders founded after the Cluniac reform of the twelfth century were allowed to take female members (the so-called second orders) but were proscribed by church law from allowing them to adopt their socially active role.[18]

Draconian as this legislation was, it proved difficult to enforce. Throughout the centuries religious women and men attempted to circumvent the papal bull in order to allow women to participate in a more active religious life. The Dominicans and the Franciscans created tertiary—or third—orders. Women like Honoria Burke in Elizabethan Ireland, for example, who wanted to participate more fully in the Dominican mission by performing charitable works outside the convent, joined these third orders.[19] They took only simple, yearly vows (as opposed to "solemn," lifelong ones) and were not considered true religious, as were their enclosed counterparts of the second order. Consequently, those taking simple vows were considered laywomen according to canon law. And because they were laywomen rather than religious, they were able to leave the convent and work outside the cloister in the same way as their male counterparts.[20] Women not associated with male orders also attempted to form new types of religious organizations which evaded enclosure. The Beguines, an incompletely understood yet significant religious movement of women with no formal organization, who lived together to perform public works of charity, flourished in parts of Europe during the thirteenth and fourteenth centuries. Early in the sixteenth century an Italian woman, Angela de Merici, formed the Ursuline sisters. The first teaching order, the Ursulines spread quickly throughout Italy and France. But as their popularity increased, many individual bishops were bothered by the unorthodox organization and lifestyle of these religious women, and eventually, in 1612, they were required to take solemn vows, forgo their work in the streets and cities of Europe, and retreat within convent walls.

In the face of almost continual pressure from religious women organizing in these novel ways, the Roman church was gradually forced to rescind the requirement of enclosure. Two new female communities in particular were responsible for forcing the church's hand. The first was the Daughters of Charity of St. Vincent de Paul, currently the largest congregation of religious women in the Roman Catholic church. The Daughters of Charity wrote no constitution, adopted no special habit, and took no solemn vows. After thirty years of charitable work and growing popularity among French women, the organization sought and received episcopal approval from the archbishop of Paris in 1655. Papal approval was finally obtained in 1688, but its scope was limited. The Holy

See acknowledged the value of a more active religious life for women and allowed the sisterhood to remain organized as it was, without the observance of enclosure. But church authorities would not go so far as to acknowledge that the Daughters of Charity was a religious organization. Rather, it was given the same legal status within the church as the tertiary orders; that is, the Daughters of Charity was regarded in canon law as a lay organization, and the sisters were considered *lay* rather than religious women.

The acknowledgment that active congregations of women taking simple vows were religious and not lay women came sixty years later: in 1749, the Institute of the Blessed Virgin Mary was approved as a bona fide religious congregation by Pope Benedict XIV. This English institute had been founded more than a hundred years earlier, in 1603, by Mary Ward. After the Roman church had declared England a mission, Ward decided to form a women's order modeled on the Society of Jesus. With this decision, she openly challenged the medieval constraints on women's orders. Ward rejected both the cloister and local episcopal supervision, hoping instead to place the new institution directly under the authority of the pope. Like the Jesuits and other male orders, she devised a system of centralized government with an elected superior general.

Ward's initiative was not welcomed by the male hierarchy. The institute was formally suppressed by Pope Urban VIII in 1631, and Ward herself was imprisoned. But as much as the male leaders might have wished for its swift demise, the Institute of the Blessed Virgin Mary refused to die. The institute was strongest in Munich, where it was tolerated until the middle of the eighteenth century.[21] Then the reigning bishop of Augsburg finally attempted to exert local episcopal control over this group of women. He applied to the Vatican to rule definitively on whether the institute was indeed a religious organization within the purview of the Roman church. If it was, then he demanded that the local bishop be allowed to exercise the jurisdictional control granted by the *Periculoso* ruling of 1299 and reinforced at the Council of Trent in 1563.

As a result of the bishop of Augsburg's attempt to bring the institute's convents in his diocese under his control, the Vatican was forced to make a ruling that proved very significant for the future development of women's religious life. In 1749, Pope Benedict XIV settled the issue with his *Quamvis Iusto*. Though the ruling upheld the right of bishops to local control over all convents in their dioceses, it approved the right of this unenclosed institute to remain organized. It also went beyond the approval given to the Daughters of Charity by allowing the sisters to remain organized as a *religious* institute. *Quamvis Iusto* consequently proved to be much more than just an approval of the Institute of the Blessed Virgin Mary. It was, in fact, a precedent-setting ruling, for by conceding the right of religious women to form a new style of religious community, it ended the era of enforced enclosure. Women who wanted to do work outside their convents could now do so. Henceforth, women who did not observe perpetual cloister were nonetheless granted canonical legitimacy within the Roman church. They did not receive the same status as those members of religious orders who took lifelong, solemn vows (they were not, for example, true "nuns"), but they were given legal existence as members of religious congregations and hence eligible for the title of "sister."[22]

Quamvis Iusto opened the door to the development of the modern sisterhoods. By 1800, new congregations of religious women were being formed all over Europe, as approval for unenclosed female religious organizations was forthcoming from the Vatican hierarchy, and as the new, socially active form of religious life became increasingly popular with Catholic women.

One of the first European women to take advantage of the opportunity afforded by the *Quamvis Iusto* ruling was an Irish woman named Honora, or Nano, Nagle. In 1775, fearing that she would not be content if confined to the cloister, Nagle decided to form the Sisters of the Charitable Instruction, later renamed the Sisters of the Presentation.[23] Organized as a new-style religious congregation, it was a new departure in the history of the religious life of Irish women. This institution marked the beginning of the growth of a powerful new movement within the Irish Catholic church—the modern sisterhoods that have been such a prominent part of Irish culture ever since.

Their numbers alone attest to this fact. Women religious increased dramatically during the nineteenth century; they numbered approximately 120 in 1800, 1,500 in 1850, and about 8,000 by 1900.[24] Not only their absolute numbers but also their relative numbers increased. In 1800, the 120 women in Irish convents represented roughly 6 percent of the total Irish Catholic workforce of priests (both regular and secular) and nuns.[25] By 1851, women religious comprised 38 percent of the total number of nuns and priests, and by 1901, 70 percent. Even with the inclusion of the approximately 1,100 teaching brothers in Ireland by 1901, nuns still numbered 64 percent of the total Irish Catholic workforce at the end of the nineteenth century.[26] Furthermore, this growth came at the very time that the overall Irish population declined by more than 50 percent.

But numbers alone do not tell the whole story. By the end of the century, women religious had created an immense network of institutions that had become indispensable to the functioning of the Irish church and Irish society. Old religious orders like the Dominicans (who became prominent educators of the daughters of wealthier Catholics) and the Poor Clares (who took up the institutional care of orphans) were revived, and dynamic new Irish congregations were formed. The most important of these, in addition to Nano Nagle's Presentation Sisters, were the Sisters of Charity, begun in 1815 by Mary Aikenhead; the Loreto Sisters (an Irish foundation of Mary Ward's Institute of the Blessed Virgin Mary), founded in 1820 by Frances Ball; the Sisters of Mercy, created by Catherine McAuley in 1831; and Margaret Aylward's Sisters of the Holy Faith, founded in 1867.[27] In addition, many European congregations, such as the Sisters of the Sacred Heart, the Daughters of Charity of St. Vincent de Paul, the Good Shepherd Sisters, and the St. Louis Sisters, were imported during the course of the nineteenth century. By 1800, the twelve houses and four religious orders in existence fifty years earlier had grown to eighteen houses and six orders.[28] One hundred years later, in 1900, there were a total of 368 convents in Ireland belonging to thirty-five different orders.[29]

These new religious establishments were by and large urban-based institutions. The overwhelming majority were located in cities and small towns,[30] with only a very few located in rural settings (most often associated with a large landed estate).[31] Convents were also overwhelmingly concentrated in the provinces of Munster and Leinster in the south and east of Ireland, the agricultural and commercial heartland of the country. Seventy-three percent of all Irish convents were located in these two provinces in 1864, and that percentage had declined only slightly to 70 percent by 1900.[32]

The importance of the work of women religious in the evolution of church and society was well understood by the hierarchy and clergy, who generally supported and encouraged the spread of the convents throughout the thirty-two counties. Yet historians have scarcely begun to explore the significance and complexity of the female orders' relationship to the institutions of Irish Catholicism. Indeed, only in the last twenty years has Irish Catholicism itself received serious scholarly attention, and that attention has been heavily focused on the male clergy and their ecclesiastical and political concerns. Moreover, as agents of the Catholic church, these women reached out into Irish society in complex and innovative ways. Yet little analytical work has been done on the impact of these women on that society.

Although the existing literature is scant, several scholars have begun to explore the Irish female religious orders. Caitriona Clear's *Nuns in Nineteenth-Century Ireland*[33] provides a sound account of the structure of the female religious communities and an overview of their role in Irish society. Although her work broke fresh ground, it persistently depicts these women as powerless instruments of the male hierarchy and fails to acknowledge their profound influence on either the revitalization of the nineteenth-century church or the emergence of a bourgeois Irish Catholic culture. Anthony Fahey's "Female Asceticism in the Catholic Church: A Case-Study of Nuns in Ireland in the Nineteenth Century"[34] and "Nuns in the Catholic Church in Ireland in the Nineteenth Century"[35] examine various changes in the nature of female orders during a period when female religious came out of the cloister and began to assume an active social-service role in ever-increasing numbers. Fahey places the Irish female congregations within the context of an expanding interest in education and social action on the part of the Catholic hierarchy throughout Europe. Fahey also assesses the effect of changes within the Catholic church on women religious in general and on Irish women religious in particular. Finally, Maria Luddy, in her study of female philanthropy during the nineteenth century, has looked closely at some of the Irish convent-run institutions and suggested that while women religious monopolized Catholic charitable enterprise, they were nonetheless an impotent and subordinate element of the Catholic church.[36]

This early work on Irish women religious, although very important, is weakened by a significant conceptual problem. Because of women's historically subordinate position in both the church and society, these scholars have assumed that women religious did not play an influential role in either. They have made it seem as if women religious merely reacted to the major social and cultural changes of their day, in particular to a need for their services identified by the Catholic hierarchy. A major task of this early research, consequently, has been to determine whether the opportunity provided them was good or bad, whether, in Clear's words, "nuns were typical or atypical of the women of their time."[37]

Two contradictory paradigms have resulted. Fahey, on one hand, sees the convent movement as having been a new and positive opportunity for some women to participate in society in a way that most women, confined to home and family, could not. Clear, on the other hand, views the role of women religious as a limited opportunity because the church kept them subjugated to its male members, causing them to internalize a sense of unimportance and leaving them unable to develop a corporate sense of themselves as influential communities of women. Hence, Clear sees them as typical Irish women.[38]

In fact, both of these assessments are true to some extent. Women religious were both privileged and subordinate. Yet to approach a study of their lives and work by focusing only on the effects of their subservience to the male hierarchy is to overlook their capacity to shape and influence the church to which they dedicated their lives. It is to ignore the possibility that they created their own opportunities, and it certainly renders it impossible to perceive their impact on the world in which they lived.

The phenomenal growth of the new religious movement for women has been assumed thus far to have resulted from the general transformation of the Catholic church during the nineteenth century. Emmet Larkin, for example, has written that the rapid expansion of the women's orders at this time was a manifestation of the revolution in devotional attitudes and practices that occurred in postfamine Ireland.[39] In other words, a changed religious culture promoted the development of the women's orders. To suggest that the modern conventual movement was principally the result of the devotional revolution is, I would argue, a serious oversimplification of the role played by women religious in this process of very significant social, cultural, and religious change. In fact, the female religious orders were a necessary component of the church's transformation. Women religious, through their intimate and influential relationships with ordinary Irish Catholics and especially young female Catholics, successfully fostered an environment for a new style of religious devotion and social behavior. Although the revolution in devotional attitudes may have helped to increase recruits to the religious life, it did not motivate the development of the women's orders. Indeed, the reverse was the case. The development of women's religious life helped to make possible the transformation of the Irish church and Irish society. As a consequence, it is impossible to discuss religious and cultural change in nineteenth-century Ireland without discussing women religious.

By 1852, the modern conventual movement had made such an impact on the Irish Catholic church that the new archbishop of Dublin, Paul Cullen, was able to say that nuns were "the best support to religion."[40] Cullen, who played so prominent a role in the centralization of the Irish church in the two decades after the famine, became convinced—and rightly so—that the women's orders were vital agents of religious reform.[41] Nuns and the convents in which they lived were fixtures of Irish Catholic culture. The architectural landscape alone attests to that fact. With the exception of the most destitute and irreligious segment of society, all social groups came within their purview. Female members of the "deserving" poor, the middle classes, and the upper classes had regular and sustained contact with these women. Boys and men, too (though to a lesser extent), were enrolled in their schools and attended their catechism classes, their sodality meetings, their temperance meetings, and the evangelical missions that they helped to organize. As a consequence, convents came to possess and exercise considerable cultural authority.[42]

This is not to deny the obvious point that women religious theoretically occupied the most inferior position in the Catholic hierarchical structure. As a cultural institution, the church played a powerful role in maintaining and disseminating a gender ideology that limited the power and range of social action of all women, including women religious. Nonetheless, Irish nuns were able to exercise considerable personal, religious, and cultural power in shaping their religious communities, the work that those communities performed, and a church that embraced their work ever more eagerly as the nineteenth century progressed.

What is so disturbing, given the influence they exerted and the religious authority they exercised, is the distortion that the lives of these women have suffered in the historical record. In some contexts, women living in convents were believed to have been virtually imprisoned there, and their family fortunes with them.[43] Convents were also thought by some to house crazed and insane women who could not function in the normal world.[44] Religious women also have been viewed as unable to find husbands.[45] Many of these notions are admittedly derived from a Protestant worldview, and yet even the nineteenth-century Irish Catholic world did not adequately acknowledge the impact these women made. Rather, male ecclesiastics laid claim to their accomplishments, as if they had conceived of and directed the work and the achievements of women religious. Many bishops, instead of supporting and encouraging religious women, were known to harbor a serious dislike of them.[46] While certainly a number of important ecclesiastics appreciated the impact of their work on the church and society, the emergence of an energetic movement of female religious orders alarmed many of the clergy. Many priests and bishops were more concerned with controlling the female religious orders within their respective dioceses than with acknowledging their contributions or encouraging their expansion.

Nuns have not figured very prominently in the secular culture either. With the exception of a few books written by women who retell the experience of their convent schooldays, women religious do not figure as popular characters in Irish literature, and their relationships with the Irish people have not been the topic of public discourse (as have those between priests and the people).[47] James Joyce does not place even a single nun among all his characters. Only once, to my knowledge, does he even mention one, and his remark is very revealing. In *A Portrait of the Artist as a Young Man*, Joyce wrote that Stephen "heard a mad nun screeching in the nuns' madhouse beyond the wall."[48]

The reasons for the misrepresentation and in some cases the invisibility of religious women's lives are complex. To a certain extent, the women themselves were responsible for some of the distortion. For example, though the women behind the redevelopment and spread of the new orders in the years before the famine were highly dynamic and outspoken, religious etiquette dictated that they either mask their assertiveness or explain it in religiously acceptable terms. As a consequence, these women appear to us on the surface as having been extremely humble and blindly obedient servants of their superiors when, in fact, they were highly resourceful and manipulative.

But the popular image of women religious that rendered them invisible was also created by others. They were strong women, and seldom has history been kind to strong women. In a social system that grants male members a monopoly of power, positive images of female authority are rare. Consequently, women religious in nineteenth-century Ireland, though they exercised considerable authority over a large segment of the population, have not been granted the right to claim that authority. Others took credit for their accomplishments, and in the process their significance has been seriously reduced. Even scholars of Irish women religious sometimes appear apologetic and defensive when they try to explain to their readers why these women were important.[49]

Religious women also had the distinction of being sexually independent from men. In a social system that engenders female sexual dependence, women who live outside the heterosexual norm are a marginalized group.[50] The result of these entrenched notions of appropriate gender roles has been that the historical consciousness has neither celebrated nor cherished the memory of these strong, celibate women. Even in Catholic countries, where there is a legitimate role for them in the church, they are not to be praised too much for the life they have chosen because there is a fine line between praising nuns and setting them up as role models for women. They are, of course, to be role models for some women, for how else would the church persuade women to join? Yet they cannot become so popular that women regularly choose this life over marriage. Hence, nuns are an anomaly. They are revered and valued, but they are also taken for granted. This book is meant to remedy this situation, for the extent and kind of religious change in Ireland between the late eighteenth century and the late nineteenth would simply not have been possible without the dreams, the ambitions, and the persistence of tens of thousands of Irish women who chose to become nuns.

TWO

Founding Women

ANGELINA GOULD TOOK religious vows in 1829 in the Presentation convent at Doneraile, County Cork. Sister Magdalen Gould, born in 1792, was a member of the great Cork merchant family of Gould. Her parents had left their native city some years previously and taken up residence in Lisbon, where they had accumulated enormous commercial wealth.[1] When Angelina Gould joined the Presentation Order, she brought with her to the convent a fortune of approximately £60,000, which she later used to found convents.[2] By the time of her death in 1869, Mother Gould had established a total of ten Presentation and Mercy convents in the diocese of Cloyne and two more in the diocese of Ross.[3] Gould accomplished this with the help of several clerical friends. At her profession, she had appointed two clergymen of the diocese of Cloyne as the trustees of her property. One of them, the chaplain of the Doneraile convent where she was professed, was an intimate friend, Father Morgan O'Brien, who faithfully carried out her wishes for almost thirty years.[4] Besides having the support of friends within the local clergy, Mother Gould also had the benevolent backing of an influential relative, the bishop of Cloyne and Ross, William Coppinger, who was a cousin both to Gould and to the foundress of the Presentation Order, Nano Nagle.[5]

This story illustrates a central thesis of this work—that women initiated and sustained the development of the modern conventual movement in Ireland. Women like Mother Gould, who founded the new orders or were involved in their early spread throughout Ireland, emerged from an energetic and determined vanguard of middle-class Catholics. They came from increasingly wealthy merchant families in the commercial centers of Munster and Leinster, especially Cork and Waterford. Furthermore, they worked within a network of active, middle-class Catholics, both lay and clerical, which was strengthened by intricate kinship ties and which was especially important in this period when episcopal and clerical leadership was still weak.

Previous scholarly work on Irish nuns has failed to address directly the question of who was responsible for this dynamic new movement of women religious. Their phenomenal growth has been assumed in the literature to have resulted from the general transformation of the Catholic church during the nineteenth century.[6] The corollary of this assumption is that the hierarchy and clergy orchestrated this reemergence of the orders and their spread throughout Ireland. Hence, the standard interpretation is that throughout the nineteenth century reforming bishops and priests initiated and managed the development of the modern conventual movement. This is the accepted interpretation not only in the hagiographical religious biographies, including those of some of the foundresses, but also in the more recent scholarly literature on the Irish Catholic church.[7] For example, in one of the best recent analyses of the class and regional origins of the reemergence of the Catholic church as a dominant force in Irish society and politics, the assumption that religious orders did not initiate their own development has been uncritically accepted. This work has reproduced the notion of episcopal or priestly initiative by asserting that "the nuns or brothers had to be asked to found a branch in a town."[8] Nuns themselves often contributed to the acceptance of this assumption by stating that they had been "invited" into a parish. The meaning of this language is significant and is discussed in a later chapter, but it is important to understand that the "invitation" was invariably a formality that actually approximated "permission" to proceed after the women had already made arrangements for a foundation.

The problem with the notion of episcopal initiative and management is that it implicitly gives credit to the Catholic hierarchy when credit is not always due and that, conversely, it robs the women involved of their self-determining role in the development of this very important religious and cultural institution. This chapter argues, then, that wealthy and well-connected women played the crucial role in the reemergence of women's religious orders and their spread throughout Ireland beginning in the late eighteenth century. These women were able to revive female religious life because of their privileged class backgrounds and because of intimate and useful kinship ties between these early foundresses and their lay and clerical supporters.

First Foundations

Contrary to current opinion, which suggests that male clerics throughout Ireland either founded or invited the various orders into their parishes or dioceses, a much more complex process was at work. In the early years of the expansion of the orders, the clergy more often acted as supporters and go-betweens than as initiators. Bishops and priests acting alone rarely pushed for a foundation in these early years. Rather, those who appeared to take the initiative usually had female friends or relatives who either wanted to join a religious community or were already in a community, which they then helped to establish. Clerical support, consequently, often depended as much on personal interests as on religious ones. Often, in fact, the new religious communities met with lack of interest or even opposition from the local clergy and hierarchy in the early years. Among the first foundations, the examples of the establishment of the Presentation, Charity, Brigidine, and Mercy orders and the founding in Ireland of the Ursuline and St. Louis sisters demonstrate clearly this complex process and the central role that women themselves played in it.

During the 1760s, Nano Nagle, who had established several illegal poor schools for the Catholic children of Cork during the previous decade, decided to establish a religious order of women to create a permanent institution for her work.[9] After Nagle made her decision, she sought the help of her Jesuit confessor, Father Doran, and his nephew Father Francis Moylan, later bishop of Cork. Nagle had become acquainted with these clergymen in France, where they were members of the large Irish Catholic community there. Records kept by Nagle's later associates stated that Bishop Moylan "warmly entered into Miss Nagle's views," and because of this he has acquired the reputation of being the guiding light for both Nagle and the new foundation. This, however, is not entirely accurate. Moylan and Doran, responding to Nagle's bold plan to establish a religious community in Ireland to educate the poor, recommended that she should found an Ursuline convent, one whose main work would be with the rich.[10] It is also recorded that Nagle, in accepting the advice of the two clergymen, did not suspect that "all this time . . . these Ursulines were intended by Doctor Moylan for the education of young ladies, and not to be devoted to the *only* and great object which she had in view, viz., the instruction of the poor."[11] Given that Nagle had been educated in France and had spent some time as a postulant in a convent there, it seems surprising that she should not have understood the work that this famous order of religious women did. And given also that these two priests knew that she had not joined a French order because she felt that she had a mission to the Irish poor, it seems surprising that they should have recommended the foundation of an order dedicated to educating ladies.[12]

There are several reasons why Moylan chose the Ursulines. First, they had a very good reputation and were respected as educators of the daughters of wealthy Irish Catholic families. Second, wealthy Irish women could be depended on to join this order readily if it came to Ireland, which is exactly what happened. Eleanor Fitzsimmons of Cork, who originally intended to join the Visitation Order in Paris, joined the Ursulines instead when she discovered that they were about to make a foundation in Ireland. Shortly afterward, Elizabeth Coppinger, a member of a "distinguished family" in County Cork, and Margaret Nagle, who were both cousins of Nano Nagle, declared their allegiance.[13] Mary Kavanagh, a member of the old Catholic nobility, the Ormonde Butlers, joined the trio when she learned that Coppinger, her cousin and closest friend, was to become an Ursuline.[14]

The third circumstance that led to the choice of the Ursulines was the fact that Mary Moylan, sister of Father Moylan and niece of Father Doran, had been educated at the Ursuline convent in Paris and intended to join the order. With an establishment imminent in Cork, she decided to return home and join the

Ursulines there. She was one of the Cork community's first two postulants and later became one of its most illustrious reverend mothers.[15]

Bishop Moylan, then, far from being the guiding light of Nano Nagle, actually frustrated her intentions by recommending an order that did not suit her goals. Because the Ursulines were popular with Cork women, including Moylan's own sister, it became the preferred order for these clerical advisors. But the order was not Nagle's choice, as she demonstrated from the beginning of its foundation in 1771. In an obituary written for Moylan at his death in 1815, a Presentation nun wrote that "he did not . . . cooperate with the intentions of Miss Nagle," and when he returned to Cork after completing the negotiations for the Ursuline foundation, "she remonstrated against this deviation from her original intention, and her arguments being unavailing, she retired from the convent."[16] Although she provided the convent buildings, the grounds, and financial support for the Ursuline foundation in the early years, she refused to join the order and lived in a small house adjoining the convent from 1772 onward.[17] Soon afterward, in 1775, she decided to begin her own order of religious women.

This decision met with opposition from both the Ursulines and Francis Moylan. The Ursulines feared that "a division in Miss Nagle's solicitude"—in other words, a reduction in her financial support for the Ursulines in the future—would damage their interests.[18] Disliking the idea of another order, they complained of Nagle's plan to Moylan,[19] who also disliked the plan. While he was supportive of Nagle's earlier intention of establishing a religious order for women dedicated to educating the Catholics of Cork, he felt that end had already been accomplished. The Ursulines were beginning to thrive. Postulants were numerous, and the school was attracting girls not only from Cork but also from all over Ireland—girls who had previously been sent abroad. He, too, feared that the stability of the Ursulines would be threatened by another community of religious women in the neighborhood, if only because Nagle's new convent might entice women to join it who would otherwise have joined the Ursulines. Moylan therefore objected vigorously to Nagle's plan for a new community of religious that he felt might compete with, and possibly imperil, the future welfare of the Ursuline convent, where his sister was quickly rising in authority.

A fight soon broke out between Nagle and Moylan when Nagle, who refused to give up "that one great object which she always had in view," began building the new convent in spite of Moylan's objections. The angry bishop confronted Nagle on the building site, "threatened to have what was erected of the building destroyed," and "ordered her to commence her work at the other end of the city."[20] In response to Moylan's tirade, Nagle threatened to leave Cork altogether and find some other place for her new order where she might secure "more encouragement to effect her purposes." Fearing that Nagle would do exactly as she threatened, Moylan backed down and left her to do as she wished. The Presentation annalist noted that "he remained ever after silent on the subject." Nagle, in the meantime, "did pursue her work, and it prospered."[21] This convent, the first establishment of the Presentation Order, did indeed prosper eventually. A hundred years later, it had become the spiritual mother house for the second largest women's order in Ireland.[22]

Daniel Murray, archbishop of Dublin from 1823 until 1852, has also been credited with sponsoring several religious orders, if not with being their actual founder.[23] The order with which he is most closely associated is Mary Aikenhead's Irish Sisters of Charity. While Murray was without doubt a strong supporter of Mary Aikenhead, and while his role in the foundation of her order was certainly important, a closer look at what happened shows that Murray's actions were not taken independently and that his decision to found a new order was not made solely on his own initiative.

Mary Aikenhead grew up in Cork city and was active in the philanthropic movement there. Throughout her teenage years, she was involved with visiting and caring for the poor in their homes. In 1804, when she was just seventeen years old, she decided to become a nun and to spend her life doing this work. At the time, she was a close friend of two influential clergymen, Francis Moylan, bishop of Cork (who had earlier unsuccessfully opposed Nano Nagle), and Florence McCarthy, coadjutor bishop of Cork and the priest who had received her into the Catholic church several years earlier.[24] It was in discussions with these two priests that she first became aware of the work being done in France by the Daughters of Charity of St. Vincent de Paul.[25] The French Sisters of Charity, as they came to be called in Ireland, appealed to Aikenhead because they were uncloistered and they cared for the poor in the community—the very work she wished to continue doing. When her best friend, Cecilia Lynch, joined the Poor Clares in Dublin in 1804, Mary Aikenhead refused to join her. Although Aikenhead promised not to enlist in any order until she had visited the Poor Clare convent, she was too impressed with the French order to join the Poor Clares. She wanted to enter a religious order but felt that those in Ireland could not match the French sisters. Although Nano Nagle's Presentation nuns were originally uncloistered and did work with the poor, by 1804 they had become an enclosed order, for reasons that are discussed in chapter 7.

In 1808, Aikenhead visited Dublin to see Cecilia Lynch. While there, she stayed with her friends John and Anna Maria O'Brien. Mrs. O'Brien, a member of the Ball family, was the leading Dublin Catholic philanthropist of the first half of the nineteenth century and an intimate friend of Daniel Murray, then curate of St. Mary's parish.[26] On this visit, Aikenhead was introduced to Murray by the O'Briens. They became almost instantaneous friends, and, as a consequence, she confided to him her aspirations for the future. She told him of her desire to join a religious order that would enable her to continue her philanthropic work with the Irish poor and of her dismay that there was no such order in Ireland.

Although Murray is popularly credited with having originated the idea of founding a new order of women religious, he certainly did not have it in mind at this time.[27] Murray did not encourage her in her goal or suggest that he was thinking of founding a branch of the French Sisters in Ireland. On the contrary, he advised her to return to Cork, where she was needed to help take care of her family.[28] Not until 1811, one year after Aikenhead had returned to Dublin freed from family responsibilities, did Murray tell her that he would bring the French Sisters of Charity to Ireland if she would head the new foundation.[29] It seems reasonable to suppose, because Aikenhead was already enthusiastic about the French order before she met Murray and because there is no evidence that Murray had any desire to make a foundation until he had become her intimate friend, that it was she who expressed to Murray a desire to see the order come to Ireland. Though it is impossible to establish definitely who first suggested the idea of the French Sisters of Charity, Aikenhead's role in actually founding a new Irish order, rather than making a foundation of the French sisters, can be firmly established.

In 1812, Mary Aikenhead and a second aspirant for the foundation, Alicia Walsh, went to the convent of the Institute of the Blessed Virgin Mary in York to undertake a three-year noviceship. They chose York for several reasons. First, although the order was dedicated to female education rather than to the care of the poor, the sisters of the institute lived an uncloistered life (having won the privilege in 1749 with the *Quamvis Iusto* ruling), which was a requirement of Aikenhead's future foundation. In addition, the York convent, like the Ursuline convent in Paris, had been for the past century a school of choice for the daughters of wealthy Irish Catholics. In fact, Aikenhead and Murray were well acquainted with the place; Anna Maria O'Brien and her two sisters, Isabella and Frances Ball, had been educated there, and Murray had several nieces presently in the establishment.

While Aikenhead and Walsh were beginning their training in the religious life, Murray attempted to secure information on the French sisters. In 1814, he sent to the superior of the York convent, Mother Coyney, a summary of the rule of the Daughters of Charity of St. Vincent de Paul, as well as an agreement that was to be accepted and signed by the foundress before the new establishment could be made.[30] He asked the reverend mother to look over the rule, observing that, with the "addition of such of your rules and customs as you and Mother Austin would have the kindness to point out, it will be abundantly sufficient for the commencement of their proposed work."[31]

Mary Aikenhead and the superiors of the York convent looked over the material and decided that the rule of the Daughters of Charity of St. Vincent de Paul would not be "sufficient for the commencement of their proposed work." First, the French sisters took only simple annual vows, which gave the institute an impermanent and less committed character than Aikenhead intended. A second objection was that the Irish foundation would be subject to the French general superiors of both the male and female branches of the order and would be required to keep three French sisters in Ireland at all times. Aikenhead came to the decision that she would prefer to adopt the York rule under which she had lived for the past several years.[32]

It is important to note that Murray himself did not feel that he could or should proceed on his own in this matter. While traveling back and forth to Rome in the spring of 1814, he was well placed to do considerable research into the plans of communal life of several European orders. But, because he had never lived in a community of women, he did not presume to dictate a plan to Aikenhead. In a letter to the York community, he professed himself ignorant of the actual requirements of a community of women and confessed that he felt "very incompetent" to form a plan. He deferred to the sisters in the matter, telling them bluntly: "I am quite certain that any [regular plan of life] that would be formed under your inspection would meet with the approbation of Dr. Troy and myself."[33] Six months later, when the sisters still had not decided whether the new foundation should be affiliated with the French Sisters of Charity, Murray implored Aikenhead and Alicia Walsh to tell him "as speedily as possible . . . your opinions on what is the best to be done."[34]

Aikenhead and Walsh answered Murray's request by objecting to the proposed affiliation with the Sisters of Charity of St. Vincent de Paul; they asked that a new foundation be based on the York rule. Upon receiving their verdict, Murray pronounced himself in agreement.[35] Thus, when Mary Aikenhead and Alicia Walsh returned to Dublin in September 1815, they began a new order, the Religious Sisters of Charity, popularly known as the Irish Sisters of Charity.

The new order was the result of close collaboration between Murray and Aikenhead. Murray played the role he did not only because he was committed to raising up new Catholic institutions but also because he was involved in extremely close relationships with the emerging and increasingly influential Catholic elite. Although Murray has previously been seen as the initiator, and even the founder, of the Irish Sisters of Charity, this is true only in the sense that he worked side by side with his friend, the foundress. Murray did not want to bring the French Sisters of Charity to Dublin so much as he wanted his friend Mary Aikenhead to establish a new type of women's order in Ireland. Murray's support was indispensable to the accomplishment of Aikenhead's dreams. Yet what were realized in the end were her dreams, not Murray's.

As in the case of the founding of the Sisters of Charity, Daniel Murray has also been credited with the foundation of the Sisters of Mercy in Dublin in 1831. Although he did suggest, among other options, that Catherine McAuley's community of charitable laywomen become a bona fide religious order, it was not because he wanted another order of religious women. In fact, the opposite was the case. Before forming the Sisters of Mercy, McAuley was involved in charity work in the city as a part of the Protestant philanthropic network active throughout the century.[36] Although baptized a Catholic, she was raised by a Protestant guardian, from whom she inherited a large fortune in 1824. McAuley decided to use this money to begin an institution that would provide overnight shelter for working women who were temporarily unemployed. She wanted to form a community of "pious ladies" who would live together in order to devote themselves entirely to this charitable work. They were, however, to be free to return to their homes when they wished. This was, in fact, a Protestant convent plan that shows the influence of her Protestant background.[37] One of her associates remarked that it was McAuley's Protestant relations, "to whom she was much attached," who "induced her to think of forming a society of ladies who would devote themselves to the practice of the works of mercy without making vows, that they might be at liberty to visit their relations and remain with them in sickness and affliction."[38]

McAuley's Society of Ladies operated on this basis for several years and attracted about a dozen women, including several nieces of the nationalist leader

Daniel O'Connell. Mary A. Doyle, one of the first to join McAuley, who was unaware at the time that the Society was to become the Order of Mercy, later commented that when the "convent" opened in 1827, "the prospect of being able to visit [her aged parents] determined them and myself in the choice of uniting with Rev. Mother in the formation of the new establishment."[39]

While its activities were limited and its budget was minimal, the institution did not attract much attention from the Catholic community. When it began to provide meals and general support during the spring of 1829, public attention focused on this institution of Catholic laywomen.[40] In order to meet the additional expenses, McAuley attempted to collect funds from the city's most prominent citizens. She sent out letters "to the wealthy of every creed," and these letters provoked an angry response from many Catholics. One of the founding reverend mothers, M. Clare Moore, later noted in her memoirs that

> from Catholics, good Catholics and rich, she got the most insulting answers. In one it ran thus: "N. knows nothing of such a person as C. McAuley and considers that C. McAuley has taken a very great liberty in addressing her. She requests that C. McAuley will not trouble her with any more of C. McAuley's [letters], etc."[41]

It is clear from this response that Catherine McAuley lacked the support of the prominent Catholics of Dublin. McAuley was not a member of the established network of active and influential Catholics, the new Catholic "ascendancy." Although she had inherited wealth, it had come from a Protestant guardian, and she herself had grown up in not very notable Protestant circles. One Mercy sister observed that "it was a galling thing to many that one who had been born their inferior in rank and fortune should now occupy a more influential position than rank or wealth had procured for them."[42] And in her memoir Reverend Mother Moore recalled that "the institution excited attention and a most unpleasant feeling among the higher rank of Catholics. . . . The foundress was sneered at as an upstart, as uneducated."[43]

The lay opposition to McAuley, though strong, was surpassed by that of the clergy. Many clergymen in the city had become supporters of Mary Aikenhead's order, established in 1815, and they feared that McAuley's new institution would be a threat to Aikenhead's. Just as Moylan had worried in Cork city thirty years earlier, they worried that McAuley's community would rob the Sisters of Charity of both vocations and charitable funds.[44] Gender-based opposition to the institution was widespread. One clergyman, objecting to both the initiative and the authority taken by a woman in founding this community of charitable women, sent her a letter addressed to "C. McAuley, Esq[uire]," which maintained that "by the mere attempt to found a new society she had *ipso facto* unsexed herself."[45] The fledgling institute did not have to endure this priest's opposition for long. According to the convent annalist, "The writer of this letter did not repeat the insult. He dropped dead in the street a few days after he wrote it, and his sudden death was by some regarded as a judgment."[46]

McAuley's most virulent opponents among the clergy, however, were the priests of the parish in which her institute operated. The administrator of the parish, Matthias Kelly, was McAuley's most outspoken and intimidating adversary. The reason for this persecution, according to the convent annalist, was that

> this gentleman had no great idea that the unlearned sex could do anything but mischief by trying to assist the clergy, while he was prejudiced against the foundress, whom he considered a parvenu. His opinions perhaps influenced the curates, by whom he was greatly beloved, for certainly they did not affect to be glad of the establishment.[47]

The nature and extent of Kelly's objections, only briefly examined here, reflected the growing concern over the changing sex ratio in favor of women within the workforce of the Irish church. Kelly objected to women's growing involvement in apostolic or parochial work, work that was formerly the sole responsibility of priests. In his opposition to McAuley, he attempted to challenge and regulate the seemingly spontaneous emergence of new women's orders. Kelly's concerns were with controlling these new orders and, in the case of McAuley's institute, with regulating a group of women who were not even in religious vows.

In July 1829, after several intimidating confrontations provoked by Kelly, McAuley moved to resolve the "problem" she had created with her bold new institute.[48] She met with Archbishop Murray and learned from him that he was not pleased with the new community. The situation to which Murray objected, according to the Mercy annalist, was this:

> All things in the new establishment were becoming too like monastic life to be permitted except under monastic rule. "The new nuns" were not religious and yet did not live like seculars. Hard labour and severe mortification marked their days, and stated periods were allotted to prayer, examen, and spiritual reading. They referred to Miss McAuley for advice and direction as to a regularly appointed superior; they had daily Mass, weekly confession, and frequent Communion, and the privilege which religious value beyond all price—they resided under the same roof with the Blessed Sacrament. They never went abroad, except to perform some work of mercy. And yet they maintained that their institute was not a convent, and that they themselves were styled nuns or sisters only playfully or by courtesy.[49]

Murray made it clear to McAuley that he had not intended to promote the foundation of another religious community. In fact, he expressed his surprise at what looked like the emergence of a new women's order. "In freezing tones and with a cold, disdainful air," he told her that he "did not think the founding of a new order was part of your plan. . . . Really, Miss McAuley, I had no idea that a new congregation would start up in this manner."[50]

With the help of Michael Blake, one of McAuley's few supporters among the clergy, a settlement was negotiated. It was agreed that McAuley and her institute would *either* "appear as secular ladies or become religious."[51] McAuley did not make her decision quickly or easily. It took her six months to make up her mind, and when she did, it was to become a nun. Although she did not decide immediately whether she and her associates would join an existing order or begin a new one, there seemed never to be any question that she would found a new order, for as one of the early reverend mothers observed, "Her property was too considerable not to form a new establishment for the poor."[52] Her property was also too considerable for her to be in any position other than that of foundress and mother superior.

It is clear from a close examination of the foundation of the Sisters of Mercy, now the second largest women's order in the world, that although Murray neither expected nor wanted a new religious order to spring up, this is precisely what happened. Although clerical pressure was a factor in the formation of the Sisters of Mercy, it was not the cause. Archbishop Murray did not request that McAuley become a nun but rather that she drop the trappings of religious life if she were not one. Neither Murray nor the Dublin clergy wanted another community of religious women. Their pressure came about because of their need to clarify the position and control the activities of these women in Catholic society. Furthermore, the support of the clergy for the already-established Sisters of Charity, whose origins, unlike those of the Mercy order, were within the most respectable and influential class of Dublin Catholics, did not guarantee support for other institutions of religious women. Rather, it was support for specific women within a specific class and for specific institutions in clearly defined and limited circumstances. Nonetheless, Catherine McAuley, lacking both lay and clerical support, managed to found what was to become a very successful new order. Her personal wealth and her willingness to work within the guidelines of the Catholic church were enough to ensure success.

Women, both lay and religious, were largely responsible for the 1859 Irish foundation of the Sisters of St. Louis in Monaghan town. This order had been set up in France in 1842 with the help of a Cork woman, Ellen Woodlock, a professed nun in the order until 1851. The foundation is a good illustration of the way women guided the new conventual movement, sometimes having literally to persuade a bishop to acquiesce in their wishes.

The event that led directly to the founding of this congregation was the passage of the Irish Reformatory Schools Act in 1858. The two leading proponents of this cause were Ellen Woodlock, who became a leading Catholic philanthropist in Ireland after she left the religious life, and John Lentaigne. Lentaigne, commissioner for industrial schools and inspector of prisons, lived in Monaghan and was eager, along with other leading Catholics in the north, to promote the expansion of Catholic institutions in the area. After working successfully for the passage of this bill, the pair decided to work to bring the St. Louis Sisters to Ireland to start a reformatory school in Monaghan.

Ellen Woodlock's first step was to visit Charles McNally, bishop of Clogher, in order to persuade him to invite the order to Ireland. Although he was not at first receptive, she did convince him to invite the sisters to his diocese to manage a government-sponsored reformatory for girls.[53] Woodlock and Lentaigne raised money to buy an old brewery in Monaghan to house the new reformatory schools and in June 1859 made a down payment on it.[54] But until it was paid for in full, they could not obtain possession. Woodlock and Lentaigne worked feverishly to secure financial support from the bishops of Armagh province for paying for the balance of the cost of the building. Lentaigne met them in Monaghan late in June and looked forward after the meeting to their support:

> I have every hope that money will be collected, as the bishops of Clogher, Derry, Down and Connor are all favourable to have it made a great provincial reformatory for Ulster. . . . I cannot tell you the result but think we shall succeed.[55]

Lentaigne was too sanguine, for though the bishops declared themselves in support of the coming of the St. Louis Sisters in principle, funds for the new institute were not readily forthcoming. Fears of Protestant reprisals led Bishop McNally even to regret the presence of a large conventual establishment in the town.[56]

The Armagh hierarchy's lack of energetic support for the new order led to both anger and action on the part of the sisters' lay supporters. When a convent had not been secured by the bishop in time for the nuns' arrival, Mrs. H. A. Lloyd, a wealthy and influential Monaghan Catholic and president of the Monaghan committee formed to lobby for the reformatory, dispatched an angry letter to the bishop:

> I am so dismayed at hearing today that the nuns are arrived and no house to put them into. I fear they will either return or go with the reformatory elsewhere. . . . I am really grieved. . . . We are certainly a poor set in Monaghan, such a church & all. I was in hopes this w[oul]d have been a new era. . . . I cannot understand the difficulties. I sh[oul]d be so glad to hear from Y[ou]r Lordship on the subject.[57]

The very next day the bishop secured a house for use as a convent by the three sisters who had arrived, two of whom were Cork women.[58] Lloyd continued her vigorous activity on behalf of the sisters. She provided money for the foundation herself and traveled throughout Ulster to collect subscriptions for the new reformatory.[59] Even so, the opening of the institution continued to be delayed. Two years later, it was still not open, and by then both the supporters of the convent and the convent's superiors were deeply concerned. Lloyd was irate. In a letter to Priscilla Beale, reverend mother of the new community, she declared herself "much annoyed at all the useless and foolish delays in our undertaking." Monaghan, she believed, was simply "not a field for being useful in, so much bigotry on one side, met with such coldness & laxity & drawing back of the other. They are not fit for nuns or anything, I sh[oul]d think."[60]

Finally, the reformatory was paid for, and it opened in 1862. Its success, as well as that of the order itself, is discussed later. The main point here is that Bishop McNally did not bring the St. Louis Sisters to Ireland. A wealthy, energetic woman who was formerly a St. Louis nun herself, in collaboration with leading lay Catholics of the day, laid the groundwork for what became one of Ireland's most successful and famous conventual establishments.

While this chapter has stressed that bishops were generally not the initiators of new orders, there was one Irish congregation whose foundation was undertaken by a bishop. In 1807, Daniel Delaney founded the Brigidine Sisters in his diocese of Kildare and Leighlin in order to provide a dependable source of teachers for the Sunday schools he had established during the previous two decades. Bishop Delaney not only founded this order but also imposed his ideas and opinions on the community in what appears to have been an unusually autocratic style. He determined the practices and customs of the convent, such as the times of rising, eating, praying, and teaching; the style of the habit; the layout of the community rooms and garden; and, most important, the primacy of the nuns' duty to his parishioners over responsibility to the women's spiritual and communal life. Delaney shaped the way of life of this order to a degree that Archbishop Murray thought unthinkable for anyone but a religious woman.[61]

Yet what is not so widely known is that Delaney was not without female influence either in the foundation of this order or in its running. From the beginning, Delaney had the active collaboration of his very close friend Judith Wogan-Browne. In the words of the Brigidine annalist, Delaney

> was much assisted by Miss Browne in forming the sisters. . . . Being educated in a convent in France, she was well acquainted with the intentions of the pious practices and customs in convents, and with much benevolence she led the sisters into the knowledge of them.[62]

Wogan-Browne, a member of the Irish Catholic community who lived in Europe and attended the courts of the Stuart pretenders to the British throne, was educated from early childhood in the Benedictine convent at Ypres. She became a close friend of Delaney while he was undertaking religious studies in Paris. When he went to Tullow as parish priest, she followed him to Ireland and took a house in Tullow in 1780. A rich woman with an overpowering personality, Wogan-Browne remained the bishop's intimate friend throughout his life and was named the executor of his will at his death in 1814.[63] She also acted as the de facto reverend mother of the congregation, attending and presiding at community chapter meetings, until her own death. Evidence of her authority is apparent in the struggle over the issue of a Brigidine boarding school. From the foundation of the order, both Delaney and the Brigidine sisters wanted to take boarders. But Wogan-Browne was opposed to the idea and was able to impose her will in this matter; no boarders were taken during Delaney's lifetime. Wogan-Browne's wishes continued to be accepted by Delaney's successor as well. In 1824, in an attempt to overcome Wogan-Browne's resistance, the Tullow convent requested permission from Bishop James Doyle to open a boarding school. Doyle wrote to the reverend mother granting the request "on condition that she could likewise have Miss Browne's consent." Wogan-Browne's consent was not forthcoming, however, and a boarding school was not opened.[64]

This order, more than any other in Ireland perhaps, owes its founding to a reforming bishop. Yet it is likely that it would not have happened at all without the cooperation and perhaps the direction of Judith Wogan-Browne. Then again, neither her influence nor that of the bishop was particularly beneficial. Structured so rigidly by a bishop and controlled so tightly by a woman who was not a religious herself, the early Brigidines failed to develop a strong sense of communal identity. Loyalty to and adoration of a founding mother created an esprit de corps that helped to draw women into orders and to make those orders known by women throughout Ireland. But this order, the creation of the hierarchy, failed to thrive as did other Irish orders. Consequently, the Brigidines did not extend beyond this diocese until the twentieth century. This example, then, is illustrative. Episcopal initiative in its purest form was not a determining factor in the reemergence of the women's orders.

Spread of the Orders

Following the establishment of the first houses, the modern women's orders gradually extended throughout Ireland between 1775 and 1850. As with the first foundations, this was a complex process that involved both cooperation from some clergy and lack of interest or even opposition from others. The story of the fourth foundation of the Presentation Order in Waterford city in 1798 is an illustration of the cooperative, kinship-based relationship that sometimes existed between women foundresses and supporting male clerics. In the early 1790s, a Waterford priest, Father John Power, heard the confession of a young female servant. Surprised and impressed by the sophistication of her religious training, he learned from her that she had been educated in the first Presentation convent in Cork city, of whose existence he had been unaware until then. Power was clearly excited about the benefits to religion that this new community of women had produced, and he wanted to see a Presentation convent established in his own parish. Power had two sisters who wished to become nuns, and after their brother's discovery of the new Irish order, they decided to join it and to use their property to make a Presentation foundation in Waterford in 1798.[65]

Even when the clergy and hierarchy were well acquainted with the new religious orders forming in Ireland, their support in the early years was not guaranteed and could not be taken for granted. Thomas Hussey, bishop of Waterford and Lismore at the time of the Presentation foundation in Waterford city, was an early defender of Catholic rights and a promoter of Catholic education. Because of this, he was expected to support the new Presentation convent. Yet when approached by Power for permission to make a foundation in his diocese, it is recorded that although Hussey "allowed" the project to proceed, he failed to provide any financial assistance.[66]

Patrick Everard, while coadjutor archbishop of Cashel from 1815 to 1821, joined other leading clerics of that diocese who had been engaged in a twenty-five-year attempt to prevent Archbishop Bray from founding a Presentation convent in Thurles out of a fund for the poor left by his predecessor, James Butler, in 1792. Everard and the others then believed that the money would be more profitably spent on the foundation of a seminary than on a convent.[67] Although Everard was a close friend of both Archbishop Murray and Mary Aikenhead, and although he supported the foundation of her Irish Sisters of Charity, his personal interest in that order did not guarantee his support for all foundations. And the Irish Sisters of Charity received little if any assistance from Archbishop Troy in Dublin, who was noted for taking little interest in the order.[68] Even as late as the 1860s, members of the clergy still resisted the incursion of women religious into their parishes. When the Irish Sisters of Charity made a foundation at Benada Abbey in County Sligo, it was recorded that "their services were neither desired [n]or valued . . . by the clergy of the locality."[69]

If the clergy and hierarchy were not the initiators of expansion in the early years of the conventual movement, then we must look elsewhere for the key to understanding the spread of the orders throughout the country. The results of a simple statistical analysis of the early foundations of the three major Irish orders demonstrate the centrality of women in the process of expansion. The Presentation Order had 32 convents by the time of the famine in 1846. Of these, 15, or 47 percent, were founded through the initiative and the money of women. By 1846 the Mercy Order had 13 convents in Ireland, of which 7, or 54 percent, were founded by women. The pattern is even more marked in the case of the Irish Sisters of Charity. Mary Aikenhead established 11 convents of her order between 1815 and 1846, and of these, 10, or 91 percent, were founded by women. A mere 4 of these 60 convents (6.6 percent) were set up directly by bishops, and just 4 others (6.6 percent) by priests.[70] While these figures are instructive, the actual ways in which women made these foundations are even more so. In many cases, the initiative to establish a certain convent in a particular area came from local women who wanted to become nuns and remain in their own neighborhood. They exerted pressure on their local clergy to arrange for the provision of a house for use as a convent, and in many cases they provided the house themselves.

The case of the Power sisters in Waterford city is an early example of women seeking hometown foundations. Ten years later, another Presentation convent was founded at Dungarvan in the diocese of Waterford and Lismore by several women of the town. These women had been living together in a quasi-religious community for several years, pooling their incomes and devoting themselves to the teaching and care of the poor. They decided to join the Presentation Order, and in 1809 their house became a convent.[71]

In 1828, a Miss O'Neil of Bandon, County Cork, informed her widowed mother that she was determined to join the Presentation Order. In the words of the Presentation annalist, Mrs. O'Neil "was determined on cooperating with the will of God in giving this exalted vocation" to her only child.[72] In order to demonstrate that determination (as well as her determination to continue living with her only child), Mrs. O'Neil decided to found a Presentation convent in Bandon for her daughter to join, with the stipulation that Mrs. O'Neil would live in the convent as well, which was a right routinely granted to women foundresses. This is a fine example of the crucial role of women in the expansion process, for this foundation was thought unlikely to succeed at the time, even by the Presentation Order itself. Superiors at the South Presentation convent, who arranged the foundation, were unsure as to whom the Bandon nuns would minister; it was commonly remarked at the time that "everyone knows there are no Catholics in Bandon and even the pigs are Protestant."[73]

Another means of expansion was through the bequests of individual Catholic women who left money for a foundation in their will; the executor was often a priest or bishop, who then made the necessary contacts and invited the order into the diocese. The Mahony bequest is an example of this pattern. In her will, a Miss Mahony left £2,650 for the foundation of a convent of Irish Sisters of Charity in

Cork city. Her brother Martin consulted Bishop John Murphy, who then formally invited the order to the city.[74] Margaret Molloy of New Ross left her house
and premises to her brother Peter for an eventual Mercy convent in that town. He
added £1,200 to the bequest and left it all in his will for the foundation.[75]

Frequently, a woman made the bequest before her death so that she could
avail herself of the right to reside in the convent. In 1799, the Cork city philanthropist Barbara O'Connell, another member of the prominent merchant family of Gould, used her inheritance to set up there a second Presentation convent.
As O'Connell approached old age, she decided to make the foundation and live
in the convent, where she died seven years later.[76]

The foundation of the Sisters of Charity at Benada Abbey in County Sligo
is also an interesting one. The owner of this estate, which was once a medieval
monastery before the sixteenth-century dissolutions, was a widow named Jones,
whose seven children all entered the religious life. When her youngest daughter
decided to join the Sisters of Charity, to avoid being left alone Jones resolved to
give the entire estate to the order for a foundation if her daughter could reside
there. Jones moved into private apartments within the convent, where she lived
until her death a few years later.[77] In 1850, the struggling Brigidine convent in
Tullow took as a boarder a woman who was "anxious to retire from business
and the world to prepare for death" when she "offered to give the convent £400,"
enough money to enable the congregation to support more sisters.[78] Charitable
bequests of this sort by lay women initiated many foundations during these early
years, including the Presentation convents in Tralee, Limerick, Tuam, and Rahan;
the Sisters of Charity convents in Dublin, Waterford, Clonmel, and Clarenbridge;
and the Mercy convents in Newry, Tullamore, Wexford, Cork, Passage West,
New Ross, and Bantry.[79]

Interpersonal conflicts within convents also led to new foundations. Personality clashes sometimes caused so much stress that the women concerned were
unable to maintain a harmonious community, which made religious life all but
impossible. In such cases it was an accepted practice among women's orders for
discontented sisters, especially wealthy ones, to establish a new convent of the
order. The South Presentation convent in Cork city experienced conflicts within
its community during the 1820s and 1830s. Convent records show great instability in the government of the convent, resulting in several unscheduled elec-
tions and requests for visitations by the bishop. One of the women involved in
the conflict was M. Joseph Hartnett. When a Limerick city woman proposed to
fund a Presentation foundation there in 1836, Hartnett was one of the sisters
sent from Cork to make the foundation. It appears that she was unable to settle
happily there either, for ten years later her family made a foundation in their
hometown of Castleisland in Kerry, where Hartnett went as reverend mother in
1846.[80] The bad blood between the Cork convent and Hartnett was made obvious in an agreement reached at the time of the founding at Castleisland. As
part of the agreement, the South Presentation community granted Hartnett permission to make the foundation, provided that she would "never claim a re-
entrance [to the Cork community] as a right."[81] This stipulation was surprising,
since convents had a regular system for dealing with unhappy or discontented

nuns that allowed them to spend time with or even to join other communities in hopes of their being able to settle peaceably into religious life somewhere. Agreements that a sister could never reenter the convent where she was professed were very rare, and this one appears to indicate the intensity of the conflict at Cork.

The older contemplative orders that had existed in Ireland throughout the penal law era began to expand as well after 1800, and these convents, too, experienced intracommunity conflicts that led to new foundations. One example is that of Sister de Sales Stuart, a Carmelite from the Ranelagh convent near Dublin. In 1823, she was supposed to have experienced a miraculous recovery from a life-threatening illness through the powers of Prince Hohenlohe, a popular Catholic figure of the time. De Sales Stuart found it impossible to remain in her convent after this affair because the publicity that surrounded her aggravated the power struggles within the convent. She left Ranelagh and during the next four years founded two new Carmelite communities.[82]

Orders also expanded because of the specific needs and goals of their communities. During the cholera epidemic of 1832, the Sisters of Charity, who cared for the sick, extended their home visits to the cholera hospitals set up in Dublin. Following that experience, Mary Aikenhead decided to take up nursing and to open a hospital of her own—St. Vincent's, the first Catholic hospital in the country. A house on St. Stephen's Green, to be used for the hospital, was purchased by a member of the congregation, F. Teresa O'Ferrall. O'Ferrall's brother, the personal physician of both Mary Aikenhead and Archbishop Murray, became chief physician of the new establishment.

Health problems, especially tuberculosis, were a continual source of concern for conventual establishments during the nineteenth century, and several congregations of women expanded in order to establish convents in areas that would be beneficial to the sisters' health. One of the first Loreto Sisters, M. Aloysia Eleanor Arthur, used a portion of her money to make a new Loreto foundation for this purpose. She asked the general superior, Mother Teresa Ball, for permission to allow her "to have a share in promoting the greater glory of our Divine Spouse by purchasing the convent at Kingstown, as it would be the means not only of gaining so many souls to God but also of reestablishing the health of our sisters."[83]

Although this chapter focuses primarily on prefamine expansion, interesting examples of this sort of pragmatic growth arose later in the century as well. In 1897, the St. Louis Sisters decided to make a new foundation after "an old bachelor friend of one of the sisters" willed a house, twenty-five acres, and £4,500 to the congregation. The sisters discussed the prospect among themselves and decided to make the foundation. Sister Aloysius, head of the Ramsgrange convent that had received the endowment, forwarded to the superior of the order her reasons for wanting to proceed: "There are advantages in having a branch house. Looking at it only as far as we ourselves are concerned, an additional work gives spirit and energy."[84]

The conventual movement was also fueled by rivalry between different orders and convents. Mother Rorke, superior of the Richmond Presentation convent in the 1840s, noted this rivalry and expressed her concern about its possibly negative effects on community life. She believed that her convent was taking too many novices, many of them unsuited to the community, because the Presentation Order had to keep up with the other convents thriving in the vicinity. Her wish to ensure the suitability of the novices by restricting entry was not popular within her community, however. The other sisters complained that she was "not anxious to have the community increase while all around [us] are."[85]

In Cork city, a rivalry developed between the Sisters of Charity and the Sisters of Mercy. Sister M. Joseph Lynch of the Sisters of Charity had a cousin who was a doctor in the town. On one of his visits to the convent, he discussed with the sisters the possibility of opening in Cork a Catholic hospital like St. Vincent's, the famous Sisters of Charity hospital in Dublin. The Sisters of Charity decided to apply for the management of the proposed hospital because, as the reverend mother of the Cork community remarked, "if we do not take it, no doubt the S[isters] of Mercy will."[86]

As the convents spread throughout the country and gained in popularity, priests and bishops increasingly sought out the services of an order of religious women for their parish or diocese. But even though a priest or bishop might want to make a foundation, this did not automatically mean that he was able to do so. The first responsibility of women religious was to their own community. Any foundation that a convent or order decided to make was undertaken only if the community making it was sure of remaining a viable entity. Convents also tried to ensure that any foundation they made would be viable as well. Hence, a bishop's wish in this matter was not a command; women religious decided if and when they would make a foundation. Ultimately, women religious controlled the spread of their orders.

Many priests who tried to bring convents to their parishes found it difficult to do so. In February 1845, for instance, William Walsh, an Irish man then serving as bishop of an English diocese, complained to Archbishop Murray's secretary, Father John Hamilton, that he was unable to find a Mercy convent in Ireland willing to make a foundation in his diocese. Walsh had been one of Catherine McAuley's few friends in her struggles with Murray and the Dublin clergy, and he was incredulous that he could not now secure a foundation.

> They have refused me at Limerick, and I am again at sea respecting the nuns. It is mortifying enough to reflect that there is hardly a priest in Ireland who did and suffered more for those good people at Baggot St. than myself, and yet the veriest stranger can get communities from them, whilst old friends are forgotten.[87]

Although Walsh felt slighted, the truth is that the "veriest stranger" could not get communities from the Mercy sisters or, indeed, from any other congregation. In 1823, negotiations had taken place between Father Peter Daly of Galway city and Mary Aikenhead over the foundation of a Sisters of Charity convent there. According to the congregation's records, "he wished matters to be carried out according to his views," which conflicted with the rules of the congregation, and so the foundation was not made.[88] In 1836, a County Galway priest who wanted a Presentation convent in his parish successfully appealed to several convents of the order to send sisters for a foundation. When the nuns arrived, they discovered that the house and financial support the priest had promised them had not been provided, and the sisters quickly returned home.[89] To cite a final example among many of this kind, during the 1850s Mary Aikenhead was approached by a Canadian bishop who wanted a foundation of her order in his diocese of Montreal. Aikenhead knew that there was already a community of religious women in Montreal who performed the same work as the Sisters of Charity. Fearing that a new community there would not thrive because of this, she refused his request.[90]

In sum, the early expansion of the conventual movement was heavily indebted to the wealth, drive, and personal goals of women. In these early days when the educated and prosperous laity was a powerful component of the Catholic community, rich, confident, and competent women provided the initiative that determined the direction taken by their orders. Furthermore, until the middle of the century, when the episcopacy began to reassert itself, individual bishops and priests assisted rather than controlled the spread of the women's orders. The idea that women religious had to be asked or invited to make a foundation in a community was a convenient myth that functioned to mask their agency and their influence on the development of both the modern conventual movement and the modern Irish Catholic church. Finally, the assumption that the phenomenal expansion of the women's orders was a result of the widespread reform within the Irish church during the nineteenth century is misleading. Rather, women with the ability and desire to do so, having taken advantage of opportunities created by the religious and social developments of their time, created and spread new religious institutions that would later prove invaluable in the reform of church and society.

THREE

Convents, Class, and Catholic Identity

ANGELINA GOULD JOINED the Presentation Order in June 1826 at the age of thirty-four. Her path to the convent had not been particularly smooth. According to an account of her life,

> she was detained in the world by a feeling of duty towards her parents for many years after she had resolved to devote herself to God in the religious state, for they were extremely opposed to her quitting the world, and her father never could be induced to consent to it.[1]

The annalist went on to describe how her father, "as some compensation for thwarting her holy designs, allowed her the disposal of the interest of her fortune (a handsome sum) in charity or otherwise as she pleased."[2] Gould chose to use the money to support philanthropic work in the city of Lisbon, where she resided with her parents. It was not until her father died and left her in control of a large inheritance that she sailed to Cork and joined the Doneraile convent, which she had once visited and where her aunt, a boarder and benefactor of the community, had recently died.

Although Gould was exceptional in the amount of money that she brought with her as a dowry (a sum of £60,000), her path to the convent was not unusual, at least not during the prefamine period. She was a member of a prominent Irish merchant family from Cork, she was convent educated and had been active in philanthropic work before she joined a religious order, and she chose a convent with which she had personal ties through a female relative. That her family resisted her choice of a religious life was not unusual either. Though it is commonly believed that Irish families willingly gave their daughters to the church, this was not necessarily the case during the period of this study.

This part of the story of Angelina Gould raises several important questions that are the focus of this chapter. First, if women like Gould initiated and sustained the conventual movement, why did they do so? Why did women found convents at this particular time? Second, why did the women who followed the foundresses into the convents want to join women's communities and in such large numbers? Finally, was the pattern of motivation and entrance exemplified by Angelina Gould a static phenomenon, or did the conventual movement over the course of the nineteenth century experience an evolution in the type of woman who joined, as well as in the motivation that brought her to the convent?

A general explanation for the growth of the conventual movement links the growth in the number of nuns to the changing social conditions of nineteenth-century Ireland, especially those of the postfamine period.[3] According to this explanation, the change in inheritance patterns, which fueled emigration and led to decreased marriage opportunities for both women and men, created a supply of women who filled the convents. In other words, "surplus" or "redundant" women reacted to changing social conditions by entering convents because it was an acceptable life option (one of the few available to women) and offered a high level of social status.[4] It has also been posited that family strategy played a part in the increase in numbers of women joining convents in the nineteenth century. It is commonly believed that daughters were willingly given to the church as a means of enhancing family status.

These interpretations lack explanatory power for several reasons. Insofar as they pertain to social and demographic conditions prevalent in the postfamine period, they fail to account for the factors that encouraged the reemergence and spread of the orders in the crucial prefamine period. Additionally, while by the late nineteenth century there is some cause to believe that families willingly gave their daughters to the church, during the early part of the century families like the Goulds often did not want their daughters to become nuns. Much evidence from the prefamine period shows that women entered convents on their own initiative, which often meant asking priests to help them enter against the wishes of their parents.[5] These popular explanations for the dramatic growth of the women's orders also fail to account for the positive and conscious reasons that women themselves had for founding and joining women's orders. An explanation that centers on women's reactions to changing social and economic structures fails to account for the impact women had on those very changes. Finally, although the reemergence of women's orders did, indeed, reflect larger changes in the social and economic structure of Irish society, the most important structural change in terms of the development of the conventual movement was not the postfamine demographic transformation but rather the emergence of an articulate and ambitious class of Catholics during the prefamine years.

Late in the eighteenth century, a wealthy, confident, and outspoken segment of the Catholic population emerged to assume a position of political, social, and religious leadership within the larger Catholic community. This group originated from the rich agricultural areas and commercial centers of mid-Munster and southern Leinster, especially the towns and hinterlands of Cork, Waterford, and Kilkenny and the city of Dublin. It included surviving Catholic landowners and strong farmers from rural areas, as well as industrialists, tradesmen, and members of the professions in the major towns and cities. Beginning in the middle of the eighteenth century, leadership in the movement to restore Catholic civil and political rights came from this segment of the Catholic population, as did leadership in the transformation of Catholic institutions that began at about the same time. To circumvent the full force of anti-Catholic legislation, wealthy Catholics from this region had turned to Catholic continental Europe for many things, including education and professional training. Connected with developments within post-Reformation Catholicism in a way that the vast majority of poorer Irish Catholics could never be, they were crucial players in the transformation of the Irish church and Irish society.[6] As leaders of the Catholic community, whose prominence and importance in politics and society increased as the nineteenth century progressed, they were determined to make their customs, behavior, beliefs, and worldview the new dominant culture of the general Catholic population.

The increasing self-consciousness and visibility of this politically and socially influential class of commercial and professional Catholics created new opportunities for its women members. Prominent among them was the ability to secure the formation in Ireland of the new, socially active religious communities for women. As wealthy, articulate, and influential Irish Catholics, these women decided that their mission was to "save" the Irish Catholic masses from ignorance and degradation, which they believed had resulted from centuries of religious oppression by the Protestant ruling class. Wealthy Catholic women engaged themselves in the culturally validated mission of philanthropic work among the Catholic poor and sought to institutionalize their work by creating, with other women, religious communities committed to the continuance of their enterprises. So motivated, they effectively and significantly participated in the social and religious transformation of Irish society that the nineteenth century witnessed. Gradually, the trickle of women entering the newly formed convents in the late eighteenth century became a flood by the final decades of the nineteenth. As a consequence, these women played an instrumental role in the development of both the identity of the nineteenth-century Catholic middle class and, more generally, an Irish identity that became inextricably linked with Catholicism. The result was a revolution in the religious and cultural landscape of nineteenth-century Ireland.

Class and the Growth of the Conventual Movement

As members of the Catholic middle classes, Irish religious women were part of a larger European process of social and cultural change that was a result of the emerging industrial and entrepreneurial class's successful attempt to dominate the social, cultural, and political structures of the day. Integral to this process of class formation and consolidation was the imposition of bourgeois values and beliefs on the "lower" classes, which was largely accomplished by the philanthropic work of middle-class women. In both Britain and Ireland at this time, middle-class women of all religious persuasions were deeply committed to philanthropic work. In England, contemporaries believed that for every woman who was the recipient of charity at midcentury there was a woman who dispensed it.[7] Though it is not clear whether philanthropy reached those same proportions in Ireland, Irish women of all religious faiths created a large number of charitable foundations during the late eighteenth and nineteenth centuries.[8] Single women and widows were especially prominent in this movement, leading efforts to establish homes for widows, orphans, and prostitutes and to improve educational and employment opportunities for women.[9]

While the desire to find some type of employment seems to have motivated this "leisured" class of women, the choice of charitable work was determined by the increasing significance of the discourse of religiosity during the century. Central to that discourse, regardless of the particular Christian denomination or sect, was the stress placed on the role of charitable work for both personal salvation and the salvation of society. This was no less true in Ireland than it was in England.[10] The evangelicals especially took up benevolent work. Given the new emphasis on the role of the individual in personal salvation, good works in the form of charity toward the poor became almost a requirement for the God-fearing.[11] In the Roman Catholic church, good works had long been proclaimed the principal method of personal salvation.[12] Hence, that church, too, was ideologically predisposed toward an expansion of charitable activity. One historian of nineteenth-century philanthropy has expressed the religious underpinning of the benevolent movement very succinctly: "Whether evangelical, High Church, Catholic, or Unitarian, all agreed: to be Christian was to be charitable."[13] She might also have added that to be middle class and female was to be charitable.

Not only did middle-class women undertake religiously endorsed charitable activity but also they came to dominate it. Distributing food and clothing to the needy, paying home visits to the sick and dying, organizing shelters for the orphaned and the elderly—these were all activities that grew out of tasks traditionally performed by women. The stated requirements of the job—compassion, sympathy, and self-sacrifice—were qualities associated with femininity. It is not surprising, then, to learn that William Wilberforce, commenting on the great involvement of women in religious charities, believed women to be "more favourably disposed to religion and to good works" than men.[14]

Not only did women's concerns and activities come to shape the appearance of philanthropic enterprise but also women in England and Ireland provided much of the necessary financial support for the work being done.[15] In a recent survey of a selected number of charitable organizations in prefamine Ireland, women were found to have contributed from 50 to 80 percent of the total funds raised.[16] In one home for the dying operated by the Sisters of Charity, women were almost its sole contributors. According to institutional records, because of their "almsgiving tendency . . . almost all who gave or left us money of considerable amount were women, and many of these widows. . . . By sums varying from units to thousands did women share their love and zeal."[17]

Because of the public's perception of female compassion and the belief that women possessed "essential" qualities of goodness and morality, middle-class women in general came to claim a certain moral authority in the nineteenth century. Wealthy, religious, well-educated, and industrious, these women, in the words of one midcentury English female philanthropist, believed themselves to be holders of "no less an office than that of instruments (under God) for the regeneration of the world."[18] While the philanthropists' specific goals for the "regeneration of the world" might not have been fully or even partially realized, their work did result in both the construction of a middle-class identity that enshrined the notion of the superiority of female morality and the fundamental recasting of the social and cultural mores of their societies.[19]

As a means of participating in what they saw as the regeneration of Irish society, then, many wealthy Catholic women, especially from the urban centers of Munster and Leinster, developed a calling to become nuns. Beginning in the late eighteenth century, they began to promote the reemergence and growth of the religious life for women, setting their sights on reviving the Catholic church and bringing the discipline of that church to the great number of Irish Catholics who remained outside its influence. The early foundresses and leaders were, almost without exception, from old Catholic gentry families or from increasingly wealthy merchant and professional families of the south and east of Ireland, which explains why convents were concentrated in this area. Nano Nagle, foundress of the Presentation Order, was of Anglo-Norman descent and a member, on her mother's side, of one of the younger Catholic branches of the prominent landowning family, the Ormonde Butlers of County Tipperary. Her Nagle ancestors were members of the Cork subgentry, with landholdings in various parts of the county and commercial and professional interests in Cork city. Joseph Nagle, the uncle from whom she inherited the money with which she founded two religious orders in Ireland, was a lawyer in Cork city. The family was also involved in the Atlantic trade; a branch of the family had emigrated to France, where they had established a commercial trading house in Lyons.[20]

Another of the foundresses, Mary Aikenhead, emerged from a similarly privileged background. Aikenhead's father was a Protestant physician and a leader of the Cork city branch of the United Irish Society. Her mother was a Catholic of Anglo-Norman descent and a member of the Stackpole family, prominent merchants in the city.[21] Mary Hennessy, one of Mary Aikenhead's first assistants, was a member of the Hennessy family who were brandy distillers in Cork.[22] The two women who were responsible for founding a total of fifteen Mercy and Presentation convents in the dioceses of Cork and Cloyne during the three decades before the famine were both members of the Gould family, wealthy merchants with branches in Cork city and on the continent.[23] One final example among many of this kind concerns the Mahony family, who owned and operated a woolen mill in Blarney. Women of this family were responsible for founding an Irish Sisters of Charity convent in Cork city and for establishing and staffing the Sisters of St. Louis, first in France and later in Ireland.[24]

Rank-and-file members, though possessed of less wealth than founders, were nonetheless from comfortable backgrounds throughout the period 1770–1870. This is evident from the quite substantial dowry amounts required to enter a convent. In the early years of the conventual movement, a typical minimum in all of the orders was £500 to £600. The dowry, if not already in the form of an income-producing instrument, was then invested, and the interest generated was used to support the woman whose dowry it was. In the George's Hill Presentation community, the general sum required was £500, and final acceptance into the community depended upon its receipt.[25] When in 1810 Ann Aylmer's family failed to pay her promised fortune of £1,000, she was denied permission to take her final vows.[26]

Although a dowry was technically required of all entrants, women were sometimes admitted without one. Most often, this was made possible by the recruitment of very wealthy women who were encouraged to bring in as much as they possessed. A novice like the English aristocrat Lucy Clifford, who brought £4,000 with her, could actually support several other women in addition to herself.[27] When Elizabeth Bodenham entered the Sisters of Charity novitiate in Dublin in 1827, she brought enough money with her to enable the order to admit her dowryless friend as well.[28]

During the postfamine period, dowry amounts declined. The £500 that was typical early in the nineteenth century became in some convents £200 to £300 by its end, a sum that was no longer sufficient to fully support a woman of the upper classes.[29] In addition, it appears that the social background of the women joining convents changed as well. In a study of two convents in the diocese of Limerick, the average property valuation of the choir sisters declined significantly between 1850 and 1880, suggesting that the "ladies" who founded the orders and were important early recruits became less important in the rank-and-file membership of the late nineteenth century.[30]

Several developments converged to produce this effect. First, during the century increasing numbers of convents and congregations joined their schools to the National Board; by the last decades of the century the great majority were receiving payments from the British state for operating their schools.[31] So significant was this source of support that by the late nineteenth century women who had been through the Mercy-run teacher's college at Carysfort, County Dublin, were being accepted into some religious houses without a dowry at all.[32] The downward movement of dowries and the subsequent decline in the wealth of the families whose women entered convents also paralleled the increasing incidence of late marriage and permanent celibacy that characterized the postfamine period. Both trends were accompanied by the spread of the women's orders, most notably the Sisters of Mercy and the Presentation Sisters, into every diocese in the country. It is tempting to assume that a causal relationship exists. Because of the increase in the number of unmarried women, the women's orders were able to grow and blanket the country. Furthermore, because the women now joining were from less affluent backgrounds, convents took root in the more rural west and north, where wealthy urban women had not already established them. In other words, because there were more women who wanted to join convents, more convents were created, and because the women were from poorer and remoter areas, convents began to spring up in the smaller towns and rural areas of the west of Ireland during the postfamine period.

Although changing social and economic structures certainly influenced the conditions of women's lives and contributed to the development of the women's orders, the relationship between their rapid growth in the postfamine period and the decline in the wealth and class status of the women who joined is not quite such a simple equation. Several factors complicate the picture. For instance, though some women may have entered religious life because of poor marriage prospects or, as was suggested earlier, as a way to boost family social status, convents could not and did not function solely as places for the growing number of single women to live out their lives. Women who entered simply to escape an unfulfilling and unmarried life at home were not assured of happiness in the convent. Sophia McCormick, for example, joined a convent of the Loreto Sisters in the early 1840s specifically "on account of being unhappy at home." She had to leave the Loreto order after several years, however, because she was not any happier there. Because her family would not take her back, she went to France, where she hoped to secure a job as a governess, believing it "better I should be happy in the world than miserable mocking God in religion."[33] In 1850, Mary Brophy was dismissed from the Sisters of Charity, where she had been professed some years earlier. The order maintained that "the poor girl had never had a religious vocation but [had] been driven into the convent by her mother."[34] According to Brophy's brother, his sister had been treated badly in the convent and had gone mad because of it;[35] the Sisters of Charity claimed that she had feigned madness because she wanted to get out of religious life. It hardly matters which version was true, for Mary Brophy was the loser either way. After the order dismissed her, her mother refused to take her back, and her family thought that her life, as well as their own, had been ruined by the expulsion. As a family strategy in the face of decreased chances of marriage, the Brophys' actions were hardly successful.

Another factor limits the persuasiveness of any interpretation that relies on the changing social and economic conditions of the postfamine period. That factor is the realization that the ability of women's religious orders to grow after 1850 depended ultimately on the fiscal strength established during the prefamine years. Perhaps the most significant reason for the decline in dowry amounts during the last half of the nineteenth century, in addition to the provision of government teaching salaries, was the effect, over time, of the accumulation of those dowries. While a woman lived, the principal of the fortune she brought with her was held in trust by the community for the production of the income on which she was able to live. Upon her death, however, that fortune became the outright property of the community. In consequence, the amount of capital possessed by Irish convents increased as its members died. When convents had been in operation long enough to accumulate money in excess of what was needed for building expansion, they were able to admit women who sometimes did not possess dowries or who possessed less than what was required to support them. The first time that the George's Hill community admitted a dowryless woman occurred in 1824, thirty years after the convent was founded. The woman's father had died and left her mother unable to pay her fortune. The chapter decided, however, that because they "had the funds to support her," they would allow her to be professed.[36] Though the increasing number of women who were able and willing to join convents was an important factor in the rapid growth of the movement in the decades immediately following the famine, this fact alone did not determine future growth. It was rather the financial security provided by the early members of an order or individual convent that enabled the increasing number of single women from less affluent families to choose the religious life.

This is further borne out by the development of the "branch" convent system of growth adopted by both centralized and decentralized orders after the famine. Mercy convents in Limerick and Roscommon, Holy Faith convents in Dublin, and Sisters of St. Louis communities in County Monaghan all expanded during these crucial decades by creating branch houses in small towns within an easy traveling distance of the parent house.[37] The unique feature of these houses was that, unlike the "daughter" house system in which a new, financially independent convent was founded by the members of an older house, these newer "branch" houses remained financially and administratively dependent on the parent community. The system appears to have been most prevalent in the west of Ireland and was the means by which new convents were begun without having to demand dowries sufficient for the support of the new community.[38] Given the realities of the funding and successful management of convent establishments, women's religious communities could not and did not accept women whom they could not support. Consequently, the new system of growth enabled the orders to take advantage of the new pool of women available for the religious life while they tapped into the considerable resources of the older convents.

The women who were drawn in increasing numbers to the Irish convents joined because they believed that they had useful work to do, both for their own souls and for Irish society as a whole. Furthermore, these women believed that theirs was an exceptional undertaking likely to have a significant impact. In the words of one eighteenth-century Presentation leader, "It is perhaps once in an age or more rarely that [God] is pleased to bless the world with the extraordinary edifying example of a Nano Nagle or a Teresa Mullaly in order to rouse our sex to a zeal."[39]

Roused to zeal, the foundresses of the women's orders were among the first to respond to both the threat of Protestant proselytism and the challenge posed by the rapidly growing number of Catholic poor. Catherine McAuley, for example, who opened her first school in Dublin in 1827, did so to provide an alternative to the proselytizing schools in the Baggot Street neighborhood that were attracting Catholic children. According to the institute's records, "stray Roman Catholic waifs" were "rescued" from the streets and taught "mainly religion" as a means of defending the Catholic community.[40] These women also attempted to increase the competence and self-respect of the Catholic community by modeling the behavior of that community on the conduct of the Protestant elite. When the Presentation convent in the north parish of the city of Cork opened an infant school early in the nineteenth century, the community remarked that it was a venture designed to counteract the effects of a similar Protestant undertaking. But the sisters defended the new innovation not only because it would be responsible for "saving the faith of many of our little ones" but also because it would "creat[e] a spirit of emulation amongst the Catholics."[41]

The goals of the women who were responsible for the spread of the orders are perhaps best illustrated by Nano Nagle, whose thoughts on the purpose of her work were particularly well documented by her order. When she returned to Ireland during the 1740s from a boarding school in France, Nagle was reportedly shocked by the great poverty and ignorance of the Catholic population she saw. According to an early chronicler of the order, "she was absolutely terrified at their wickedness. . . . Oaths, imprecations, resentment, envy, and dishonesty were so habitual amongst them."[42] Nagle quickly developed the opinion that the source of the "vices" she witnessed in them was their ignorance of religion. Given that church institutions capable of tackling these problems were virtually nonexistent, "she conceived the most earnest desire of striking at the root of all their evils by providing them with the proper means of instruction."[43] As the Presentation annalist remarked,

> she saw the pulpits deserted and the voices silent which should have thundered aloud with all their energy. . . . She was shocked to see the work of God thus chained down by injustice and the little ones crying out for bread. . . . With such incentives, nothing could deter her.[44]

Nagle set up her first school in Cork city during the 1750s,[45] and there, according to her chronicler, she "assembled thirty wicked children."[46] Within several months, two hundred of those "wicked" children were flocking daily to this novel and clandestine Catholic school. Although many of her prominent Catholic friends, afraid of detection by the authorities, accused her of "misguided zeal" and "inconsiderate piety," she carried on her work with little or no community support until 1757, when one of her schools was detected by the Protestant authorities. The discovery proved to be a test case for Cork Catholics of the Ascendancy's will to enforce the penal laws. When her brother learned that she was operating a Catholic school, Nagle recounted, "he fell into a violent passion and said a vast deal on the bad consequences which may follow. His wife is very zealous and so is he, but interest blinded him at first."[47] What Nagle's family and Catholic associates feared was "the persecution which [her defiance of the penal laws] might bring upon the family and even upon religion itself." Nagle chose to defy the law and risk the consequences. "Far from being deterred by such obstacles to the work of God, [she] rather extended than confined the range of her exertions."[48] The authorities, as it turned out, did not prosecute Nagle for operating her Catholic schools; consequently, her family and other influential Catholics in Cork city soon began to support her work.[49]

Nagle continued to operate as many as seven schools in Cork with the help of paid teachers until 1769, when, after a period of "heavenly communication," and supported by a generous settlement from her uncle's estate that allowed her to enlarge her vision, she "conceived the noble idea of perpetuating the good work she had begun."[50] She decided to secure a religious order from France to staff her schools and tend to the sick poor, and in 1771 the Ursuline foundation was made.

Nagle and other women like her viewed forming religious orders to carry on the work of their charitable organizations as a sure means of making their social work more effective and of achieving greater permanence than otherwise would have been possible. The significance of this motivating factor was expressed quite nicely when Mother Mary Francis Tobin wrote to the foundress of the Presentation community in George's Hill, Dublin: "You wished to have a religious establishment as the only means of rendering your schools permanent, and you now enjoy it."[51]

There is no question that the many women who followed the foundresses into the convent in the early years, though they expressed less exalted motives for doing so, believed that they had important charitable work to do. In fact, the chance to do significant, valuable labor was perhaps the single most frequently stated reason why women wanted to become nuns. A letter from one young woman seeking information about the Sisters of Charity is representative of many such letters of inquiry sent to Irish convents in the nineteenth century. This woman, a friend of Archbishop Murray, who was acting on her behalf, was said to be "very anxious to enter a religious state that would afford her active occupation."[52] The three women who founded the Presentation convent at Dungarvan in 1809 had reportedly been "desiring for a long time to devote themselves to the service of God and the good of their neighbor" by forming a permanent institution which would allow them "to spend their time instructing the poor."[53] As we have already seen, Angelina Gould, whose relatives were reportedly "remarkable for their zeal to promote the interest of religion and . . . the poor,"[54] was a generous supporter of Catholic charities while she was living in Lisbon. When she assumed control of her inheritance, not only did she join an order that would keep her involved with the poor but also she chose to use her enormous wealth especially for the purpose of "propagating and extending" those women's orders that ministered to the impoverished.[55] These women, then, as members of the articulate and influential Irish middle class, created a new role for themselves by taking an interest in the condition of the Irish Catholic masses. But in creating this new social role, they were also reformulating the social hierarchies of Irish society, for their institutions and their work became a crucial part of the identity of the wealthier Catholic classes, a segment of the population that would grow ever more influential in Irish social, cultural, and political developments as the century progressed.

Women Religious and Nineteenth-Century Class Formation

When discussing the philanthropic work of these women, scholars commonly emphasize motives of compassion, empathy, and concern for the poor. Certainly, women religious were genuinely concerned to alleviate the misery experienced by the impoverished members of their society, but that concern was not simply altruistic. Middle-class women's work with the Catholic poor was also part of the formation of a new class-based Catholic social system in which certain groups of Catholics would eventually form a new ruling elite. As the Catholic community became increasingly more significant in the political and cultural life of Ireland during the nineteenth century, the hegemony of the Protestant Ascendancy gradually weakened. Readying itself to take the place of the old Protestant ruling class was the Catholic elite. Part of the process of defining itself as an elite was the business of creating and maintaining a well-defined and well-ordered modern class system within the Catholic community. That women religious were conscious of this process is made clear in an explanation of the function of her Dublin schools written by Catherine McAuley in the early 1800s:

> In these schools five hundred poor girls may daily experience the blessing of religious instruction, and being practised in various branches of industry, come forward, shielded from all the ills incident to ignorance and idleness, prepared as Christians to discharge *the duties of the humble state in life to which it has pleased God to call them.*[56]

In their work with the poor, these women were consciously shaping and reinforcing class divisions.

That the new women's orders were intimately involved in reinforcing class divisions was apparent not only in their attitudes toward the lower classes to whom these women ministered but also in their attitudes toward those women who wanted to join convents but who were not members of the more privileged Catholic classes. Although Irish convents were primarily the stronghold of the middle class, they also attracted women of the lower classes. Typically from farming or poor urban backgrounds, these women were allowed to enter but as "lay" sisters who took nonbinding vows as opposed to the "choir" sisters who took solemn, life-long religious vows. Such women typically comprised from 10 to 20 percent of the total number in a community, and they took responsibility for the domestic duties of the convent (i.e., cooking and cleaning for the rest of the sisters).[57] Along with the elevated status that religious vows brought to these women in society at large came the understanding that they would hold an inferior status within the community. While this class distinction (not finally eliminated until the church reforms of the 1960s) has now become an awkward and embarrassing memory for many orders as well as a regrettable, if not reprehensible, feature of women's religious life in the eyes of some scholars,[58] the system nonetheless provided opportunities of a sort for poorer women. As employment options contracted throughout the century, especially in cottage and textile industries, women who needed work moved increasingly to the only positions left available to them—those of service. Among these service positions, practically speaking, were situations as lay or domestic sisters in convents.

Although the religious orders themselves did not classify lay sisters as servants,[59] many lay sisters themselves considered theirs to be a servant's life. This was made evident by the common problem faced by religious orders of former lay sisters suing convents for unpaid wages. One notorious case was that of Miss Gaynor, formerly Archbishop Murray's housekeeper, who left a Mercy convent in America and proceeded to sue the convent for her wages.[60] Although this particular case occurred in an Irish convent on the other side of the Atlantic, it was a thorny problem in Ireland as well. The Mercy convents in the diocese of Elphin experienced enough trouble with former lay sisters demanding back wages to devise a contract that all women joining the order in that capacity had to sign. In the agreement, these women declared that they understood that they had "been admitted into this congregation of the Sisters of Mercy for the purpose of performing domestic duties, such as servants perform in secular houses," and they promised "to make no claim whatever for my labour or services in the congregation should it unfortunately happen to me to leave it by my own free will or on the demand of my superiors."[61]

But the fact that poor women understood this to be domestic service does not mean that they saw lay sisterhood in a religious order as a disagreeable option. As much as we may disapprove of the class-based hierarchy in convents of the time, it appears that acceptance into a convent as a lay sister was still seen as desirable by some women without sufficient means or class status to enter as a choir nun. One woman who lived on a farm in County Cork with her brother made repeated trips to the Sisters of Charity convent in Cork city, begging admittance to that community as a lay sister. So anxious was she to get off the farm that she told the convent superiors that "she would be content to wait for months provided she had any hope."[62] Furthermore, joining the lay sisterhood may have offered laboring women a chance at advancement into supervisory roles that would not have been open to them in secular service. Usually, women were admitted as lay sisters only after working for a number of years as servants in the convent.[63] Once she proved herself reliable and trustworthy, a woman applied to become a lay religious; with this advancement went less labor and more time for solitude and prayer, not to mention the responsibility of directing the convent's servants. Ellen Daly, a lay sister in several convents in Cork city in the years before the famine, regularly supervised servants in her role as a lay sister. When she came to the Sisters of Charity convent, however, her mother was very disappointed to learn that she would not have that right there. According to the congregation's records, her mother even came to the convent to complain about it. Other convents, Mrs. Daly protested, "did not ask lay sisters to work so hard. Would [they] have no servant to be under Ellen? She always had a servant under her."[64]

One should not exaggerate lay sisterhood as a chance for advancement because the benefits were certainly ambiguous. For women who accepted or acquiesced in their inferior status vis-à-vis the choir nuns of the community, being a lay sister may very well have been better than most could have hoped to have done with their lives. But for many, the experience of oppression within convent life was traumatizing; acceptance or acquiescence became impossible. The records of the Sisters of Charity provide telling examples of two such women. In 1844, two of the order's convents were the recipients of visits from a former lay sister who had lost "her reason." Believing herself to be the Queen of England, she began to regularly monitor what was happening in the two communities. According to the convent account, this woman, Sarah Kenny, had been a totally uneducated but very likeable domestic sister who had asked and received permission to be instructed to read and write. But in the annalist's words, "it did not tend to happiness. Her bane was vanity. She became dissatisfied with her subordinate position, which ended in her losing her reason."[65] Eight years later, in 1852, the order recorded the death of another domestic sister, Mary Paschal Kane, of the Stanhope Street convent in Dublin. An orphan, Kane had grown up in the convent's House of Refuge and had been accepted into the community as a lay sister in 1830. The rest of the story reads much like that of Sarah Kenny:

Unfortunately for her, she shortly after heard that a sister of hers had entered a Visitation convent in America as a choir nun. This made an entire revolution in all her ideas. She no longer valued her holy vocation. She felt degraded by being a domestic sister—she could not be happy if she were not raised to the first class. In short, she lost her reason.[66]

The records do not describe the struggles in which Kenny and Kane must have been involved between the first realization that they might accomplish more with their lives and the discovery that they were locked into an inferior position within the convent based on their unchangeable class background. But whatever caused them to lose their sanity, if indeed they did, a hard-and-fast rule of convent life in Ireland was illustrated by their lives—that sisters of the second degree (lay sisters) could not and did not become sisters of the first degree. Any woman who aspired to such a thing was open to the charge of being "crazy." The barrier was impenetrable; social mobility was not a feature of convent life in nineteenth-century Ireland. In fact, the opposite was the case. A hierarchy based on class was constructed and maintained in the great majority of Irish convents. Any woman who hoped to move across class boundaries was clearly dashing her head against the proverbial brick wall. Convent life as a new and highly respectable option was only for women of the right class or the right attitude. Laboring women of poor urban or rural backgrounds were accepted only so long as they did not attempt to undermine the system. The conventual movement, though it provided personal options for many women, was intimately involved in the dynamic of nineteenth-century Catholic class formation. Consequently, women's religious life mirrored and reinforced the rigid, class-based social structure of the wider society. All Catholic women had the choice of joining, but the underlying purpose of religious life at this time was its social and political mission aimed at transforming Irish culture. The idea was to provide poor, ill-educated, and irreligious women (according to middle-class standards) with the education and religion they lacked; it was not intended that these women should aspire to become ladies (or choir sisters) regardless of their virtue or holiness.[67]

Though this book is concerned primarily with evaluating the material basis for women's religious life and its impact on Irish society and culture, it must be emphasized that women did not long remain in religion without a sense of spiritual purpose. The ultimate justification of the new congregations, regardless of their dedication to charitable work, remained the attainment of eternal salvation for their members. One of the early leaders of the Presentation Order reminded the lay foundress of the George's Hill community, a Dublin philanthropist, of the centrality of spiritual purpose in a letter written in 1795. "My dear friend," she declared, "you could never have proposed to yourself to get religious who would be content to devote themselves entirely to the instruction of others and neglect their own perfection."[68] Catherine McAuley expressed the primacy of spiritual salvation in the following way: "To devote our lives to the accomplishment of our own salvation and to promote the salvation of others is the end and object of our Order of Mercy."[69] The belief that she had a "supernatural" vocation, then, was an essential feature of the woman who entered a religious order throughout the century. In the modern active orders, laboring on behalf of the poor not only became the method by which women religious participated in the creation of a "modern" Irish Catholic identity but also became the most favored method of gaining spiritual perfection. Although it was important to these women that they work to alleviate the misery of the impoverished, their labor was ideally meant to be a means to an end and not the end in itself.

In sum, the rapid expansion of Roman Catholic convents during the nineteenth century and the swift increase in the number of women who joined them owed much to the emergence of a wealthy, commercially based Catholic middle class in Ireland. If the growth of the conventual establishment was a correlate of any social phenomenon, it was the rise to prominence of a Catholic elite. In the process of expanding its social and political influence, that elite increased its attention to the growing number of destitute Catholics in both the towns and the countryside. The formation of religious congregations provided the women of this class with a vehicle for extending their influence. Furthermore, religious orders provided a socially accepted structure within which they were able to institutionalize their achievements. Although much emphasis has been placed on the feelings of compassion and altruism that motivated the socially active women's orders, an uncritical acceptance of these motives begs the important question of the larger meaning of their work in Irish society. I have begun to argue in this chapter that the philanthropy of the Catholic women's orders was more than simple altruism. Rather, these orders were part of the drive of the emerging middle class both to define itself and to reshape the Irish world in its own image. One way in which this was accomplished was through the philanthropic work of Catholic middle-class nuns. Consequently, membership in these orders proved to be the most culturally privileged position women could hold in nineteenth-century Ireland.

FOUR

Intimate Boundaries

MOTHER MAGDALEN GOULD died in 1869 in the Youghal Presentation convent, which she had founded with her inheritance earlier in the century and where she had been a revered figure for many years. Under her leadership the convent had become particularly successful through its ability to offer a stable, peaceful, and fulfilling life for the women who entered there.[1] In death, she was mourned by many, but no one felt the loss more keenly than did her community:

> Sorrowfully do we record today the lamented death of our beloved, revered, and saintly Mother Angelina Gould, called in religion Mary Magdalen, which took place in this convent on 5 March 1869. . . . However much may be said in praise of the virtues and character of our loved departed Mother, it could scarcely do justice to her memory in the eyes of those whose privilege and happiness it was to live with her. . . . We would gladly pay her here, if we were able, the tribute she deserves, for there are some amongst us . . . who account it the greatest privilege of their lives to have known and conversed with her.[2]

This obituary, like Gould's life, is remarkable in several ways. Its main aim was not to laud the great deeds accomplished by this founding mother, a common feature of such obituaries, but rather to express the loss the community felt on her death. Perhaps even more significantly, it was a clear statement that for many women in the Youghal convent one of the most meaningful aspects of their lives was having lived with this woman.

This is in clear contrast to popular ideas of convent life. Women were said to "quit the world" when they took religious vows, breaking off ties with home, family, and friends. Convents were commonly believed to be places where women lived solitary lives of prayer, mediated by brief periods of recreation in walled gardens, and where they worked in relative isolation, both from one another and from other communities of women religious.[3] These notions of

convent life were far from accurate, however. One prominent Presentation superior, Mother de Pazzi Leahy, stated this quite clearly: "A maxim of the world
is that persons enter a monastery without knowing each other, that they live
there without loving each other, that they die there without regretting each other.
Thanks be to God," she insisted, "there is no truth in it."[4]

The impact of Gould's life on her community serves to illustrate the central
point of this chapter: the lived experience of women religious was far richer than
a reading of the constitutions and rule books would suggest. Moreover, although
there existed a centuries-long legacy of constraints imposed by the institutional
church, that lived experience was defined and shaped, to the greatest extent
possible, by individual convent mothers in the interests of themselves and their
spiritual daughters. Financially secure and autonomous communities, such as
Gould's, with competent, well-loved, and well-respected women within the
community and in leadership positions, were able to create a meaningful and much-
sought-after community life for increasing numbers of women in nineteenth-
century Ireland. While not all convents achieved the degree of harmony that
Gould's did, the successful convent mother attempted to maximize not only the
spiritual life, but also the personal, intimate life of their communities. Regular
communal life, when successful, offered a style of living found highly desirable
by many Irish women in the nineteenth century.

Spiritual Mothers and Daughters

The primary religious and cultural justification for the great numbers of women
joining active orders throughout Europe at this time was the achievement of
personal salvation. This meant that a primary goal of religious communities was
to provide a meaningful spiritual experience for its members. With this goal in
mind, religious orders for women had developed a system of regular access to
clerical advisors such as chaplains, who provided daily masses in the convent
chapel, and confessors, who heard the sisters' confessions and gave them spiritual advice and direction.

Important as priestly ministration was, however, over the centuries convent
mothers had become spiritual directors themselves, overseeing the community's
daily regimen of spiritual exercises and rituals and, generally, taking great responsibility for the spiritual lives of their members. From the time that women entered
the convent, they were engaged in a sort of spiritual tutoring by the mothers of
the community, especially the mother superior and the mistress of novices. On
entrance, a woman gave to the superior an account of her life, including any "inclinations" or "weaknesses" that the superiors should know about so that they could
help the woman in her striving for perfection. This was a woman's first experience with a practice known as the "examination of conscience" or "manifestation
of the interior." Throughout the two-year-long training period in the noviceship,
women were encouraged to "approach their mistress [of novices] to make their
manifestations with uprightness and simplicity and perfect confidence."[5] The
manifestation was meant to keep convent leaders apprised of the feelings, doubts,
and transgressions of each member of the community. It also functioned to rein-

force the mother superior's spiritual authority. Once professed, women repeated these manifestations, or examens, to the mother superior at regular intervals throughout their entire religious lives, "so that with maternal care and solicitude, the superior may be the better able to remove her from danger." The custom of the examination of conscience encouraged an intimate spiritual relationship between convent superiors and the women in their care. It was a relationship in which some women exercised considerable spiritual authority over others. In doing so, these women assumed the very powerful role of religious mediator.[6]

Mother superiors grounded their authority as mediators in religious holiness. Mother Magdalen de Pazzi Leahy, who was responsible for codifying the customs, practices, and principles of the Presentation Order during the early 1840s, believed that convent mothers were analogous to the "great apostle" Peter, who was responsible for the spiritual nurturance of his disciples. Like the Presentation mothers, he saw himself as "a nurse who caresses her children and who nourishes them with her milk because they are not as yet capable of digesting more solid food."[7] She also suggested that, like Peter, convent mothers were selected by God to direct the sisters in their care. Leahy directed that novices "shall pay great respect to their mistress and in all things shall obey her with perfect submission, she being the person whom God has given them as a guide in the way of virtue."[8]

Probably the most striking claim made by convent mothers in justifying their right to mediate the spiritual lives of the women in their communities was their identification with Christ himself. In the obituary of one of the leading mothers of the Presentation convent in George's Hill, Dublin, Sister Mary Paul Higgins was eulogized for her successful inculcation of the spiritual preeminence of the convent mothers. The George's Hill annalist wrote of Higgins that "as mistress of novices, she stressed to novices the need to rely implicitly on convent superiors, viewing Christ in their person."[9] Obituaries were a particularly forceful way of imbuing convent mothers with religious authority, for they functioned as the means not only of acknowledging the special qualities of the deceased but also of reinforcing the values of the community by choosing those qualities that were to be stressed. In this respect, Higgins's obituary was a strong proclamation that the Presentation Order viewed its superiors as the equivalents of Christ on earth.

This conviction existed in orders other than the Presentation, although it was not accepted by the Mercy sisters. Catherine McAuley, who was a novice under Higgins before she began the Mercy Order, felt that this ideology created relationships within the convent that were too hierarchical, which was, indeed, the net result. It is highly significant, however, that the one order on record as objecting to such claims objected to them because of their effects on community life and not because the claim was radical in itself. Asserting that convent superiors were the equivalent of Christ on earth was tantamount to proclaiming women to be members of the priestly class. This fact was not lost on male church leaders. By the late nineteenth century, the right of convent superiors to act as spiritual directors was proscribed by the papacy specifically because these women came too close to performing rituals reserved to priests. The examination of conscience, for example, was banned outright in 1894, when it was declared a female usurpation of the priest's role in the confessional.[10]

The notion of convent mothers as spiritual advisors was a concept embedded in the basic organizational and disciplinary principles of communal life for women. Convents were governed by a well-defined hierarchy of "spiritual mothers" who led and "spiritual daughters" who followed and obeyed. The concepts of "mother" and "daughter" were representations of those with authority and influence in the convent and those without. That respect and obedience were owed to convent mothers was a fundamental principle of convent life, vigorously inculcated from the moment a woman entered. Mother Leahy in Cork was particularly emphatic in her use of the mother-daughter metaphor as a characterization of ideal authority structures. About the "respect, the submission, the holy tenderness which a novice owes her who is immediately charged with her direction" Mother Leahy had much to say:

> She is your mistress, she is your mother, and what is more, she is a mother whose tenderness might be disputed with her who has given you birth. . . . I content myself with saying that if you owe much to one because she has given you life, you do owe, and you will for ever owe, much more to the other, because it is to her, after God, that you are indebted for all your happiness.[11]

Relationships between spiritual mothers and spiritual daughters, then, were firmly grounded in the complementary concepts of motherly authority and filial obligation. This basis of monastic organization and discipline was very old; spiritual parenting that presupposed the obligation of spiritual direction was a fundamental principle of the early monastic founders.[12]

Ideally, religious women were also united by bonds of motherly devotion to convent leaders. Besides learning to respect and obey their convent mothers, women were encouraged to love them as well. Guidebooks like those Mother Leahy wrote stressed this ideal repeatedly. Convent obituaries, those great teaching tools, routinely celebrated women who had been devoted to their superiors. When a woman showed "veneration for her superiors" or when "her love for her superiors was very great," later members of the community learned about it.[13]

Although in many cases the love and devotion resulting from this sort of inculcation was artificial, mechanical, and not deeply felt, the point here is to demonstrate what made convents attractive places for women to live out their lives. Though there were often mediocre and uninspiring women in positions of leadership, there were also many other women, like Angelina Gould, who truly inspired love and devotion among the members of their communities. Charismatic women like Gould possessed certain qualities that made it inevitable that they would be chosen to lead their communities. Often, they remained in positions of authority for their entire lives. Reverend Mother Carroll, who was in and out of the superiorship at the Presentation convent in George's Hill, Dublin, for almost thirty years, was loved by the sisters there for her care of the community. She was respected for her "marvellous capacity for dispatching business, strong intellect, [and] clear and solid judgment." She also earned their affection because "she did not believe [that] God required rigid fasts, long prayers, or extraordinary things" of the sisters. Rather, she believed that "only common community life," in which strong and healthy members devoted themselves to a common goal, was required of the sisters.[14] Mother Mary Tobin, one of the Presentation Order's most beloved superiors, was said to have shown "prudence and wisdom and all the rare qualities necessary for those who govern well."[15] She worked hard to instill this ideal in other mothers of the congregation as well.[16]

Convents with charismatic leaders tended to thrive because they became dynamic places for women to spend their lives. One such leader was Mother Genevieve Beale, founding mother of the St. Louis sisters in Monaghan town, who in her twenty years of superiorship helped the community to grow from just four sisters at its establishment to forty-nine by the time of her death in 1878. The energy and enthusiasm this woman brought to her community is evident in a letter she addressed to the congregation in 1874. A stirring, spiritual pep talk on the occasion of an upcoming retreat, it bid the sisters to

> pray hard that the spirit of God may direct all concerned, that each may return to the old work or take up the burden of the new one with fresh spiritual rigour and earnestness. . . . Dieu le veut! [God wills it!] A fitting device in every religious, old or young, grave or gay, senior or junior. Dieu le veut! In the petty crosses of everyday life, as in the heavier ones, which are the portion of some souls, Dieu le veut! In the schools, in the kitchen, in the laundry, in authority or in lowliness, in health or in sickness, at Monaghan, Bundoran, or in a far off land, let our rallying cry be ever and always "Dieu le veut!"[17]

Perhaps the most-loved convent head in Ireland during the nineteenth century was Mother Catherine Walsh of the Irish Sisters of Charity. From the earliest days of the founding of that order, she was known as "a universal favorite."[18] Women in Sisters of Charity convents throughout the country never ended a letter to each other without speaking of her or sending their love to her. Sisters who left the order never forgot her, and several went on loving her for decades afterward.[19] Women who were dismissed often left without seeing her because they did not want to face her. It was said that her mind was full of literature and "works of genius," which made her the "great charm" of the community's social interaction. One sister, in an attempt to communicate the love her community felt for her, observed: "When the sisters returned from the mission wet and weary, she would meet them with the greatest concern, one time relieving them of their wet cloaks and shoes and taking them to dry, at another time taking their turn to read at dinner." If she thought that a sister was not eating enough to sustain her labor, she would send up food to her "with an order to eat it."[20] This woman, one of the founding mothers of the Sisters of Charity, managed to combine authority and nurturing in such a way as to render her one of the best-loved and most successful Irish superiors of the nineteenth century.

At the very heart of religious communities during the eighteenth and nineteenth centuries, then, was a relationship between women which was modeled on that of mother and daughter. Daughters in religion relied on their spiritual mothers for daily spiritual sustenance, direction, and protection. The source of female authority within the convent was rooted in this parenting role that was a

long-standing traditional source of authority for monastic leaders. The practice
of spiritual mothering was both accepted and guarded by women religious.
Furthermore, it was the primary means these women employed to ensure the
smooth functioning of the community from within and to protect it from as-
saults from without.

Friends and Family

Religious women also experienced a distinct, nonspiritual, personal life that has
not as yet been fully appreciated. It has been suggested by other writers that Irish
women religious, controlled and dominated by episcopal authority in all aspects
of their existence, led relatively isolated and restricted lives in religion.[21] While
serious constraints (which are discussed later) did, indeed, exist, lived experience was substantially more complicated than this theory implies. An understanding of convent experience requires that we take notice of the ways in which
women attempted to challenge and expand the boundaries that surrounded and
limited their lives. A closer look at the world of the convent shows that women
religious enjoyed a multifaceted intimate life. Moreover, this life often existed
in contradiction to the ideology of religious life.

According to the ideology of female monastic establishments, women who
took religious vows were obliged to disconnect themselves physically and emotionally from family and friends, as well as from each other, to devote themselves to a life of the spirit. Rule 8 of the Sisters of Charity, commonly designated by the community as the "Holy Eighth," is a good example of this ideal:

> Each one who enters into this congregation, following the counsel of our Lord
> Jesus Christ, "He who shall have left father, house, or lands for my sake, shall
> receive a hundred fold, and possess life everlasting!" (Matt. xix, 29), must reflect
> that she is truly to leave father, mother, brothers, sisters, and whatever she
> possessed in the world. She must even consider that sentence addressed to
> herself: "Whoever hateth not father, mother, etc., and even his own soul,
> cannot be my disciple" (Luke, xiv, 26). She must therefore carefully divest
> herself of all carnal affection for her kindred and change it into that which is
> spiritual: loving them with that affection only which well-ordered charity
> requires; that being dead to the spirit of the world and to self-love, she may
> live to Jesus Christ our Lord, whom she has chosen in place of parents, rela-
> tions, and all other things.[22]

Although this rule particularly addresses attachment to relatives, it was meant
to discourage any personal attachment that drew a sister's attention away from
her devotion to God. The Sisters of Charity reiterated the ideology of detachment in a more general way: "Let them [the sisters] endeavour to seek God in
all things, divesting themselves as much as possible of the inordinate love of crea-
tures."[23] Very simply stated, close relationships with other individuals were seen
as hindering a woman's relationship with Christ and her community. According to the ideology, close relationships ought to have been discouraged.

In fact, close friendships and loving relationships existed between members
of religious communities and friends and family both within and outside con-

vent walls. Furthermore, a certain degree of attachment was accepted and even encouraged as natural and beneficial to religious life. In practice, then, the convent's task was to negotiate the boundary between the ideology of the rule books and the demands of its members. The result was a set of informal rules governing acceptable intimate relationships, which were defined by convent leaders and made clear to the members of the community through their spiritual direction. Convents thus accepted a great deal more personal affection and attachment than a reading of the official rules might lead one to believe.

According to those rules, once women joined convents, they ended their involvement with friends and families. The question that needs to be asked is whether practice was faithful to prescription. Did reverend mothers, in fact, actively discourage women in the community from maintaining contact with friends and family, and did women themselves then break off ties with home? The answer is no. Practice was not faithful to prescription.

To begin with, when they joined convents, women were often accompanied by their siblings. In the early years of the conventual movement, two, three, and even four sisters frequently joined convents together and not always with their parents' blessing.[24] In the Ursuline community in Cork, of the 56 women who joined the convent during its first 50 years (1767–1817), 20 (36 percent) had siblings in the convent. In addition, there were several sets of cousins and also aunts and nieces.[25] The result was a community in which more than 50 percent of the women were related to at least one other woman in the convent.[26] During the first 50 years of the Presentation convent in Cork (1775–1825), 44 women entered, and 13 of them (30 percent) were siblings. Again, there were aunts, nieces, and cousins residing together as well.[27] At the Presentation convent at George's Hill, founded in 1791, 27 women were professed in the first 50 years. Of those, 6 (22 percent) were siblings.[28] And at the first Mercy convent, begun a little later in 1827, 88 women entered during the 20 years before the famine, of whom 19 (22 percent) were siblings.[29]

Later, as convents became established in an area, a feeder system developed between convent school and cloister, which meant that novices were likely to know one another from school or know other women already in the community when they entered.[30] Consequently, the number of siblings who entered a community together declined somewhat over time, although it never ended completely. During the second 50-year period (1817–1867) of the Ursuline community in Cork city, for example, the number of siblings entering fell from 36 to 15 percent.[31] Siblings entering the South Presentation convent also fell to 15 percent of the total number of entrants during that community's second 50 years (1825–1875).[32] In Dublin, the situation was similar. Between 1841 and 1891, no siblings were professed at the Presentation convent at George's Hill,[33] while 16 percent of the 129 women who entered the Mercy convent in Baggot Street during the years 1847–1877 (completing its first 50 years) were siblings.[34]

Not only is it clear that siblings regularly entered religious houses together but also it is evident that siblings and friends influenced one another in the decision to undertake religious life itself. Teresa O'Brien, one of the first Brigidine sisters, exerted considerable pressure on one of her siblings to join the struggling order. On her deathbed in 1808, she asked her mother to allow her sister Mary to enter the young community, and "her sister, though without an idea of doing so before her sister's request, entered the convent a few months after and piously persevered."[35] The influence of friends and family was also clear in the decision of the Presentation mother, Mary Columba Brophy, grandniece of Cardinal Cullen, to become a nun. Brophy, it was stated, came from "a family of nuns; consequently, her desire for the religious life was no surprise."[36] Finally, in a description of her early convent life, St. Louis Sister Mary Stanislaus Kehoe credited a friend's example for her decision to become a religious: "What made me think of it was a young friend who was a couple of years older than myself entered [*sic*] the French Sisters of Charity in William Street. Before this I had never thought of the future, but now I said, this is what I would like."[37]

Much evidence also exists to suggest that detachment from friends and family who did not join the convent was not achieved either, and it was not praised by the women themselves as a particular virtue when it did occur. In fact, the opposite was the case; women were often praised specifically for their continued devotion and attachment to their families and friends. Obituaries regularly acknowledged with admiration the woman who was "devotedly" or "deeply attached to her family."[38] While on her deathbed, one sister who was noted for being very "fond of her family . . . particularly of her younger sister Helen," was said to have told Helen (who was herself a nun in the same order) "to keep an eye to them at home."[39] One of the best-loved nuns in nineteenth-century Ireland, Mother Catherine Walsh of the Sisters of Charity, earned a special mention for family devotion on the occasion of her death. A native of County Wicklow, Walsh was reportedly "an enthusiastic patriot" whose family had been arrested and imprisoned during the rebellion of 1798. The events of that year dispersed the family and its property, but Walsh attempted for the rest of her life to hold together what was left, earning her a rebuke from Archbishop Murray for "excessive attachment."[40] Her community, however, in sympathy with Walsh's pain, both honored her with the retelling of this story and acknowledged the importance of family relationships in the lives of the sisters.[41]

Upon entering a convent, women corresponded regularly with family and friends. Although there were holy times of the year when they were discouraged from writing, and though in some convents women were not allowed to write to someone more than once a month, letter writing remained a vital means of staying in touch with the world. Unfortunately, most of this evidence, once in the possession of religious orders, has not been preserved except in the cases of the founding mothers and the few reverend mothers who did not have their personal letters burned when they died. Collections of family papers containing letters from daughters in convents are rare as well, probably because, with the exception of landlord papers, family documents have not been systematically collected, deposited, or catalogued in Ireland.

One family collection does exist, nonetheless, which contains hundreds of letters from two religious daughters and one niece of the nineteenth-century historian John D'Alton.[42] Eliza D'Alton, a novice in the Presentation convent at Clane and later a professed nun in the Dominican convent at Drogheda, maintained a regular and voluminous correspondence with both of her parents while they lived. In this way, she was kept informed of all family events and problems, and she forwarded her opinions on the manner of their solution. She remained involved in the measures her parents and her brother took to improve their health, she commiserated in the financial embarrassment of her uncle's family and approved of measures taken by them to solve the difficulty, she introduced her family to priests with whom she wished them to become better acquainted, she asked her family's help in securing positions in service for former convent pupils, and she passed along recommendations on convents and convent schools suitable for joining and attending. In addition, she kept her family informed of her life in the convent, her health, and the health of a family friend who was also in the Clane convent. She assured them that she was happy, enjoying her favorite pastimes of singing and drawing.[43]

The D'Alton correspondence also shows that Eliza expected regular visits from her family. Her mother visited her often, bringing personal gifts of linen and other cloth to be used as garments, as well as gifts for the community, such as a modern bathing machine which she called a "shower bath."[44] Visitors often came in the summer, and among them Eliza expected to see not only her parents but also her brother and sisters and her best friend.[45] Although the visits were most frequent in the first few years she spent in the convent, her father continued to visit her regularly, though not frequently enough for Eliza, until his death in 1865.

Family visits to the convent were a regular feature of the life of all orders at this time. Visits were made for pleasure, for business, and to see sick or dying relatives. At the Presentation convent in George's Hill, visiting friends and family members came at all hours on any day of the week. One frequent visitor to the convent during the 1840s and 1850s was William Walsh, later archbishop of Dublin. Walsh's mother was a sister of Reverend Mother M. Ignatius Taylor, and as a child, he and his mother called on the community regularly. The annalist affectionately remembered Walsh playing "tig" around the back parlor table with the sisters while his mother visited with her reverend sister.[46]

By midcentury, the Dublin hierarchy attempted to restrict the hours during which visitors could be received, but these attempts met with resistance. Although the sisters technically accepted the restriction of hours, they managed to insert an escape clause. Like taverns which, according to a strict code of hospitality, never closed to those who were traveling or far from home, convents similarly refused to limit the visiting hours of out-of-town guests or those who had "business" with the sisters. It appears as if visiting remained a "problem" in this convent, to judge by the fact that it continued to be a topic of discussion and was criticized by the hierarchy during several subsequent episcopal visitations.[47]

Centralized orders seem to have avoided priestly interference in their visiting customs because the affairs of their individual convents were not subject to the same degree of scrutiny as were decentralized orders like the Presentation sisters. In determining visiting policy, convents with a central motherhouse sought, if necessary, the guidance of their general superior. The St. Louis sisters did not enforce a strict visiting code on their houses at all. One reverend mother from the Ramsgrange convent had to write to the general of the order, Mother Francis Xavier Finnegan, to find out what the visiting customs were at Monaghan, whether they limited the time of visits, and whether a second sister was required to be present. She added that they themselves did not require a second, and because most of their visitors came from so far away, they were allowed to "stay as long as they please."[48]

Finally, although the official justification for limiting contact with family members was that continued attachment hindered a woman's spiritual commitment, a practical reason led communities of women to maintain this principle, to which they did not always seem to adhere, when it suited their needs. An ideal of detachment from family members encouraged loyalty and obedience to convent leaders, fostering within the community the acceptance of the authority of the new mother figure, the mother superior. That both elements were goals of the ideal of detachment, devotion to Christ, and devotion to convent mothers was expressed beautifully by Eliza D'Alton in a letter to her mother just before she was professed in the Dominican convent. Responding to her mother's expression of pain at the thought of no longer having her daughter in her home, Eliza assured her mother that she, too, would feel pain. Yet her sorrow would be compensated by "Him who can be *all* to me. . . . Nor can I ever miss the kindness of a mother whilst I have such as my dear Mother Raymond."[49]

That attachment to family had the potential to compromise the authority of convent mothers was borne out by the prominent St. Louis superior, Mother Finnegan. Believing that the parents of one of the sisters in the Monaghan community were interfering excessively in the life of their daughter, she drafted a letter to them requesting that they cease their interference. In answer to their repeated visits and inquiries about their daughter's health and position in the convent, Finnegan decided to clearly remind them of her authority over their daughter:

> It is not well for parents to trouble themselves concerning the health of the children they have given to religion, their superiors being more solicitous than any relative could be as regards their subjects. Besides, it is injudicious for parents to interfere with religious superiors.[50]

I do not wish to imply that these women experienced the same degree of involvement with their families as they would have, had they not taken religious vows. Indeed, women were separated from family in some rather painful ways. They did not go home for holidays, which seemed to have especially disturbed their parents,[51] and as a rule they did not go home when a loved one was dying. Furthermore, personal contact could be maintained only if family members visited the convent, for women were not free to return home except in unusual circumstances. Continued contact thus depended on how willing family members were to make regular visits to the convent. Letitia More-O'Ferrall, whose family vehemently objected to her joining a religious order, weighed this fact very carefully before she entered a convent: "I am very certain when I once bid adieu to my family, it will be forever, as they will never favour me with a visit. Being so fully aware of this made me at first endeavour to banish from my mind all idea of becoming a nun."[52] Yet evidence shows that even though contact with friends and relatives decreased, it did in fact continue. Moreover, such contact was vital to the women, and the threat that it might have to end, as in the case of Letitia More-O'Ferrall, could cause women to seriously consider not joining at all. Perhaps the best indication that women were expected to remain involved with friends and family outside the convent is the fact that the rare woman who lived up to the ideal of total detachment was seen as an object of pity. Sister Mary Teresa Paul Higgins, celebrated within the George's Hill Presentation community as an exemplary mistress of novices, was nonetheless thought odd in at least one respect. Her obituary recorded the fact that, unhappily, "her visitors were few."[53]

It is clear, then, that women religious did not become "dead to the world." They continued to remain attached and to maintain regular, if attenuated, contact with their families. Moreover, when family attachments were actively discouraged by the convent leadership, it was often because they lessened devotion to the reverend mothers, not the sister's devotion to Christ. Although they no longer lived in a traditional family setting, they continued to engage in a considerable amount of communication and exchange with the world outside the convent. A popular anecdote that nicely exposes the reality of the relationship between women religious and the world in which they lived goes something like this: "If you really want to know what's going on in a town, go to the convent and the nuns will tell you."

Sisters in Religion

An essential element of the religious life for women was the attraction that convents held for some who desired primarily to live in a community of women. The story of Elizabeth Bodenham, a well-educated writer and member of an upper-class English Catholic family, illustrates this point. Bodenham was thrilled about the reemergence of convents in the English world and decided that she wanted to join the Irish Sisters of Charity, which she did in 1826. In one of her letters to the foundress seeking admittance, Bodenham declared that she intended to renounce all literary pursuits so that she could devote her time "either in attending to the concerns of my own salvation or in serving the poor to the best of my ability."[54]

It was not long, however, before Aikenhead realized that her professed desire to relieve the poor was feigned. One Jesuit friend and advisor of Aikenhead's reported that on a visit to Ireland, which included a stop at the Jesuit seminary at Clongowes, Bodenham had commented to the priests there that she was glad to be leaving Ireland in the dark so that she did not have to look at the country and its people.[55] Aikenhead was also disturbed by this literary woman's desire to improve the congregation's library by boxing up her considerable collection of books and bringing them with her to the convent. The problem was not that she showed "a bit of bluestockingism."[56] Aikenhead was an intelligent and competent woman and, like other religious leaders, tended to welcome those qualities in her members. In fact, when Aikenhead's Jesuit advisor objected to Bodenham because she was a "silly" literary lady who could not even sew, Aikenhead did not welcome the implication that ladies (who were the backbone of the women's orders) were somehow questionable subjects.[57] What Aikenhead worried about was Bodenham's alleged commitment to active social work. As it turned out, she did not particularly like the hard labor undertaken by the sisters and was not interested, as a rising leader in the community, in expanding the range of that work. What did interest her was community life, and to enrich that experience she devoted her energy to the social and intellectual life of her religious sisters. After ten years in the order, however, Aikenhead decided to dismiss her. The foundress believed that Bodenham had overstepped a boundary; in valuing the community life of the sisters to the extent that she did, Bodenham had attempted to redirect the order away from its primary mission of philanthropic work.

The dismissal of Bodenham was a great blow to the Sisters of Charity. She was an attractive and engaging woman, well liked by most who knew her; she was wealthy and brought much of her wealth with her to the convent; and she had influential relatives in high places, including an uncle who was an English cardinal. For the years that she worked on building a rich and meaningful intellectual life for the women in the Stanhope Street community, Bodenham was rewarded with their affection and loyalty. When she left, more than a dozen other women left with her. Among them was Margaret Aylward, who would later found the Sisters of the Holy Faith.[58]

The story of Elizabeth Bodenham illustrates that some women joined convents specifically to live with other women. There were many reasons why women chose to live communal lives together. Some women, for example, joined convents because they had grown up in a religious institution and knew no other life. One early leader of the Sisters of Charity, Mother Lucy Clifford, had been orphaned at the age of eight and sent to the Augustinian convent at Newhall in England, where she lived until she was eighteen. Although she lived for a few years after that outside convent walls, she very quickly decided that she wanted to live her life as a nun. The Sisters of Charity commented that "it did not appear that the world had ever had any attraction for her."[59] Women without families or other connections in the world frequently sought to find community with religious women. In 1848, Anna Maria Leix applied for admittance to the Presentation convent at Richmond, County Dublin. To the reverend mother of that community she wrote: I have very little property, only £200, but I am allowed £12 a year until I am of age. . . . I am an orphan and I have but few friends. I trust, dear Rev. Mother, to your kindness and charity that you will do something for me."[60] Others, often elderly, disabled, or widowed women, sought refuge in convents, especially in the early years. The Presentation convent at George's Hill accepted Mary Aylmer, a member of a prominent Dublin Catholic family, into the community when she was "advanced in age" and considered her a valuable addition to the community.[61] In the 1830s, the Carmelite community at Delgany, County Wicklow, voted to admit a fifty-year-old woman who had been a frequent visitor to the convent and whose "manners" the sisters enjoyed "very well."[62] In 1859 a young disabled woman and member of the Irish Sisters of Charity died and left her considerable inheritance to the order.

Mary Barry had been crippled by a childhood disease and was unable to do any work in the community. According to the order's records, on her deathbed Barry stated that the community should consider her fortune a token of the appreciation she felt for their having taken her in.[63]

While little explicit evidence of marriage avoidance exists, it is also fairly safe to assume that some women joined religious communities to avoid marriage. In valorizing women's community life, women religious frequently expressed disdain for the married state. Eliza D'Alton, who joined the Presentation convent in Clane, County Kildare, in 1851, expressed this disparaging attitude toward marriage in a letter to her family. In response to the news that an old friend of hers had recently married, D'Alton observed, "I was quite shocked at your information regarding Miss Talbot. Perhaps if she had been in Clane convent, she would not have been so soon metamorphosed into a married woman."[64] And when Miss Stewart, reportedly a beautiful and talented woman whom the community loved very much, left the South Presentation convent in 1842, the annalist declared that since Stewart had left, she had married and "has lived a most miserable life."[65]

Widowed women also sought out convent communities in the early years. This fact is reflected in the average age at entrance, which during the first two decades of the nineteenth century ranged from twenty-seven to thirty years— the highest average age during the entire century.[66] Widows were especially heavily represented in the prefamine period. As we have seen in an earlier chapter, those with money used it to found and join convents in considerable numbers, sometimes bringing minor children with them.[67] In the years when convents were struggling to gain a foothold, their financial support was vital. Vital as well was their contribution to community life, for they were seen as great social assets. Armed with rich life experience, these women were entertaining companions and widely welcomed. In 1824, for example, the widowed Mrs. Wilmerding, whose husband had been an officer in the British army and a veteran of the Napoleonic wars, joined the Presentation convent at Maryborough in Queen's County. She rose to leadership in the convent and was a favorite personality in the community, entertaining many women over the years with her war stories, including that of Waterloo, which she had personally witnessed.[68]

By midcentury, after the orders were well established, widows came to be seen as less desirable than they had been earlier. New community members, drawn more and more from the network of convent schools, were younger and less experienced than in the early years of the movement. Again, the overall decline in the average age at entrance indicates this trend. Between 1825 and 1850, the average age at entrance in the large Irish orders declined to 24 to 27 years (from 27 to 30 years between 1800 and 1825), and those average ages fell even lower, from 22 to 24 years, in the two decades after the famine.[69] As the conventual establishment became more regularized, independent and worldly women became somewhat suspect, and their popularity as members of religious communities declined. By midcentury one reverend mother of a well-established convent went on record as being opposed to widows in religious communities for reasons which, just a few decades earlier, had made them very popular:

I have a holy horror of the convent becoming a "widows" house. . . . The knowledge these holy widows have of the world and all that passes and, above all, what did pass long ago, now revived from recollections and circumstances, leaves little room to doubt that a party of widows are not likely to keep alive the religious spirit in a convent or preserve religious harmony.[70]

As in the case of Elizabeth Bodenham, religious mothers had to carefully negotiate the boundary between community life and spiritual or apostolic life. Valuing the quality of a community's social life too much could result in valuing the quality of its religious life too little. Consequently, during the second half of the nineteenth century, widows came to be seen as a threat rather than as an advantage to community life in general.

Once women had entered the convent, they related to one another primarily as sisters in religion. Women were encouraged to form bonds of sisterly love with the other women of the community, and from this custom has come the common form of addressing women religious as "Sister." The cultivation of this relationship was an important means of ensuring the smooth functioning of the community. In her book of advice for new entrants into the order, Mother de Pazzi Leahy explained a woman's ideal relationship to the other women in the community:

Your first duty to them . . . is to love them sincerely. . . . They are your real sisters because they are your sisters in Jesus Christ. You all wear the same livery, you combat under the same standard, you aspire to the same recompense, you all walk by the same way to arrive at it. If on the way you wound each other, it is certain you will retard your march. . . . Besides, what happiness can you feel in living always with persons whom you cannot bear, and who in all probability cannot endure you? It is said, and nothing is more true, that without charity cloisters become a hell, and with charity they become a true paradise.[71]

Leahy stressed what was probably the most important reason for creating a strong bond between women in a convent. Although the community was united in its reason for existence, many different women of many different temperaments and backgrounds were attempting to live together, sometimes for the greater part of their lives. Promoting sisterly feelings was not so much an essential means of fostering love as it was a means of keeping peace in the community. To some extent, religious communities were modeled on the supposed harmony attainable in a family or kin network, and it was hoped that creating bonds of sisterhood would help women to accept and tolerate women whom they might not ordinarily like. Furthermore, it was hoped that developing a strong ideal of sisterly love would serve to create artificial bonds of loyalty and obligation similar to those experienced within kinship networks. "The ties which bind us to each other as sisters" ideally resulted in caring and nurturing feelings among all women in the community.[72] In addition, sisterly affection was also promoted as a kind of nonsexual love. Thus kisses and embraces were made acceptable when motivated by "sisterly" feelings, and statements such as "I give you a sisterly embrace" were ubiquitous in conversation and correspondence between women religious.[73]

Sisterly affection, then, was one of the fundamental relationships cultivated within the convent. It involved no natural feelings of affection or camaraderie. Rather, it was meant to create a powerful principle that would persuade women to overcome aversions toward and conflict with other women. Ideally, the result would be a peaceful, harmonious, and charitable environment in which to live, work, and pray.

Women religious not only were involved in intimate relationships with sisters within their own communities but also established extended networks of contact with other communities. These networks, which were maintained by visiting, by receiving sisters as visitors, and through written correspondence, operated at two different levels. First, they functioned as a source of advice and assistance in the working life of the active orders. Second, and more important for the present discussion, these networks served as the basis of a structured social life that sustained the many women who had chosen to "quit the world."

Women religious seem never to have missed an opportunity to visit one another. Whenever they had to travel from one convent to another for reasons of health or business, they took the opportunity to visit other communities of women. Sisters making new foundations regularly visited other convents in the town or vicinity that they were leaving as well as in the area of the new foundation. In 1818, the South Presentation convent in Cork city sent three sisters to make a foundation in Doneraile. Before they left, they spent a day of visiting and recreation with the Cork Ursuline community.[74] In 1825, before the Ursuline community moved to its new convent in Blackrock, County Cork, the Ursuline and Presentation communities exchanged day-long visits with each other. Because the nuns did not know just when they would have the opportunity to see one another again, these visits were major celebrations in the lives of the women, recorded and remembered for years afterward.[75] When Mary Aikenhead and five Sisters of Charity came to Cork city in 1826 to begin a new convent, one of the first things they did there was to visit the two Presentation convents. These occasions were especially pleasurable for Aikenhead, who was a native of Cork and had many friends and acquaintances in Cork convents.[76] In 1834, the Blackrock Ursuline community attempted a foundation in America. Before they left Ireland, the women pursuing the foundation visited both Presentation convents in Cork city and then stayed with the George's Hill community in Dublin while waiting to sail.[77] In 1841, the Sisters of Charity founded a convent in Waterford town. The Ursuline and Presentation sisters already had convents there and invited the newcomers to visit them when they arrived.[78] One final example is the 1855 visit of several sisters from the Paris convent of the Order of Our Lady of Charity of Refuge with the Presentation sisters in George's Hill. Among these sisters, who were on their way to their new foundation on the north side of Dublin at Drumcondra, was Sister de St. Anne Carroll, a sister of the George's Hill community's reverend mother, Mary Bridget Carroll.[79]

Sisters also commonly exchanged visits for health reasons, either to find "a change of air," to visit sick or dying siblings or aunts in other communities, or to stay in another religious house while visiting a distant town or city seeking medical advice.[80] During the first half of the century, visits to other parts of the country for a "change of air" were a standard remedy for ill health. Kate Doran, who was professed in the South Presentation community for the foundation in George's Hill in 1798, returned several years later to recover her health in the convent where she had been professed and had many close friends.[81] One Presentation sister spent the summer of 1822 at the spa in Mallow, County Cork, for a change of air. Although it is not clear if this sister stayed in a convent in the vicinity, the annalist did note that the woman's family joined her there and that a very pleasant and health-restoring visit resulted.[82] In 1860, Mother Mary Agatha Cullen, a sister of Archbishop Cullen, left her Presentation convent in Kildare to spend several months at the Clondalkin convent for a "change of air." On her way to Clondalkin, she stopped for a visit of several days with the Dublin sisters, where she received visits from her many Dublin friends.[83] Cullen's stay with the George's Hill community was followed by a visit from two Loreto sisters, who had come to see an aunt of one of the sisters, Mother Clare, who was dying. Mother Clare was also visited frequently during this year of her death by another niece, Kate Doyle, a member of the Sisters of St. Vincent de Paul.[84] Later in the century, visits to doctors in distant towns and cities, especially Dublin, rivaled the change-of-air visits in frequency. In 1867, two Presentation sisters from Clonakilty, County Cork, stayed a week with the George's Hill community while one of the sisters sought medical advice in the city. A little later in the year, the mother superior and a companion from the Presentation convent at Cashel spent a month at George's Hill while the former received medical treatment from a Dublin physician. The year's visits were ended with that of Mary de Pazzi from the order's convent at Listowel, who spent one week with the community while being treated by an "occulist" in the city.[85]

Indeed, religious women were on the move continually as their orders spread throughout Ireland and the world during the century. In rapidly expanding orders like the Sisters of Mercy or the Presentation sisters, which were sending out women almost continually to make new foundations, the women regularly moved from one convent to another. In 1855, two Presentation sisters who had been unhappy on the San Francisco mission sailed back to Ireland. Before returning to their own convent in Midleton, County Cork, they stayed at the George's Hill convent, sharing news and stories of California with their Dublin sisters.[86] Shortly after they left, two Ursulines were given extended hospitality by the George's Hill sisters. The Ursulines had come back to Ireland from an overseas mission to spend some time recovering from undisclosed "difficulties" before returning to their posts.[87] In 1867, two more Presentation sisters from the San Francisco convent spent a week at George's Hill before going to visit other convents in the country in search of novices for the California mission.[88]

Perhaps the best illustration of the degree to which women were moving around the country comes from an examination of the work histories of the sisters at the first Mercy convent in Baggot Street. During the first fifteen years of the existence of this congregation, eighty women joined the Baggot Street community. Of that number, fifty-four went on to head or staff new convents of the order as it expanded. Half of these founded two, three, or four other convents, and one woman, the famous Mother Mary Clare Moore, was a founding mother of ten new Mercy convents. The number of women moving to other convents might have been greater still if death had not prevented them from doing so. Fifteen of the eighty women died within the first few years of their religious life at Baggot Street, and many of the women who moved to only one other convent died shortly after that first move.[89]

Women religious visited women in other convents whom they knew or loved. Often, the presence of a particular friend or relative established one convent as part of another's network of "friendly" communities. Women religious also regularly visited the mother houses of their congregation in order to "absorb the spirit" of foundresses like Nano Nagle, Mary Aikenhead, or Catherine McAuley. In addition, houses where foundresses had spent their noviceships became special places for their orders. The George's Hill Presentation convent, where McAuley had done her noviceship, became a regular visiting spot for any Mercy sister going to Dublin on business or leaving the country on a foreign mission.[90] The Ursulines, who continued to maintain a special relationship with the Presentation nuns because of their common foundress, regularly visited houses of that order when they traveled.

The exchange of visits was a treasured practice, and details recorded in convent records show how collective memories of mutual hospitality were developed and have been maintained even to the present day.[91] Examples of this particular facet of the life of religious women abound throughout the entire century. The impression is given that there was never a time when nuns were not on the road to somewhere to enjoy the company of other religious women. This does not mean that religious women traveled around the country as freely or as frequently as middle- or upper-class secular women.[92] Nor did women religious have the freedom to choose when they would visit friends or other communities of women. Rather, the custom of visiting was grafted onto traveling necessitated by nonsocial reasons. Yet the point here is that women religious manipulated their seemingly austere and isolated lives in ways that enhanced and enriched them. If it is true that the exception proves the rule, then the story of the life of Sister Mathias, a member of the Sisters of Charity convent at Donnybrook in Dublin is truly illustrative of both the regularity and the importance of traveling and visiting. On the occasion of her death in 1886, the congregation's annalist had this to say: "Strange to say, she occupied the same cell for 40 years, never having slept out of the same convent except for a few nights during the illness of her sister."[93]

Particular Friends

The world of the convent was a female one, and in that world women sought satisfaction of their desire for intimacy with other women. One of the most compelling attractions of convent life was the opportunity it provided for the lifelong companionship of close women friends. Particular friendships, as they were commonly known, were widespread in Irish convents in the eighteenth and nineteenth centuries. In contrast to the traditional rules concerning close personal friendships discussed earlier that actively discouraged attachment, it is clear that nuns were permitted and even encouraged to love one another as sisters and mothers. However, what is not so well understood is that they were also permitted to love one another as particular friends.

Particular friendships or attachments were relationships of intimacy long associated with convent living. Recent writing on particular friendships in both contemporary and historical contexts has highlighted their sexual dimension.[94] In fact, the term "particular friendship" is frequently used interchangeably with lesbian relationship. Whether these terms can or ought to be used synonymously depends on how one chooses to define the term "lesbian" and on whether one chooses to apply the term to women before that sexual label was either a cultural category or a personal identity that women could adopt—that is, before at least the late nineteenth century.[95] While the issue of sexual categorization—and, specifically, the determination of whether particular friendships can be claimed as part of lesbian history—is certainly an important one, what is more important in terms of the present discussion is to explore the full range of intimate expression that was evoked by these relationships. By broadening the terms of the discussion beyond naming or claiming, a more nuanced understanding of the depth and complexity of intimate relationships between women in nineteenth-century Irish convents will emerge.

Particular friendships were homosocial, intensely homoemotional, and at times homoerotic relationships. Some were undoubtedly sexual, and at that point they were, according to the language of the church, labeled "unnatural" or "criminal" and were vigorously discouraged. Yet, between celibacy and overt sexual acts existed a wide range of intimate relations that reflected and often fulfilled women's desires for emotional and physical intimacy. As John Boswell stated in an appeal to broaden the terms of discussion of the history of sexuality, "most of the drama of sexuality in any individual's life has to do with nonphysical aspects of human interaction: affection, attraction, devotion, jealousy, passion, restraint, desire, sublimation, transformation."[96] The historical record left by women religious in nineteenth-century Ireland makes clear the immediacy of this drama in their lives.

From the earliest years of monastic development, religious communities, grounded in the notion of communal and companionate existence, promoted loving friendships between sisters or brothers as essential to successful community life.[97] During the eleventh and twelfth centuries, at the same time that clerical marriage was being suppressed, several leading churchmen in England, including St. Anselm and Lanfranc, wrote sympathetic defenses of the intense and emotional friendships that they believed to be an integral part of monastic living.[98] Perhaps the fullest expression of the nature of friendship in monastic communities was contained in the book *Spiritual Friendship* written by the twelfth-century monk Aelred, abbot of the English Cistercian monastery of Rievaulx and advisor to Henry II.[99] Aelred asserted that human love and friendship within religious communities were good and natural and that each religious needed someone within the community with whom they could be spiritually and personally intimate. "He is entirely alone who is without a friend," wrote Aelred.

> But what happiness, what security, what joy to have someone to whom you
> dare to speak on terms of equality as to another self; one to whom you can
> unblushingly make known what progress you have made in the spiritual life;
> one to whom you can entrust all the secrets of your heart.[100]

According to Aelred, such a friend inspired a kind of love that helped each to
know divine love.[101] Aelred encouraged his monks to develop close and intimate friendships, which he called holy companionships. Such a companion would
have been one's "particular friend."

Although there is no indication that any of the medieval writing on monastic
love and friendship was known or read in Irish convents during the nineteenth
century, if it had been, convent mothers would likely have agreed with its sentiments. They valued friendship between the women in their communities. They
thought that the women in their charge, especially while in the novitiate, would
and should bond with one another and share their innermost thoughts, hopes, and
fears. Mary Francis Allingham, one of the founding mothers of the Holy Faith
Order, wrote that "it is good to be spiritually attached to a person, that is, to love
them because they are good and beloved by God and because they aid us in the
way of salvation. This is a very lawful attachment and even pleasing in the sight of
God."[102]

However, the notion of intense spiritual or particular friendships had im-
plications that were quite serious for the celibate lifestyle, for they had long been
known to result in sexual intimacy between community members.[103] From the
earliest days of monastic life, women were cautioned against this possibility. For
example, in a letter written in 423 to his sister, a professed nun, Saint Augustine
was explicit in his warning that sexual intimacy was not to be tolerated within
the community:

> The love which you bear one another ought not to be carnal, but spiritual:
> for those things which are practiced by immodest women, even with other
> females, in shameful jesting and playing, ought not to be done even by mar-
> ried women or by girls who are about to marry, much less by widows or chaste
> virgins dedicated by a holy vow to be handmaidens of Christ.[104]

In time, those "things" that were "practiced by immodest women" with one
another came to be called "unnatural" or "criminal" acts by church leaders, who
believed them to be "against nature," "contrary to human custom," and a violation of divine law.[105]

Particular friendship in convent communities, then, was problematic. A
particular friend could be the source of deep spiritual fulfillment, but she could
also become a partner in the breaking of religious vows. Consequently, convent
communities had to struggle to resolve this seeming contradiction. As a result of
that struggle, we find, as one historian has put it, "the curious coexistence of
particular friendship and its interdiction."[106] Thus, the task of making sense
of love and intimacy within the convent lies in examining the historical problem of how nuns reconciled the contradiction of encouraging and valuing intimate and loving friendships with a life vowed to celibacy.

Nano Nagle, Founder, Sisters of the Presentation. Copy of Charles Turner's engraving in the British Museum. Source: South Presentation Convent, Cork.

Mary Aikenhead, Founder, Sisters of Charity. Source: Sisters of Charity Convent, Sandymount, Dublin.

Catherine McAuley, Founder, Sisters of Mercy. Source: Sisters of Mercy Convent, Baggot Street, Dublin.

Margaret Aylward, Founder, Sisters of the Holy Faith. Copy of a sketch by Esther Eustace. Source: Sisters of the Holy Faith Convent, Glasnevin, Dublin.

South Presentation Convent, Cork. Source: South Presentation Convent, Cork.

Sister Clare Agnew and her students, 1840. Source: Sisters of Mercy Convent, Baggot Street, Dublin.

The Orchestra, Sisters of St. Louis Convent School, 1925. Source: Sisters of St. Louis Convent, Monaghan.

Chapel, Sisters of Charity Motherhouse, Milltown, Dublin. Source: Sisters of Charity, Sandymount, Dublin.

Study Hall, Our Lady of Mercy Teacher's Training College, Baggot Street. Source: Sisters of Mercy Convent, Baggot Street, Dublin.

Mary Byrne, Rose Kelly, and Sarah Hurst. Students of Our Lady of Mercy Training College, 1902–1904, Baggot Street and Carysfort Park, Dublin. Source: Sisters of Mercy Convent, Baggot Street, Dublin.

Because of its foundational nature, the notion of spiritual friendship continued to be central to communal life, but by the sixteenth century the framers of religious rules began to make a clear distinction between spiritual and personal attachment. Saint Francis de Sales, whose teachings were widely read and enormously influential in Irish convents in the nineteenth century, refined the concept of love in order to enable religious communities to distinguish clearly which variety could lead to breaking the vow of chastity. One Irish sister noted these distinctions in her spiritual exercise notebook:

> According to St. Francis de Sales, there are three kinds of love, natural, supernatural, and sinful. Natural love is the affection we feel for those who are endowed with certain fine qualities and talents which attract our esteem and admiration, such as sweetness of temper, sincerity, readiness to oblige, and such like. Such love cannot be called either good or bad, virtue or vice, only in as much as it is dignified by exalted motives which make it meritorious, or by evil motives which would make it sinful. Supernatural love [is] that by which we love the creature . . . as the child of God, who desires that we should love our neighbour for His sake. This too is holy and the result of great virtue. Sinful love is that which inclines us to form an inordinate attachment for any unlawful or criminal purpose.[107]

While Aelred had advanced the idea of spiritual intimacy and the companionship of souls, de Sales suggested that the motive for choosing one's companion of the soul was the chief criterion in determining whether it threatened the rule of chastity. Love, either natural or spiritual, when coupled with "criminal" intentions—in other words, the desire for sexual intimacy with another member of the community—was sure to lead to sinful love and, thus, the breaking of religious vows.

In general, much evidence exists to suggest that a major concern of women's communities in Ireland in the nineteenth century was the tension that resulted from attempting to reconcile love and affection between women with the threat to celibacy which that love posed. Negotiating this fine line was a difficult task, and it is more than likely that some women crossed over it, entering into sexual relationships with other women. Despite the fact that, historically, church leaders had reviled same-sex physical relationships in monasteries particularly because of their unnatural or criminal nature, that reputed criminality is not what appears to have troubled the women's communities themselves. It was not so much whether the object of their love was a woman but, rather, that the relationship threatened their vow of celibacy, their spiritual peace within the community, and the well-being of the community itself. The main challenge convent mothers faced in developing a workable model of particular friendship between members of a religious community, then, was in reconciling the contradiction of valuing close, loving friendships between women with a life vowed to celibacy.

There is no question that women's religious orders, as a matter of course, attempted to dissuade their members from becoming involved in particular attachments with other sisters. The Sisters of Charity, routinely invoking the "Holy

Eighth," moved women from one convent to another in order to prevent them from becoming too attached to one another.[108] The Sisters of Mercy also proscribed the formation of these friendships:

> As the love and union of religious persons should be founded not on flesh and blood or on any human motive, but on God alone . . . the Sisters of this institute shall not admit any particular friendships, attachments, or affections among them.[109]

The Presentation Order was no different in its attitude toward particular friendships. Its notable mistress of novices, Mary Teresa Paul Higgins, was eulogized by the George's Hill community for her efforts in achieving "the attainment of high perfection" among the sisters. To accomplish this, she forcefully warned her novices "against particular friendships, the bane, nay, the very scourge of religious communities."[110]

Irish convent leaders objected to particular friendships for two specific reasons. First was the awareness that these friendships could result in sexual relationships. Irish nuns were taught to recognize this possibility. One woman, in a notebook she kept especially on this issue, remarked that particular friendships tended to get out of hand. Rather than remaining well within the bounds of spiritual love, they often led to feelings of "inordinate" love for another woman. While inordinate love was not in itself a sin, it was only a short step away from "sinful" or sexual love. She maintained:

> Inordinate love exposes a religious to the danger of losing the grace of God. . . . The reason for this is obvious . . . on account of the nature of this passion which excites violent temptations.[111]

To guard against the temptation of physical intimacy, orders proscribed certain behavior. Excessive touching, entering another woman's cell without knocking, and socializing in pairs rather than in larger groups were all prohibited. No order escaped these codes, which attempted to end all "undue familiarity."

The second reason why these intense attachments were thought to be the "scourge of religious communities" was their destructive effect on the community. Intense, loving friendships were said to produce "innumerable idle and inconsiderate words, murmurs, jealousies, anger, flattery, hatred, and calumny." Furthermore, convent morale was soured by "feelings of contempt, rancour, ill-will, and animosities."[112] Sisters excluded from these intense and romantic affairs often felt bitter and neglected; such feelings led to factions and divisions within the community. The Presentation convent in Kilkenny got off to a very shaky start in the first decade of the nineteenth century because of the relationship between the superior and another woman in the convent. In this case it was particularly destructive because there were only four sisters in the young community, and the other two became quite disaffected. They complained to Mother Tobin, the dominant figure of the early Presentation Order. She penned one of her famous letters of advice to the Kilkenny superior, Mother Mary Joseph McLoughlin, addressing directly the harmful effects of "this great attachment between you and De Sales." She warned her of the risk of creating a situation like that at the Ursuline convent in Thurles, where a particular friendship between Mother Tobin's sister and another nun in the community had caused a serious scandal. "You can and ought to remedy it," she wrote.

> If not, it will end badly, and we will have a Thurles house in the order. . . . You will be like Mrs. Morgan and Mrs. Tobin, and thus you will be a divided house which can't stand. . . . It is on you it will fall heavy, and if it reaches the publick, all will see that former accusations were not groundless, and the credit of your house will be gone.[113]

Yet in spite of all precautions and prohibitions, these relationships flourished. Particular friendships in Irish convents were widespread and frequent. And what is even more perplexing, there seems to have been a model of particular friendship that was acceptable, and sisters who followed that model were often respected and admired for their loyal and long-standing relationships.[114] Admittedly, under certain conditions, particular friendships could destroy the ability of a group of women to develop any sense of mutual community life, but under other circumstances close, loyal, and loving relationships were seen as one of the best things that convent life could offer. If women were able to love one another while continuing to fulfill their spiritual obligations (or in other words, if loving another woman enhanced their spiritual state rather than disturbed it), then that love was considered a good and natural experience. Furthermore, if love for a particular woman did not interfere with a sense of responsibility to the community, with the accomplishment of the sisters' duties, or with their obligations to maintain sisterly affection for all members of the community, then particular friendships were actually praised.

An especially close friendship developed between Mary Aikenhead and her devoted assistant, the second superior general of the Sisters of Charity, Mother Magdalen McCarthy. Like Aikenhead, McCarthy was an extremely intelligent and competent woman, and they were said to have been drawn to each other very early. McCarthy was elected to office shortly after her profession in 1831 and rose to the superiorship of St. Vincent's Hospital by 1836. She remained in that office for almost twenty years, in close companionship with Aikenhead, and helped her to run the order as a member of what became known as the "inner council" until Aikenhead's death in 1858. The convent annalist who recorded the story of the close and life-long collaboration between these two women noted that from the time of their first meeting in 1829 "a strong and holy friendship was cemented."[115] Before Aikenhead died, she named McCarthy to succeed her. She became the order's second general superior and remained in that office until her death in 1875.

Often, friendships were well established before the women entered the convent. Among the pioneering Ursuline sisters, for example, was Mary Kavanagh, who joined the Irish community because her best friend, Elizabeth Coppinger, had done so, and she could not envision life without her company.[116] In 1809, the three women who founded the Presentation convent at Dungarvan—the Misses McGrath, Collins, and Hearne—did so because they were "determined upon living together."[117] And in 1825, lifelong friends Jane Carroll and Eleanor

Hughes, both in their fifties and longtime friends of Mary Aikenhead, decided to live out their lives together as Irish Sisters of Charity.[118] Hughes, who because of her general infirmity was unable to do any work in the community, provided the dowry for the pair, a sum of several thousand pounds, while Carroll provided the labor power. After sixteen years of life together in the Stanhope Street convent, Hughes died, and it was recorded that on her deathbed she said to Carroll, "Well, Mary Bridget, if I have any interest with God, you shall not remain long after me." Overwhelmed with loneliness and grief, Carroll followed Hughes to the grave just two months later. The annalist who recorded the story of Carroll and Hughes added a final detail meant to demonstrate the fineness of Carroll's character. In spite of her grief over Hughes's death, Carroll had continued to work ceaselessly among the poor and literally died in harness, falling sick while on the mission one day and expiring the next.[119]

The story of Jane Carroll and Eleanor Hughes was not an isolated incident. Many Irish women throughout the eighteenth and nineteenth centuries joined convents with close and intimate friends. There they expected to reside in each other's company, working and praying together until they died. There is no doubt whatever that the deep friendship between these two women (certainly a particular friendship if there ever was one) was accepted and even admired by the Stanhope Street community. But the message of the obituary amounts to more than that. By placing this story in the permanent record of the community, it also acted as the model for loving and loyal friendships between women in the community. The message was that, devoted as she was to Hughes, Carroll had continued to be a vital part of her community and had earned the respect and friendship of other women in the convent. Although friendships such as these were obviously emotionally successful ones and were held up as models in the community, we can know nothing whatever about their sexual content. We know only that they were regarded as successful. In other words, these women were able to love one another without causing disruption to the rest of their community or apparent spiritual distress to themselves.

This was not the case, however, with other particular friendships. In 1825, Sister Mary Xavier Holmes died in the Stanhope Street Sisters of Charity convent. For several years before her death, Holmes had apparently struggled with her feelings for another nun in the community, Mary Weldon. It was said in the convent that Weldon's character "fascinated all who came within its influence," and Holmes was just one of those who were smitten. Although the annalist recorded that Holmes "was intensely fond of Sr. M. F. Weldon," she did not say that her feelings were reciprocated. Holmes decided to suppress her attraction for Weldon, and, according to the convent record, "she denounced what she considered faulty in her."[120] It is apparent that this relationship was considered inappropriate by her community, for the tone of this story is one of strong support for her decision to attempt to suppress her feelings. It is not clear, however, exactly why it was improper. The annalist did not condemn the fact that Holmes was attracted to Weldon or think it unusual or shocking that many other women were attracted to her. The point emphasized in this story is that Holmes was one of many, that her affection was probably not returned, and that she wisely thought her love "faulty" and decided to subdue it. While this same order praised the loving mutual relationship of Sisters Hughes and Carroll (who entered the convent in the same year that Holmes died), the congregation was not prepared to praise one-sided, uncommitted, or emotionally unstable relationships.

It appears, then, that religious communities of women attempted to develop standards of appropriate and acceptable loving relationships. With the Sisters of Charity, the standard seems to have been based on mutuality and continued ability to function within the community as a whole. Other standards existed as well. One Holy Faith sister, troubled by her attraction to another woman in the convent, believed that she had behaved in a "too familiar" manner with the woman. To overcome her anxiety, she resolved to adopt a style of behavior more acceptable within her community. The code of behavior she was determined to follow dictated that "we must avoid all familiarity, that is, we must have a respect for each other and observe a certain reserve which even the most attached sisters will often observe towards each other."[121] The message here is that it was acceptable to be "attached" to another sister, but that it was not acceptable to demonstrate that affection, at least not openly.

Although these standards were meant to help women to love one another in ways that supported the success of the community as a whole, there were painful personal struggles involved in attempting to live up to those standards. The stories of two women will make this point clear. In 1882, Mary McPhillips was a troubled postulant at the St. Louis convent in Monaghan. Notes she made on her progress toward eventual profession as a religious show that from the time of her entry she had difficulty managing her feelings toward another member of the community. Early in her noviceship, she asked, "Am I disposed to cut the tie between myself and [blank space]?" The relationship caused her much spiritual disturbance. Guilt over the degree to which she loved this woman prevented her from developing that close personal relationship with God that was one of the goals of convent life. She wrote: "Let us ask ourselves, is there any man, any woman, or anything to which we are attached and which is an obstacle to our end? Let us have the courage to remove it."[122]

In 1886, McPhillips, now a professed nun, appeared more troubled than ever at her inability to reconcile the demands of convent life with her own desire. In that year she drafted a long treatise on "sinful love," which was the result of an examination of conscience, probably undertaken with the mother superior. Six times in that year, from April through August, she copied it over, word for word. The thrust of the essay was that inordinate or excessive love within the convent leads almost inevitably to "violent temptations" and ultimately to the commission of mortal sin through "unlawful or criminal" behavior—in other words, sexual intimacy with another woman.[123] In this essay she described the struggle involved at the boundary of acceptable love:

> A violent attraction draws her heart to the creature while a spiritual insensibility removes it far from God. In this state she will think with pleasure on the object of her affections, delight in conversing with her even when separated from her, rejoice in her society. She will no longer feel any desire to converse with God; she will find great difficulty in the recollection of His

Divine Presence. Thoughts of the person to whom she is so devotedly attached will distract her at prayer, and internal recollection will either be entirely neglected or will have become distasteful. Hence it is evident that God will no longer dwell in this divided heart with many venial sins.[124]

Again, one of the main reasons why love out of control was such a great fear for religious communities was that it left women in spiritual conflict. Given the fact that the major justification for women living a religious life was spiritual fulfillment, if an intense attachment had the effects just described, the convent experience could be very disturbing for both the women involved and for the entire community. But besides the fear that intense friendships withdrew a woman's attention from her religious duties, these passions led to violation of the vow of chastity. Inordinate love, McPhillips observed,

predisposes [the woman] for the commission of mortal sin. How many sinful thoughts and guilty imaginations are entertained with complacency in the hearts and minds of those who are under the influence of this passion. . . . It is as impossible to entertain deliberately inordinate love in the heart for any length of time without committing mortal sin, as it would be to keep a serpent in our bosom and escape being bitten.[125]

It is not possible to determine how successful McPhillips (later Sister Gonzaga) eventually was at resolving her conflict. She wrote nothing more on the subject, or at least there is no extant written material after 1886. The struggle, however, cost her much time in preparing for her profession. In a process that took her compatriots three or at the most four years to complete, she took six. Yet it appears that she came to some sort of modus vivendi, for she remained in the community until her death five years later in 1891.[126]

In 1890, just one year after the death of her great friend and the foundress of the Sisters of the Holy Faith, Margaret Aylward, Ada Allingham died in the mother house at Glasnevin on the north side of Dublin city. William Walsh, then archbishop of Dublin, sent a surprised letter to the superior of the order, Mother Vickers, which expressed his shock at her death. Most people had expected Allingham, not Vickers, to head the congregation after Aylward's death. Certainly, she was the only one, besides Vickers, who Walsh thought was "fit" to head it, and now to his great surprise she was dead not long after the foundress.[127]

That Ada Allingham, known in religion as Sister Mary Francis, did not take over the Holy Faith Order in 1889 did, indeed, come as a great surprise to many. But there were personal reasons why she did not do so, and I would suggest that they centered on her lifelong devotion to the foundress of that community. Allingham was Margaret Aylward's first companion in the creation of the Holy Faith Sisters in 1859, joining Aylward when she was still in her teens. Aylward was in her forties at the time, and the relationship between the two was very different from that of Mary Aikenhead and her first assistant, Mother McCarthy. It is clear from letters that Aylward sent to Allingham while she traveled around Ireland raising subscriptions from the hierarchy for the support of her orphanages that Aylward directed and guided Allingham, as if she were her child, in every detail of the running of the new community.[128] It was also recorded that

Allingham suffered great loneliness when Alyward was away on these trips.[129] When Aylward was at home, the two were inseparable, and tradition has it that they spent most of their time together in a private area of the convent away from the rest of the community.[130]

It appears that Allingham, like McPhillips, struggled greatly with her affection for Aylward, and those struggles were recorded in a diary she kept from 1864 until 1876.[131] In the early years, Allingham was concerned with determining whether the attachment she felt was excessive and how that attachment was best expressed. Attachment to a person was excessive and displeasing to God, she recorded, "if you feel great pain at another being preferred to you or at the absence of the object of your attachment, or if you find yourself constantly thinking of that person and recalling their looks and words." Perhaps having decided that her attachment was not excessive, she proceeded to make resolutions on the type of behavior to which she would attempt to conform. She decided that she need not be totally "reserved" or passive in her affections for the other sister, "but although we may be gay and affectionate, we must avoid all familiarity."[132] At first she seemed to have resolved her conflict over her feelings of excessive love, but entries in her notebook in the final years show that she had, in fact, grown deeply troubled. By 1875, Allingham was suffering from regular bouts of depression, and the source of her mental state may perhaps have had something to do with the last resolution that she recorded in her notebook. On 31 December 1875, she resolved "to renounce that attachment and [its] satisfaction if it due [sic] to cost me the last drop of my blood."[133]

Fourteen years later, Aylward died and Allingham was passed over as the new superior of the order. It appears to have been a decision made within the governing body of the community itself. Allingham, the community's beloved spiritual director, Father Gowan, and Sister Vickers reached a mutual decision that the future of the order would be best served under Vickers's leadership. Allingham declared herself unfit for the office, a move that surprised the Irish Catholic world, and quietly sickened and died shortly afterward. From the material that has been preserved, it is impossible to know the exact reasons for Allingham's abdication. Perhaps, as only the convent leadership would know, she remained debilitated by periods of depression. Or perhaps years of the kind of close and exclusive attachment with Aylward that apparently characterized their relationship and that, to judge from Allingham's last entry in her diary, may even have resulted in violation of the vow of chastity, made Allingham an unpopular or unwilling candidate as leader of the large and growing community. Whatever the reason, Ada Allingham strove for many years to reconcile that most serious of problems—how much love was too much love.

It is obvious, then, that upholding the vow of chastity was a clearly defined task of religious communities at this time and that, as in earlier centuries, the boundaries of that vow were constantly being assailed. In at least one nineteenth-century Irish congregation, sexual intimacy between women, or "unnatural love," was technically grounds for dismissal.[134] It is not clear, however, whether any woman was ever dismissed for this offense. While many women were asked to leave for one reason or another, I was unable to find even one case in the records

of more than twenty convents during a period of 150 years of a woman depart-
ing specifically for this reason. And yet the evidence shows that women experienced considerable tension in loving members of their communities. Though
women experienced intimate relationships with one another, it was only when
they themselves became troubled and their troubles affected the community's
peace that something needed to be done.

This, then, is perhaps the kernel of the meaning of love between women in
the convent. Close and exclusive relationships were, indeed, both allowed and
forbidden. The varieties that love might take, as well as instructions detailing
what was appropriate in the convent context, were explicitly defined and taught
by the superiors of the community. In the noviceship and later, in the process of
regular manifestations of conscience, women learned to love one another in ways
compatible with convent life. The rule seems to have been that if a woman could
personally reconcile her affection for another woman with her spiritual vows
and religious existence, and if she could do so without threatening the sisterly
and motherly relationships that held the community as a whole together, then
particular loving friendships were judged acceptable and even admirable results
of convent life. But if a woman could not love another without shattering her
spiritual peace or that of the community, then particular friendships were truly
"the scourge of religious communities." For many, it was a tortuous journey of
discovery.

Clearly, the female world of the convent was a far richer and more complex experience than contemporaries or recent writers have recognized. Roman
Catholic convents had provided for centuries unique conditions in which women
lived their entire lives with other women, in communities bound by complex
ties of obligation, obedience, and love. It was a way of life shaped by centuries
of tradition but adapted and modified to suit the demands and aspirations of the
nineteenth-century women who lived the experience.

That experience was grounded in a female world of companionship and
intimacy. It offered women a viable alternative to the married state. In contrast
to popular notions about the reason women joined convents, it is certainly safe
to assume that joining a convent represented a conscious desire on the part of
some women not to marry as much as it did a response to the inability to marry.
That women themselves were conscious of their choice is evident in the language they chose to represent their life decision. Women stated repeatedly that
they were "quitting" or "leaving" or "withdrawing" from the world. While this
language has its roots in the medieval period, it might be argued that it was more
appropriate to the older style of religious life than it was to the new-style orders
that remained active in society. Yet, women religious continued to define themselves as existing in another sphere, removed from what they called "the world."
It is perhaps an indication that what was meant by "quitting the world" had more
to do with choosing to live in a world of their own—in other words, to live in
a manner not associated with women's traditional lives and work. Quitting the
world, then, as the term was used by the women themselves, had less to do with
maintaining contact with that world than it did with providing a justification—
or, perhaps more accurately, a representation for the meaning of their lives.

Mother Leahy knew that "the world's" belief that women "enter a monastery without knowing each other, that they live there without loving each other, that they die there without regretting each other" was a mistaken one. In fact, Irish convents in the eighteenth and nineteenth centuries provided female space in which women were encouraged to love one another as mothers, as daughters, as sisters, and as friends. The manner of expression of that love was explicitly defined and regulated by the superiors of each community. The ideal was to create an effective community held together by love between women. For some, that love was one of the best things that convent life offered.

FIVE

Cultural Authority

JOHN TROY, ARCHBISHOP of Dublin, helped to orchestrate the city's first public profession ceremony for women religious in 1802 at the Presentation convent in George's Hill, Dublin. To "add to the solemnity" of the occasion, Troy invited the city's priests to attend, as well as the country's bishops and archbishops. The first to arrive in town was Doctor Dillon, archbishop of Armagh. The country's Catholic elite and the close friends and relatives of the Presentation sisters were also invited. According to one of those professed that day, "Our chapel, before 8 o'clock, was as crammed as it could be. Fainting and almost suffocation was the consequence to several. . . . Many, particularly the priests, were much struck and pleased by the ceremony."[1]

The event, which was specifically designed to impress on Dublin Catholics the sacred and exalted nature of the religious life for women, was an overwhelming success. Regardless of the private sentiments individual priests and bishops might feel toward the new conventual establishments, the episcopacy did expect public respect to be demonstrated toward these women. Female monasticism had, after all, been a legitimate and integral part of the Catholic church since its earliest days. Though at the turn of the nineteenth century, the phenomenon of female religious houses was still a novelty in Ireland, bishops who did not actively promote the reemergence of the orders nonetheless actively encouraged deference and reverence for the women once they began to appear on the religious scene.

The consequences were enormous. In Catholic Ireland during the nineteenth century, the religious life for women became the most privileged position that a Catholic woman could hold, for women in religious orders secured for themselves the right to help construct and reproduce the new dominant culture. From 1800 to 1900, nuns were able to play a pivotal role in effecting those religious and social changes associated with the "modernization" or "embourgeoisement" of the period. As a consequence, the religious life became the principal vehicle by which female influence and authority were expressed. In order to exert that influence, however, women religious first had to secure the cultural authority to do so.

Status and Cultural Authority

By virtue of their position both within Irish society and within the Catholic church, the women who entered convents throughout the period of this study possessed considerable social status. We have already seen that the women who joined convents in the prefamine period were from extremely privileged class backgrounds. Even after midcentury, when women of less wealth were enabled to enter, the daughters of poor farmers and urban laborers and artisans were not represented among the members of religious communities except as domestic or lay sisters. The status of women religious was amplified by the fact that religious communities were often landlords. Houses, farms, and other income-producing property were a fairly common form of dowry payment. Charitable donations from lay benefactors also came with regularity in the form of real property.[2] As landowners, convents acquired tenants. In some cases, such as the large estate that Eleanor Arthur brought with her to the Loreto Order, the community acquired middlemen and subtenants.[3] Consequently, landownership gave convents and their members "rank" or "station" in the upper echelons of Irish social structure.

By midcentury, the social and religious significance of the women's orders was becoming apparent, especially among wealthy and influential Catholics. In 1840, before leaving the country for a foundation in England, seven Sisters of Mercy stopped for a visit at the South Presentation convent in the city of Cork. While visiting this convent, which just forty years earlier had been prosecuted when its members began wearing the religious habit, they participated in a public profession ceremony attended by the "principal Catholics" of the neighborhood. According to the Presentation annalist, the public gathering of these two religious orders was a source of pride in the city, an event that "wonderfully pleased the very numerous assemblages of persons who were present."[4] Ten years later, Nicholas Murphy, a prominent Catholic figure in Cork city and a nephew of the late bishop of the diocese, had occasion to express the high degree of respect the Catholic leaders of the town felt toward its religious women. In a letter to Dean John Hamilton, Murphy described the various Catholic enterprises blossoming in that city, most of which had been commenced by religious women. "You will, I am sure, read with pleasure," he declared, of "these God-like institutions, the Sisters of Charity and Mercy."[5]

Male members of the church also acknowledged and articulated the significance of women religious in their lives. One bishop from Macon, Georgia, wrote a poem in honor of the deceased Genevieve Beale, superior of the Sisters of St. Louis in Monaghan and the bishop's first and well-loved teacher:

What a joy to think in exile
Of the blessings that our Lord,
By her hands in richest plenty

On our people hath outpoured;
Of the children led so sweetly
Into learning's useful ways,
While religion's light around them
Shed its sweet and gentle rays.

Of the wanderer and the erring
That she harboured, that she saved,
For the sorrows that she solaced
Of the trials that she braved;
Of the nuns she gathered round her
In that old monastic town,
Holy sisterhood well worthy
Of its ancient bright renown.[6]

Many priests and bishops corresponded regularly with their old teachers, and
many attributed their vocations to them. One particularly touching tribute came
from Father John Quicky to Mother Mary Callaghan, superior of the South
Presentation convent in Cork city. In an 1813 letter to his friend, he professed,
"Did you know how much good your kind letters do me, you would write to
me more often. You began my true spiritual instructions in Cork; you continue
it by your letters. The Holy Ghost never speaks more sweetly, more efficaciously
to my heart than by you."[7]

Religious women also came to be held in esteem by the common people in
both the towns and the countryside. All accounts of the reestablishment of the
women's orders include some description of the crowds that gathered in awe
and wonderment to see the new "walking" sisters as they went about their business among the people. When the Sisters of Charity founded their rural community near the town of Clarenbridge, County Mayo, in 1844, they were readily
welcomed by some people who referred to them as "the blessed women from
Clarenbridge." Those who were more suspicious of strange visitors opened their
doors to the sisters once they learned who they were. One sick man, alone in his
cottage with an infant son and a three-year-old daughter while his wife was away
trying to "earn something for their support," refused to speak with the sisters
until they told him that they were "nuns from Clarenbridge."[8]

To know a nun well enough to ask her to speak on one's behalf or to have
a nun in the family was to be in a fortunate position, indeed. One man found
begging in County Mayo assured the authorities of his respectability by telling
them that he was related to a priest and a nun.[9] Women religious were valuable
character references and were often asked, for instance, to write letters of rec-
ommendation, or "characters," for various individuals seeking employment. Men
applying for positions in business and the civil service asked nuns to recommend
them.[10] So, too, did women seeking jobs as governesses and servants. One woman
who was trying to get back on her feet after having spent time in the North
Dublin Union workhouse was able to obtain help through a personal recom-
mendation from her sister, a Carmelite nun for twenty-five years.[11]

The consequence of this combination of secular and religious status was public support and public trust. Both were available to the new sisterhoods in great abundance. The Sisters of Charity, for example, relied on this support to help them finance the building of St. Vincent's Hospital, the first Catholic-run institution of its kind in Ireland. In an appeal for funds, the community stated that they felt "certain" that they incurred "no risk in thus fearlessly commencing an undertaking naturally attended with considerable expense." Because they had been "already made ministers of the charity and benevolence of individuals to a very considerable amount," they did not think it "presumptuous" to expect that in enlarging "the range of their usefulness" they would "be cheered on by a still more liberal share of public confidence and support."[12] In 1844, almost two decades after the opening of St. Vincent's, several prominent Dublin Catholics asked the Sisters of Mercy in Baggot Street to consider opening a second Catholic hospital in the city. In their letter, the men articulated the trust they placed in the institutions of women religious. They fully expected that another Catholic hospital on the north side of the city would "attain the same success" as St. Vincent's had on the south side. That institution was, according to the men, the "most convincing proof of the advantages which an hospital under the care of a religious community has over all others." The advantages included "the confidence" felt by "all classes" that the needs of the sick poor were being "scrupulously and kindly attended to." The appeal to the Sisters of Mercy concluded by stating that it was because of the "deference which the sick poor of this city feel for such an institution over similar ones under lay management that we aim to found one under your guidance."[13] The public trust of the wealthy and the deference of the poor were clear indicators, then, of the cultural authority that had been invested in these women by the middle of the nineteenth century.

Expressions of Cultural Authority

Invested with that cultural authority, religious women were able to gain access to the Irish people, poor and rich alike. Until approximately 1850, out-of-doors relief was the principal method of providing care to the sick and poor. Each of the 7 Irish Sisters of Charity convents in Dublin typically visited from 50 to 200 people a week. A sick person was usually visited 3 times a week for 2 to 8 weeks, but 3 weeks was typical. Consequently, in 1850 each Dublin Sisters of Charity convent visited, on average, from 850 to 3,400 individuals during the course of that year. If one uses a conservative average figure of 1,500 individuals visited per year, it was easily possible for these 7 convents to have visited more than 10,000 people in 1850.[14] In 1850, 78 convents (of a total of 91) provided some type of poor relief. The 42 Presentation convents, bound as they were by enclosure, did not visit individual dwellings but rather gave food and clothing to persons who came to the convent door.[15] There were, however, a total of 28 Mercy and Sisters of Charity convents in Ireland in 1850 that specialized in home visitation. Even by a conservative estimate of 700 individuals visited per year (which 7 Sisters of Charity convents exceeded),[16] these 2 orders between them could have visited at least 19,600 people in 1850. Their impact was undoubtedly even greater, however, for family members also came into contact with the nuns while they visited. If such relatives included 4 persons per household, those 28 Mercy and Sisters of Charity convents alone would have been in sustained and intimate contact with at least 78,000 poor Irish Catholics in 1850.

Although out-of-doors relief continued to be part of the work of the Sisters of Charity and the Sisters of Mercy, from the 1840s, institutional care for certain groups of people was on the increase. Orphanages, asylums (for the blind, the aged, the homeless, the mentally impaired, and the morally deviant), industrial training schools, reformatories, and hospitals and hospices all appeared in increasing numbers after 1850. As a general rule, the various orders did not specialize in any particular type of institutional care but tended, instead, to open institutions that individual convents of the order felt well-suited to staff and manage. Remaining flexible was important; women religious could then respond quickly to new needs and opportunities. Consequently, most Irish convents were engaged in a multitude of activities. The Sisters of Charity, for example, not only were busy with their extensive home-visitation service but also ran primary schools for children, night classes for adults, several asylums for prostitutes and drunken women, a training school and employment service for domestic servants, an asylum for the blind, several hospitals, and a hospice for the dying. Nonspecialization was the rule during the first half of the century, when only about 10 percent of convents specialized in any one area, and this was still the most popular way of operating in the second half of the century. As late as 1900, 63 percent of all convents were still engaged in more than one enterprise.[17]

In multipurpose communities, women were assigned to staff the various convent institutions. In a typical convent of fifteen to twenty-five members during the second half of the nineteenth century, labor power would have been distributed roughly as follows: two women, the convent superior and the mistress of novices, would have been occupied in managing the community and would not have been engaged in any other task except on an emergency basis. Typically, two or three women would have been elderly and no longer able to work. In 1865, there would have been two, three, or even four women in the novitiate and therefore not yet assigned permanently to any one task. Two or three women would have been lay sisters and responsible for the domestic chores of the convent. Finally, eight to twelve women would have been responsible for managing and staffing the convent schools and institutions. Five to seven would typically have been teachers and three to five would have operated one or another of the noneducational enterprises. In the few convents that did specialize, for example, the Sisters of Charity community which ran St. Vincent's hospital in Dublin, all of the sisters able to work would have been employed in the one specialized activity.

Among the earliest institutions developed by the women's orders were orphanages and asylums. There were a number of convent-run orphanages in Ireland before 1850 (including the large Presentation one at George's Hill, Dublin, which housed more than a hundred children, and the Poor Clare orphanage at Harold's Cross, Dublin), as well as small asylums for widows and homeless people.

These institutions increased in number and in size after 1850. By 1864, according to Caitriona Clear, 11.2 percent of the approximately 200 convents were operating asylums and orphanages.[18] That translates into roughly twenty-two convents in all of Ireland conducting institutions of this kind. Although convents sometimes managed more than one asylum, this figure, I believe, is probably too low. Without looking at the records of each of those 200 convents, it is impossible to arrive at a total number of institutions or individuals served because published directories of the time are quite unreliable for information about convents.[19] Published biographies of the foundresses, centenary publications, and diocesan histories regularly fail to mention all of the institutions operated, particularly those for widows and homeless men and women.

Concrete evidence, though incomplete, suggests that more than 22 convents were operating orphanages and asylums. The 27 convents in this study that were in existence by 1870 operated 16 different asylums (see Appendix). In addition, the Mercy Sisters opened 30 orphanages around the country between 1850 and 1875.[20] If we add to these 16 asylums just half of the total number of Mercy orphanages founded by 1875, or 15, we already have 31 convent–run asylums and orphanages, or roughly 15 percent of all 200 convents. I feel quite confident in speculating that 20 to 25 percent (roughly 40 to 50 convents) were operating orphanages and asylums of one type or another by 1864.

Convents availed themselves of the opportunity to run government-funded institutions whenever possible. After the Reformatory Act of 1858 was passed, some convents applied to the government to open reformatories for girls aged five to sixteen. The reformatory movement never really caught on, however. Between 1858 and 1865, the government funded ten reformatories housing 756 youthful offenders.[21] Five reformatories were opened for girls; four of those were operated by Catholic nuns.[22]

More successful was the government-financed industrial-school movement aimed at alleviating childhood vagrancy. The first industrial school to come in to operation after the passage of the Industrial Schools Act of 1868 was the Lakelands School begun by the Sisters of Charity in Sandymount, County Dublin, in 1869. By the end of the first year twenty-one more schools had been opened, eighteen of which were for Roman Catholic girls and were operated by convents. Approximately one hundred children were committed to each institution and taught a trade (for girls these included needlework, weaving, and dairying), and the products made were then sold. This program proved popular; the government's expenditure limit of about £30,000 per annum for the support of 2,300 children was exceeded within the first two years, and financial restrictions on the program were dropped when it became clear that the schools were turning a profit.[23] Although women religious were the first to seize the opportunity provided by the government, male religious orders also opened residential schools for vagrant boys. By 1899, there were 8,422 children in seventy-one industrial schools throughout the country.[24] Convents conducted twenty-two of those schools, housing more than 3,000 girls.[25]

From 1865, convents began to take up nursing, managing their own private hospitals and health care facilities, as well as providing nurses at state institutions. As noted earlier, the first foray into institutional health care had come in 1834, when the Sisters of Charity opened St. Vincent's Hospital in Dublin. St. Vincent's, which joined five Protestant voluntary hospitals in the city, was the first to provide care specifically for the Catholic population.[26] It was enormously successful. In its first decade, it admitted 500 patients per year, a number limited only by available bed space. In addition to inpatient services, St. Vincent's operated a dispensary (the nineteenth-century equivalent of an outpatient clinic). In 1838, 5,100 people were treated, and the number grew to more than 15,000 per year in just four years.[27] The Sisters of Mercy followed the Sisters of Charity into hospital work in 1861, when they opened the Mater Hospital in Dublin. Other hospitals were opened in Belfast, Cork, Limerick, and Dublin in the last four decades of the century. Nursing became a major occupation of the sisterhoods, especially the Sisters of Mercy, when they began to nurse in state-aided hospitals. The precedent was set in 1861, when the Limerick board of guardians won permission from the poor-law commissioners to hire Sisters of Mercy to nurse in workhouse hospitals. These hospitals, formerly a relatively insignificant part of the workhouse system, were becoming increasingly important centers of public health care. For example, on 4 January 1851, almost 29,000 patients were registered in 163 Irish workhouse hospitals, a number that was just 14 percent of the total workhouse population of 206,500 on that day. When the number of people seeking admittance to the workhouses declined in the 1850s and 1860s, the workhouse hospitals became relatively more important. In 1872, there were 16,600 patients in the hospitals or 34 percent of the total workhouse population of 48,700.[28] As the number of people entering workhouses declined, the former workhouse fever hospitals gradually developed into a broad-based system of public hospitals. It was in these hospitals that nuns began to work in 1861. By the end of the nineteenth century, roughly half the workhouse hospitals were staffed with nuns, principally Mercy sisters. As a result of their work in both public and privately owned hospitals, hospices, and dispensaries, 81 (or 22 percent) of the 368 Irish convents in existence in 1900 were engaged in nursing.[29]

Finally, women religious became significant contributors to the developing nineteenth-century Irish educational system. Throughout the century, 75 to 85 percent of all convents conducted schools.[30] The results of an inquiry into the state of education in Ireland in 1825 showed forty-six convent schools for girls among a total of 2,470 settled schools with permanent buildings and staff.[31] Furthermore, because of larger enrollments these schools, which accounted for just 1.9 percent of the total number, represented 4.5 percent of total enrollment (or 7,600 of 168,000 pupils).[32] As many as 121,000 of the pupils enumerated in the inquiry were attending the Kildare Place schools (the state-funded schools of the time) or Protestant proselytizing schools, two sets of institutions of which the Catholic church did not approve. Those academies the church did sanction were the 422 schools run by the parish clergy and religious orders, which were attended by some 47,000 Catholic pupils.[33] Convents operated 11 percent of these Catholic schools (for both boys and girls) and attracted a little more than 16 percent of the total enrollment.

After passage of the Stanley's Education Act of 1831, the government developed a comprehensive national school system. Each religious denomination was empowered to manage its own schools, but to receive state aid it was obliged to use nonsectarian textbooks provided by the government. Religion could be taught only at a designated period of the day. If convent schools abided by the rules, they were permitted to enter the system. By the late 1850s, 75 percent of all convent elementary schools (or approximately 110 schools) were attached to the National Board.[34] These schools represented 2.2 percent of the total number of national schools for boys and girls. By 1880, 205 convent schools were in the system, representing 2.9 percent of the total. By 1890, the number had grown to 301, or 3.9 percent of all national schools.[35]

Their relative importance within the system was greater than these numbers suggest, however. Enrollments at convent schools (and also at schools conducted by male orders like the Christian Brothers) were much greater than at the ordinary national school. In 1850, the enrollment of a typical convent school was 3.8 times greater than that of the average national school, and by 1900 convent schools were larger by a factor of 5.6. Furthermore, convent schools were able to secure higher attendance rates. In 1860, average daily attendance at all national schools was just 32 percent of those enrolled. Convent schools, meanwhile, maintained a average daily attendance of 38 percent during that year. The pattern continued into the later decades of the century. By 1890, while the overall daily attendance rate within the national system had risen to 46 percent, the daily attendance at the convent schools was 51 percent. If we adjust for larger enrollments and higher attendance rates, then it becomes apparent that convent schools were of considerably greater significance within the system than numbers alone imply. In 1860, for example, though convent schools represented just 2.3 percent of the total number of schools, they accounted for 11.3 percent of the average daily attendance. By 1890, convent schools accounted for 3.9 percent of the total but 16 percent of those attending on a typical day.[36]

Even these adjusted National Board figures do not tell the whole story, however. Several other factors must be considered in assessing the issue of impact. First, in these figures, convent schools are considered as a portion of all national schools, including Protestant ones, rather than as a percentage of Catholic national schools only. The proportion of Catholic schools run by the nuns increases when the figures are calculated this way, though not substantially. Second, many convents operated more than one school. Those schools that joined the national system were often former "poor schools." Convents frequently operated pay schools for wealthier girls side by side with their national schools. In addition, a number of orders like the Dominicans, the Loreto Sisters, the Ursulines, and the St. Louis Sisters operated "superior" schools, which provided secondary education for Catholic girls. Although the 1901 census reported that only 2.8 percent of Catholic girls (or 7,100) received a secondary education, 91 percent of them obtained their education in convent superior schools.[37]

Convent schools affected the educational system in one other very powerful way. Although the national system had "model" schools for training its teachers, the Catholic clergy, who managed all of the Catholic national schools not conducted by nuns, increasingly refused to hire lay teachers who had been trained in them. Rather, they preferred teachers trained in the convent superior schools. As a result, in 1862 the Irish bishops adopted a resolution stating that "Catholic teachers are not to be sent to model schools."[38] By the 1870s, 75 percent of all Catholic lay teachers were being trained in convent schools like the Baggot Street training college. The Mercy Sisters, taking advantage of the growing distrust of the model schools, specialized in this work and gradually secured the right to train all female national schoolteachers. Their training college at the Baggot Street convent (later Carysfort Training College) was the first convent superior school to be formally approved as a national school system training college in 1883.[39] Consequently, though the nuns did not manage all Catholic girls' national schools, by the 1880s they were training all teachers in such schools.

Almost from the moment they opened, convent-run schools, orphanages, industrial schools, and asylums filled to capacity, making admittance a privilege. With the exception of reformatory schools, admission was voluntary. Individuals asked, and usually paid, to be admitted. In gaining access to the nuns and in acknowledging their authority, the people of Ireland, especially the poor, expected benefits for themselves and their children. In 1851, for example, a widower asked that his fourteen-year-old daughter be admitted to a training school run by the Stanhope Street Sisters of Charity convent in Dublin. "I hope you will pardon me for trespassing on your valuable time," he pleaded in a typical appeal for admission, "but this is, by your kind influence, with respect to getting my daughter for a while into Stanhope Street convent." He continued:

> She is a good healthy girl, 14 years of age, attentive to her religious duties, anxious to learn, but deficient in a knowledge of general work that would enable her to earn her bread. Having lost her mother at the age of 4 years, at this period of her life it would be an invaluable blessing to her to have the advantage of those good ladies' instruction and relieve my heart from a heavy load of anxiety concerning her.[40]

In the case of convent-run penitent or "Magdalen" asylums, drunkards, prostitutes, and other women living beyond the moral pale of society either sought admittance of their own accord or were brought to the nuns by friends and family.[41] In both cases, the institution performed a vital social and cultural function. For many women, the asylum functioned as a temporary shelter during hard times when they could find no other source of support. For their families, moreover, these asylums, managed by the arbiters of female morality, offered a cure for perceived moral failings. Convent-run Magdalen asylums functioned as models, if not enforcers, of the dominant moral standard. Families sought out these institutions to help them control and reform errant members. Many inmates of St. Mary Magdalen's penitent asylum in Dublin were there because their families thought they were "an embarrassment" to them.[42] In the mid-1860s, a widower with five children brought his eldest daughter, Mary Hanlon, to the asylum when he learned that she had been charged with "misconduct." While she was there, he visited her often, encouraging her to follow the nuns' tutelage. Eventually, she returned home, reportedly a "reformed" girl.[43]

Perhaps the greatest authority exerted by women religious was over Irish children. The most extensive of all the many works undertaken by these women was the religious and secular education and training of children, and in this work they assumed the right not only to supervise but also to control their charges. In many cases, this authority challenged that of their own parents. This was as true in the prefamine period as it was in the last half of the nineteenth century. One revealing indication of their unrivaled authority occurred in Kingstown. There in 1839 Father William Walsh addressed an impassioned letter to Dean John Hamilton, asking him if it was true that the Sisters of Charity were considering coming to the town. He and the other priests ardently hoped that it was so, believing that only a convent would be able to counteract the destructive effects of a local proselytizing school. Catholics in Kingstown were apparently allowing their children to attend a Protestant church school, and the local priests were appalled. One Sunday at Mass, Walsh found himself unable to contain his anger. "I read the parents a lecture which I trust they will never forget. But alas! Of what avail is all this if we are to have no female school and no means to combat the insidious, persevering efforts of the wealthy bigots who swarm in this place."[44] The only means of combating Protestant proselytism that this priest thought effective was the establishment of a convent and school. Walsh had little confidence in the ability of the Catholic parents of the town to keep their children in line, but he had every confidence that the nuns would do so, even in the face of parental apathy or opposition.

Parental influence was often overtly discouraged in preference to that of the nuns. This was most obvious in convent-run institutions like orphanages, industrial training schools, and reformatories. In the reformatory system, circumvention of parental influence was built into the institution. Begun in 1858 and modeled on reformatory systems recently established in Europe and America, these Irish institutions aimed to reform juvenile offenders in the hope that they could be dissuaded from continued criminal activities. Private religious charities built and managed sectarian institutions that were licensed by the government. Children under the age of sixteen were maintained at the government's cost for one to five years. The managers of the Ulster Reformatory School for Catholic Girls conducted by the St. Louis Sisters in Monaghan believed that one of the excellent provisions of the new law was the fact that these young offenders were placed "in a safe asylum where, separated from depraved parents . . . they can be formed to habits of industry and virtue." Furthermore, the law required that parents contribute to the "training" of the child whom they had "neglected or corrupted."[45]

The belief that juvenile crime was the result of parental corruption was firmly held in all the Catholic reformatories. Consequently, the sisters discouraged contact between the children and their parents by asking the government to send their charges to reformatories far from their homes. Doing so decreased the chances that parents would be able to take advantage of their right to visit their children periodically. According to one inspector of reformatory schools, the nuns believed that "from these interviews the morals and peace of mind of the child is not improved."[46] Some orders went to even greater lengths to circumvent parental influence. In order to permanently separate released inmates from their parents, the Mercy sisters in Limerick routinely assisted their most promising charges in emigrating.[47] The St. Louis Sisters did likewise with favored children to prevent them from returning to their families when their time in the institution was completed.[48]

Women religious asserted their greatest authority over orphans, those children without any parents or lacking parents able to care for them. Prevalent were instances when a surviving parent, often a woman, requested that a convent-run orphanage take children whom she could not support.[49] Most vulnerable were children whose living parent was either a Protestant or "deemed" unfit in some other way. In such cases, a nun's authority directly challenged that of the parent. When a collector for Archbishop Daniel Murray died, leaving two small daughters and a "drunken" wife, Dean John Hamilton paid for the girls to be admitted to an orphanage run by the Carmelite convent in William Street, Dublin. Although we do not know whether the children wished to live with the Carmelites, it is clear that the girls' mother did not wish them taken from her. She was able to get her children back only when a friend abducted them from the convent.[50]

Women religious did not assume such rights without the implicit consent of the Catholic community. An important question to consider is just what the larger Catholic population—or at least its lay and clerical leaders—thought of the practice of taking orphans. That they highly approved of the prerogative of these women to raise children despite the existence of a living parent was made manifest in the notorious case of *the Queen v. Margaret Aylward*. In April 1858, Margaret Aylward, who had just begun the formation of what was to become the Holy Faith Sisters, enrolled a four-year-old girl named Mary Mathews in her orphanage. The young girl had been brought to St. Bridget's by Mary Jordan, who had received the girl from her father, Henry Mathews, just before he had died. The girl's Protestant mother, Maria Mathews, had left her husband and two of the couple's three children and taken a job as governess to the governor of the West Indies, giving the couple's youngest child to Protestant relatives in England. Because he was ill, Henry Mathews reportedly lived in fear that his wife or her relatives would try to take the two older children as well. Some months later, he died in Sir Patrick Dun's Hospital in Dublin, but not before declaring to his employer, Mary Jordan, and several members of the hospital staff that he did not want his children to be returned to their mother but wished them to remain in Ireland and to be raised as Catholics.

Ensuring that children of mixed marriages remained Catholics was a monumental concern of the time. When the Catholic parent died, priests, nuns, and lay Catholics worked together to see that the children continued to practice the faith. If this was in doubt, the children were cajoled or coerced into convent-run orphanages. Not surprisingly, then, Mary Jordan, who now had the children, sought advice from a priest, Edward McCabe (later archbishop of Dublin), who advised her to send the children into Catholic institutions. He recommended that the daughter, Mary Mathews, be taken to St. Bridget's orphanage, run by the highly respected Margaret Aylward.[51]

At the time that the girl was admitted, Aylward knew that her mother had returned from the West Indies and intended to come to Dublin to demand to have her children given to her. She located her son and took him out of the home where he was residing. When she came knocking on Aylward's door looking for her daughter, Aylward refused to hand over the child. In fact, Mary Mathews, whose name Aylward had changed to Mary Farrell, was not living with Aylward but had been sent to live with a nurse in the country. Shortly after Maria Mathews had demanded that Aylward return her daughter, the child was "mysteriously" taken from the nurse; Aylward claimed to have no knowledge of the abductor and, when requested by a court order to do so, could not produce the child. Two years later, Aylward was found guilty of contempt of court and sentenced to six months in the Grangegorman prison for women.[52]

Margaret Aylward defended herself, though unsuccessfully, by declaring that she was upholding Henry Mathews's dying wish that his child remain a Catholic. Furthermore, she argued that the girl's mother had abandoned her daughter by going to the West Indies against her husband's wishes, thereby invalidating her parental rights. A trial of a similar nature, the Moore case, was being decided at the same time, which caused Aylward to hope that she might have grounds within the British legal system for her actions. At issue in the Moore case was whether a mother possessed a natural and inalienable right to custody of her children, and, if so, what acts could result in the loss of that right.[53] Aylward hoped that the court would rule in her favor if the Moore decision either denied a mother's natural guardianship over her children or set aside that right for any reason. But the Moore case upheld the rights of the mother. Aylward, with the support of leading Dublin clerics, still refused to produce the child whose return the court demanded. Consequently, she was sentenced to prison for contempt of court.

The incident outraged Protestants, who accused the Catholics of virulent proselytism. The Catholic community, however—or at least its vocal elite members—condoned Aylward's actions and came to her defense. The Catholic press was especially vocal in its support.[54] A committee of Catholic supporters was formed, headed by Ignatius Kennedy and the Reverend Edward McCabe, and sent out circulars and appeals for financial assistance in meeting court costs and continuing the work of Aylward's orphanage. One of the circulars insisted: "Miss Aylward interfered with no parental right. She received the child from the hand of the guardian solemnly appointed by its dying father."[55] Archbishop Cullen defended her publicly at a meeting he called in January 1861 that was attended by many of the Irish bishops.[56] Letters and demonstrations of Catholic support even included a gift and a message from the pope.[57] When she was released from prison, her orphanage was more popular than ever and was organized on a permanent basis with the formation of the Holy Faith Order. Aylward herself became a celebrity and traveled around the country raising funds from illustrious churchmen and prominent Catholics. Mary Mathews was, in fact, never returned to her mother. She was taken out of the country, placed in a convent in Belgium, and eventually became a nun.

The most important element about this story is the fact that the Catholic hierarchy and leading members of the Catholic community defended Aylward's decision to keep the girl. The power of this religious woman cannot be denied. Aylward and other women religious like her claimed the right to raise this poor woman's child. The Catholic public did not think that Aylward had done anything that any other nun in charge of a Catholic orphanage would not also have done. The editor of the *Morning News* stated this point clearly:

> There can hardly be a shadow of doubt that had any other lady occupied the same position as Miss Aylward did in regard to St. Brigid's Orphanage, she would at this moment be spending her Christmas holidays within the walls of Grangegorman Penitentiary.[58]

Though the court did not agree with her belief that she had a right to keep the child, Aylward proceeded nonetheless on her own course in opposition to British notions of parental rights. In that decision she had the backing and undoubtedly the collusion of other members of the Catholic community. Thus was her cultural authority, as well as that of all women religious leaders, clearly confirmed. By the postfamine period, then, to be a nun was the most culturally privileged position an Irish woman could hold.

SIX

Transforming Catholic Culture

IN 1800, SHORTLY AFTER they first began to wear their religious habits on a regular basis, the women of the South Presentation convent in the city of Cork were prosecuted for what was still a penal-law crime. In the court case that resulted, however, the magistrate dismissed the charges against the women. His reasons for doing so were contained in the following statement which he made to the court:

> I have heard all the arguments adduced for drawing upon them the severity of the law and still, I must confess, it seems to me unreasonable for us to meddle in so unimportant a matter as that of the ugly costume in which these ladies choose to dress. And what evil can possibly ever be the result of a set of helpless, friendless women assembling together to say their beads and drink their cup of tea?[1]

This man's opinion of the significance of the Presentation Sisters proved to be highly unimaginative. Though most would concede that no "evil" resulted from the congregation of Catholic "ladies" in convents, these women eventually did exert an enormous impact on nineteenth-century Ireland, which this member of the Protestant Ascendancy at the turn of the century failed to foresee.

Ireland in 1750 was a Protestant country dominated politically, socially, and culturally by a small Anglo-Irish elite. Standing in sharp contrast to this ruling class was the largely impoverished, malnourished, illiterate, disaffected, violent, intemperate, superstitious, and nominally Catholic population of subtenants and landless laborers.[2] Just one hundred years later, by the late 1800s, the situation was considerably changed. The political and social hegemony of the Protestant Ascendancy (once thought unassailable) had been challenged by an increasingly wealthy, well-educated, ambitious, socially disciplined, and notoriously devout Catholic population. The institution of Protestant landlordism was nearly defunct, and the beginning of a sophisticated Irish Catholic nationalist campaign to end British colonial control over the island was less than twenty years away. This transformation was fueled by the growing influence of the wealthier members of Catholic society, principally from the south and east of Ireland, which included both large tenant farmers and affluent commercial and professional Catholics.[3]

The increasing prominence of this group was part of that nineteenth-century process of social, economic, and demographic change discussed earlier. During this century, cottiers and landless laborers declined precipitously in number. The decimation of the poorest of the rural people was accompanied by the decline of their distinctive culture, a culture characterized by decidedly unorthodox religious practices, the almost exclusive use of the Irish language, and expressive and unreserved cultural customs and mannerisms.[4] In contrast, the increasingly prosperous and prominent farming classes, as well as the urban commercial and professional classes of the south and east, were part of a very different culture shaped by a more anglicized worldview and more exposed to a broad range of influences, including that of continental post-Tridentine Catholic orthodoxy. The ethos of the wealthier Catholic classes of the south and east gradually replaced the prefamine, Gaelic culture of the rural areas, especially of the north and west. It was the destruction of this traditional culture and the construction of a new, bourgeois Catholic culture that occupied so much of the time, energy, and money of both women and men of the wealthy Catholic classes. What the Cork magistrate failed to foresee in 1800 was the role that women religious would play in constructing the cultural beliefs, practices, and attitudes that underlay the emergence of the modern Irish Catholic state.

Constructing the New Religion

Although much has been written in the last ten years about the characteristics of both traditional Irish culture and the bourgeois Catholic culture that replaced it, the interface between the two cultures has remained relatively unexplored. Despite the scarcity of research, there seems to be a consensus that popular beliefs and customs were not assaulted by the institutions of reformed Catholicism so much as they died a natural death.[5] The decline of traditional patterns of behavior and popular religious customs is generally seen as having been the result of "changes in the outlook and aspirations of the Catholic laity."[6] The question that has not yet been addressed is how such changes in outlook and aspirations occurred. The result of my exploration of the interaction between nuns and the people of Ireland in the nineteenth century suggests that those changes did not take place without considerable effort on the part of the wealthier Catholic classes. While the poorer, rural members of the Catholic laity may, indeed, have changed their outlook, their choices were clearly and aggressively defined by the purveyors of the new and increasingly powerful Catholic ideology. Consequently, the process of cultural change was not quite so benign as some writers would have us believe. I do not want to suggest that popular culture is ever easily assaulted, but I do believe that religious belief and practice was contested territory in nineteenth-century Ireland.

The wealthy and ambitious Catholic classes who underwrote the reforming Catholic church did actively attempt to rewrite the meaning of Irish Catholicism, and prominent in that process were women religious.

Employing a multitude of conversion techniques, women religious set out to instill new feelings of piety and to spread a new system of outward symbols that reflected that piety. The authority possessed by these women to mold and influence others was aimed, first of all, at their families and friends. Women religious worked persistently to ensure that those within their family and social circle adopted the new codes of religiosity. One Sister of Charity who was on her deathbed in 1851 reported that her worst worry when dying was not having been able to influence her father to attend the sacraments regularly. Having decided to make one last effort, she sent him a long and final letter on the subject. According to the community annalist, her letter had "the desired effect"; her father adopted the new devotional practice of frequent and regular reception of the Eucharist.[7] Eliza D'Alton, daughter of the Irish historian John D'Alton and a member of the Dominican convent in Drogheda, put almost continual pressure on her father to attend to his spiritual duties.[8] Early in her convent life, she reminded him yearly of his Easter obligation to attend mass and receive the sacraments (which he seemed too willing to ignore); she requested that he attend mass on the anniversary of her mother's death, if not for his own soul, then for the benefit of her mother's; she worried that he did not respect the church's holy days of obligation; she advised him on the custom of having masses said for the soul of her mother; and she informed him that she believed that his excessive regard for his "literary pursuits" was robbing him of a deeper understanding of "a more real and substantive immortality."[9] Later in her life (and his), she devoted one letter entirely to preparing him for his imminent death, convincing him finally to adopt a more regular and diligent style of religious practice. She recommended that he begin to say the rosary weekly and also suggested that a favorite spiritual advisor of hers should come to advise him on appropriate religious practice.[10] Her suggestions and advice were delivered with confidence and authority. Significantly, she had the power to influence, for toward the end of her father's life, Eliza D'Alton was gratified to learn that he was finally "receiving spiritual attention" on a regular basis.[11]

In spreading the new religion among the people, women religious promoted rituals and elaborate ceremonies, believing that ceremony made the religious message more attractive and the desired change more permanent. In order to end the ages-old belief, which was particularly common in country parishes, that young people under the age of seventeen or eighteen were exempt from attending mass or receiving the sacraments, women's orders developed ambitious programs replete with pomp and ceremony aimed at encouraging children as young as seven to receive the sacrament of the Eucharist, a practice that soon became the norm. Nuns not only instructed children at their own convents but also visited nearby chapels several times a week. Once a year the Sisters of Charity at Benada gathered together all the children they were instructing for a grand first-communion ceremony at one of the chapels, which the nuns decorated elaborately for the occasion. Afterward, they provided a breakfast for the group, which

never numbered fewer than a hundred girls and boys. The trouble taken to create a memorable occasion produced what the women called a "good effect" on
both the children and "their parents likewise."[12]

Singing, too, was encouraged and became an increasingly important part of
the new piety. According to one convent annalist,

> [singing] not only attracts [the children] to religious instructions but their
> parents likewise. . . . For profane ballads, hymns on various religious subjects
> are substituted at many of their social meetings. [Through song] the most
> essential truths [are] conveyed to the minds of some it would hardly other-
> wise reach.[13]

Another popular custom cultivated by religious women that appeared on
the cultural landscape by midcentury was the Christmas crib. Convents began
to display these scenes annually and recorded that "great devotion was excited"
by the new custom. People came from far and near, and their numbers increased
every year.[14] While the crib was on display, women and men crowded to the
convent, where they were treated to religious instruction and advice.[15] One
convent annalist remarked confidently that "many a sin was avoided during those
evenings" when men would otherwise have been in the public house.[16] One
man who traveled fourteen miles to view a life-sized crib at the Clonmel Sisters
of Charity convent went home and told his parish priest about the display, and
the priest soon came to see it, too. The children from the poorhouse were invited to visit the crib, and a dinner was provided for them afterward. The great
value of this new custom, according to the Clonmel sisters, was that "these occasions always afford favourable opportunities for instruction and advice."[17] New
religious knowledge filtered into the countryside, as all who came received teaching "on the subject of our Blessed Lord's nativity."[18]

Popular devotions, such as those of the Sacred Heart of Jesus or the Month
of Mary, were introduced and spread throughout Ireland by the women's orders,
sometimes before a book in English even existed about the devotion.[19] The
Confraternity of the Sacred Heart was first begun at the Presentation convent in
George's Hill in 1809, and over the next eighty years almost 10,000 members
were enrolled. Obligations included frequent reception of the sacraments and
special devotional practices.[20] Convents learned very quickly that the people took
special pleasure in having their names enrolled in convent books and thus regularly linked the advocacy of new religious practices with special societies or
sodalities requiring formal registry.[21] In the Sodality of the Immaculate Heart of
Mary managed by the Cork Ursuline community, 1,600 men, women, and children signed its registry book between 1841 and 1868. Each member was required
to perform specific devotions to Mary, which included reciting the litany of the
Blessed Virgin Mary every Saturday in preparation for Sunday mass and saying
the Ave Maria every single day.[22] In the Guard of Honour, the most elite Catholic organization for men, regular religious practice was expected, and social deference to church leaders demanded. The Sisters of Charity tell an instructive story
of a Guardsman from the Donnybrook convent sodality. This man, who traveled
frequently on business, informed the nuns that he would not be back in town on

the following Sunday in time to attend mass at the local church. The sisters suggested, and he agreed, that he attend mass in a different parish on his way back into town. When the man next visited the sisters, he told them the result of his efforts to avoid missing Sunday mass. Apparently, he had arrived late at the church and was shocked when the officiating priest turned around on the altar and publicly reprimanded him for his tardiness. After hearing the story, the nuns advised the man to return to the parish and apologize to the priest for being late. According to the sisters, this was the "Christian way of acting, [and] above all, the Guardsman's." The convent annals recorded that the man did as the nuns urged.[23]

Religious culture was also transformed through the widespread use of a variety of sacred items to alter personal circumstances, modify behavior, and promote miraculous healing. In 1860, the motherhouse of the Sisters of Charity at Harold's Cross in Dublin began an association for devotion to the Sacred Heart of Jesus and enrolled members who were then enabled to purchase a sacred lamp. When prayed to, the lamp was believed to encourage Jesus's intercession on behalf of the petitioner. The reported power of the oil lamp set off a frenzy of religious devotion in Dublin. In just four years, more than 6,000 members (most of whom seem to have been women) were enrolled, and the record of miraculous cures allegedly produced was a long one. One young woman, for instance, bought a lamp to pray for work for her father, who she expected "would take to drink" without it. Not long after, he obtained work. Another young woman, who was thrown out of her house by her father, bought a lamp, lit it, and prayed that he would learn to control "his unbending temper." It is recorded that, before long, he came to her and asked her to return home, "promising in future to be a good father to her." Still another woman, who was married to a man who for twenty-five years had not once approached the sacraments, was promptly rewarded when she bought a lamp. Although it was known that he "abhorred" what he called "preaching women," he agreed to go to see the nuns at Harold's Cross, who then prepared him to receive the sacraments. A Dublin convent, short of funds for completion of their buildings, received a large bequest just a few days after they had begun to pray before the lamp. One woman who ran a lodging house that was failing because of a lack of business lit a lamp, and, shortly afterward, lodgers reportedly began returning. The lamp proved enormously popular with Dublin women, who used its reported power to help them control such material conditions as their physical and financial security. When the miraculous lamp was credited with having healed a paralyzed girl, requests for admission to the association arrived from all over the country, and an agent had to be employed to handle the sale of the wildly popular lamps.[24]

Knowledge of the Lourdes miracle spread quickly, and Marian grottoes became a ubiquitous feature of convents throughout the country by the early 1860s. Convents made it a point to obtain water from the Lourdes shrine and used it to produce cures. One infant girl with a large lump on her spine was brought to the Sisters of Charity Clarenbridge convent by her mother and was reportedly cured after the nuns blessed her with the water. Learning of this miracle, many other mothers brought their crippled children to the convent, and several other cures were reported.[25]

Relics were a particularly popular sacred item that women religious used to help bind the people to the church. Relics were often applied directly to the body, as were amulets and charms, to promote healing of body or mind. This practice appears to have been quite common in rural areas, though it was also frequent in towns and cities. The Clarenbridge Sisters of Charity found that the application of their relic of Saint Edward produced numerous cures. "The relic of St. Edward is marvelous," exulted one sister in the community. "Over and again we have seen people cured. . . . It seldom if ever fails."[26] One man who experienced a complete recovery from a debilitating disease through the nuns' physical application of this relic reportedly was so impressed that he quickly became a "practical" Catholic, in other words, a Catholic who attended mass weekly and went regularly to confession and communion. Soon he became even more serious about religion; he joined the Guard of Honour and encouraged other men in the area to join as well.[27]

Pieces of wood, believed to have come from the cross on which Christ was crucified, were probably the most common relic used by women religious. When the Clarenbridge Sisters of Charity learned of a poor and seriously ill young woman who, though nominally a Catholic, was not practicing her faith, they employed the powers of this relic in their attempt to bring the girl firmly within the Catholic fold. When the sisters visited her, they took with them a relic of the true cross, and when they placed it on her body, she reportedly got immediate relief. Impressed by the effect of the treatment, she received the sacraments and became a practicing Catholic. According to the Clarenbridge community, this relic was "famed" for the many such cures it had effected in the Galway area.[28]

Although the widespread use of relics and other sacred items in this way may at first seem to conflict with the image of nuns as the vanguard of a reforming Irish Catholic church, this is not the case. Widespread acceptance of magical practices and beliefs was, in fact, one of the distinguishing features of both the older, Gaelic traditional culture and the modern Irish Catholic culture that supplanted it. Traditional popular religion abounded in devotional practices that were magical in nature, the most common of which was the pattern or patron. Patterns, according to James S. Donnelly Jr., were "a combination of penitential pilgrimage, quest for magical healing, and boisterous popular festival in honor of the local patron saint."[29] During the seventeenth and eighteenth centuries, thousands—sometimes tens of thousands—of people gathered at the innumerable sacred places spread throughout the country. Water from holy wells, pieces of sacred trees, sacred stones, and relics and images of saints were employed to cure disease, prevent accidents and mishaps, and control the many irrational forces of nature.[30]

Magical practices were not a feature of only traditional culture, however. The modern brand of Catholicism that the Irish upper and middle classes implanted beginning in the late eighteenth century was itself replete with customs and rites of a magical sort. The magical or supernatural power of relics, medals, holy water, and pilgrimages to heal, restore, and safeguard was an important and orthodox element of Roman Catholicism.[31] These sacred objects approved by the church, as well as sacred church rituals, were sanctioned by the clergy and used by religious and laity alike to bring about cures and prevent mishaps in much the same way as the sacred objects of traditional popular religion had been.

So common and necessary were these relics that they were frequently given as gifts by episcopal friends or superiors. It was especially common to present a new convent with a relic or two when it opened. The more influential friends a community had, the greater was their supply of relics. The Presentation convent in George's Hill, Dublin, was in proud possession of "many" relics given them by Dr. Nicholson, archbishop of Corfu, who was an uncle of one of the community's early sisters.[32] Wealthy lay Catholics also gave relics to convents as gifts. Mrs. Redington, a patron of the Sisters of Charity convent in Clarenbridge, County Galway, furnished that convent with several outstanding reliquaries (one as large as three feet by four) that held "innumerable relics of saints. Another shaped like a standing cross contains a portion of the True Cross and relics of the instruments of the passion." These were the relics the sisters used so effectively in their missionary work.[33]

It should come as no surprise that such practices were such an important component of nuns' work. These customs were an orthodox part of post-Tridentine Catholic culture, and they were also a deeply ingrained part of popular, prefamine Catholicism. Consequently, the use of relics and other sacred items proved to be a very influential way of establishing the authority of the institutional church, not to mention the authority of the nuns themselves. As a result, the Irish orders were able to secure the people's acceptance of the new religious culture that was being overlaid upon the old. One scholar has suggested that the crucial element in the success of the reformed Irish church was its ability to reconcile the magical and the rational elements of religious belief.[34] If this is true, then Irish nuns, in using relics and ritual to such great effect, gained the people's trust and helped to convince them to accept the dictates of the reforming church.

Another important tool that the women's orders used in helping to spread modern devotional practices was the "mission" conducted throughout the country by about a dozen male religious orders during the middle and later decades of the nineteenth century. Convents, which as a general rule were on good terms with male religious orders, cultivated long-standing friendships with the men and often collaborated with them in the management of the mission. They helped with local arrangements and often provided food and accommodation for the priests who led the mission. In remote rural areas, they also provided chalices, vestments, and other religious articles from their own richly supplied convent chapels. In some instances, they even initiated the mission itself. In County Sligo in 1866, for example, the Sisters of Charity at the Benada convent suggested to their Jesuit friend, Father Daniel Jones, that he conduct a mission to "rouse the people to a greater appreciation of . . . the advantages the establishment of a convent of Sisters of Charity" in the area had put within their reach.[35] Jones agreed to the proposal and arranged for four Jesuit priests to come and direct the two-week-long event. Catechism classes were conducted by the Jesuits, religious hymns were taught, masses were said in one of the parish churches near Benada Abbey, and benediction was given every evening. Two major processions were organized, one to the Blessed Virgin Mary and the other to the Most Holy Sacrament. Hymns were sung at all the devotions, which, according to the sisters, "contributed to make the people take a greater interest and be more attracted to attend."[36] In all of these events, the nuns were deeply involved. They handled much of the organization, provided supplies for the services and processions that the poorly equipped chapels did not possess, took care of all the altars, and fed the Jesuits and the other attending priests at the convent. When the mission ended, 300 adults had been confirmed, many of whom had received their first formal religious instructions in the Benada convent. Incentives were included for continuing to practice what they had just learned. Those who continued to confess regularly and communicate at mass received a plenary indulgence for kneeling before a crucifix and reciting five paters and aves every month. Those who regularly said prayers before a crucifix received a seven-years indulgence, and one hundred days could be remitted from one's time in purgatory by saluting the crucifix with the aspiration, "Praise be to Jesus Christ for ever and ever, Amen."[37] The event was thought such a success in promoting the new religion that seven years later the sisters held another mission. This time they invited the coadjutor bishop of their diocese of Achonry, Francis J. MacCormack, to conduct the mission, and he came himself to lead it. The agenda was similar to that of the earlier mission, but this time much larger numbers of people participated, with 1,000 men, women, and children receiving the sacrament of the Eucharist. The mission ended with a procession in honor of the Blessed Virgin Mary and a mass at the convent. The crowds were so great that the sermon had to be preached outdoors.[38]

Home visitation was a powerful means of spreading the new religious orthodoxy. Though home visits had the ostensible aim of relieving the bodily or "corporal" wants of the sick, poor, and dying, they were primarily meant to provide religious instruction and encourage piety and devotional conformity. Although convent records present these visits as having been pleasant and benign, they could actually be quite intrusive. Examples abound of the way these women were able to influence—and sometimes even intimidate—the people in their locality through access to their homes. In 1863, a Clonmel woman came to the Sisters of Charity convent there to inform the nuns that a man in the neighborhood whom the sisters knew well was about to die while in the midst of a raging feud with his sister and brother-in-law. One of the sisters on the sick mission went to visit this man and encourage him to "forgive all" rather than risk dying with the sin of anger on his soul. The man refused, professing instead a "deadly hatred" of his sister and her husband. "Were they to presume to come to my wake," he was reported to have cried, "I would start up to strike them and the blood would gush out of my nose." Shocked, the attending nun informed him that as far as she was concerned, his feelings were "incompatible with salvation." With the fear of damnation before him, he was, reportedly, soon reconciled with his sister and brother-in-law. The nuns took great pride in this manifestation of their influence, counting it as one of their successes: "Thus was this poor soul snatched from perdition, and the grace attached to the ministries of our holy vocation illustrated in a manner truly striking and consoling."[39] Another man who lived in the vicinity of the Sisters of Charity convent in Cork city insisted on dying without the presence of a priest. The man's servants, who were reportedly "too timid about crossing him," informed the nuns of his decision. Sister Mary Wyse, appalled by such behavior, declared that she was not too timid. She went to his house, "insisted on the priest being sent for," and stayed with him until he had received the last sacraments.[40] The Sisters of Charity in Clarenbridge, County Mayo, were prepared to go to almost any lengths to influence the devotional practices of the people in their neighborhood. During the 1860s, one old man who refused to receive the sacraments became their special cause: "We made some calls at his house, but as soon as he saw us, he always shrank away through the back door and hid. However, there was nothing for our success but pursuit, so we followed him from field to field." The man tried to hide behind a large stack of grain, but the women found him and there they began their conversion:

> While one sister was talking to him, part of the corn stand gave way. A huge stone fell down so near the other sister that it seemed very miraculous how she was not hurt by it. The effect upon the poor man was thrilling; he softened down immediately, allowed himself to be conducted to a seat, where between English and Irish he was made aware of the danger his poor but precious soul was in, and without a good confession he would undoubtedly burn in hell for ever! He was deeply impressed, moved to make great promises which he kept, may God be praised.[41]

He continued to receive the sisters' visits and was soon prepared for confession and Holy Communion. The community annalist recorded that in time he became "a holy old soul with the grace of God beaming in his face, and the change has continued."[42]

Another important vehicle for the spread of modern devotional practices was the burgeoning number of convent-run institutions. Saint Vincent's Hospital, the first Catholic institution of its kind, founded in Dublin in 1834, was believed by both the Sisters of Charity and the leaders of the Catholic community to have great religious impact on the tens of thousands of people who sought care there each year.[43] In contrast to secular hospitals, St. Vincent's provided help not only for the body but also the soul, and in many cases the care of the soul was thought more important. Many who were refused entrance to the hospital by the doctors because their illnesses were not deemed serious enough or because they were terminally ill were nevertheless admitted by the sister in charge for her own set of reasons. One young woman who, according to hospital records, had been "drawn into sin" was now dying and repentant. "By a look of such entreaty and a few words of such sincerity . . . she so gained upon the sister," reported the annalist, "[as] to be allowed in." The sisters did not regret the decision to admit her over the doctor's refusal, for by the time she died two weeks later, she was reportedly "reconciled with God" and expired "most happily."[44] In fact, the managers of this hospital, at least from a reading of their community annals, seem to have taken much more pride in their spiritual successes than in their physical ones. "Many who had long been strangers to religion . . . looked forward to St. Vincent's as the port wherein their wrecked and shattered spiritual life should be repaired," remarked the annalist. One such stranger whose spiritual life was restored was a Dublin tradesman who was brought to the hospital in 1864 after falling from a scaffold. This Irish Catholic man made his first communion at the age of forty. When he recovered from his injuries, this religiously reformed tradesman reportedly became a "happy and highly thought of" member of society. He continued thereafter to live "in strict confidence with his employer, in peace and happiness with his family, and giving edification to his fellow workmen."[45]

Women religious were not only instrumental in constructing a new devotional code among Catholics but also deeply involved in the rampant proselytism of the nineteenth century. While Protestant proselytism is a well-known phenomenon, less frequently discussed are the proselytizing tactics employed by the Catholic community. Though Catholics may not have felt the need to lure Protestant children into their schools in the same way that Protestant religious groups enticed Catholic children, the subtler Catholic proselytism was undoubtedly more effective.[46] This was due in no small part to the fact that women religious were actively engaged in the business. From the earliest years of the conventual movement, the nuns delighted in bringing converts into the fold. Late in the eighteenth century, the South Presentation convent in Cork was reportedly inundated with Protestants whom the sisters instructed in the Catholic faith. One member of the community, a postulant for the Dublin foundation that was to be made in the following year, remarked in a letter to the Dublin foundress: "We are crowded with old and young women sent by his Lordship [the bishop] and the priests for instruction, the greater part of whom are Protestants." That the conversion of Protestants was a valued aim of the Presentation Order was also expressed by Sister Doyle: "The new proofs we experience every day of the great good of our labours is an additional cause of gratitude for us."[47] When the Presentation Order made their Bandon foundation, they feared that it might not succeed because of the high concentration of Protestants in the area. They were soon gratified to discover, however, that great numbers of people came to the convent to seek the nuns' care, and many of them were Protestants:

> Crowds of adults have presented themselves to receive instruction, and most zealously have their spiritual and corporal wants been attended to. . . . Innumerable souls have returned to God, and many Protestants have sought for instructions and have embraced the Catholic faith. The harvest has been great for the nuns, whose good fortune it has been to be employed as workers in the vineyard of the Lord.[48]

While the Presentation Sisters, because they observed enclosure, relied on converts to come to them, the Sisters of Charity took a more active role in seeking new members of the church. The Clonmel community recorded how they engaged in what was a very common method of conversion. During the 1860s, this community paid regular visits to the poorhouse hospital. To discourage proselytism, the women were permitted to speak only with individuals who were legally registered as Catholics with the poor-law guardians. On one visit to this particular hospital, the sisters noticed a Protestant man in a bed nearby who seemed to be listening to what they were saying to their Catholic patient. Although the sisters professed not to "attend to any but Catholic patients," the convent annalist noted that they "of course did not lower their voices." The man soon registered himself as a Catholic with the authorities, and the Sisters of Charity began to visit him as well.[49]

Perhaps nowhere were reformed religious practices and attitudes more powerfully inculcated, however, than in convent-run institutions that catered to children, especially convent schools. It was there that children and their families were exposed for the first time to the discipline of the nuns. In the schools of the Sisters of Charity in Gardiner Street, Dublin, children were first subdued before they were taught. Begun during the 1820s by Sister Mary Xavier Hennessy, these schools were considered by many to be the most successful convent schools in Dublin. By drawing on the experience of several educators of the time, Hennessy created a system of school management that provided a superior education in a strictly disciplined environment. One of the strongest influences on her was the new male teaching order, the Christian Brothers, whose discipline she thought sound, though their students did not appear to her to be well-taught. After deciding to try their system of school management, based on the popular Bell and Lancastrian system famous for its use of student "monitors" as teachers, she sought out the head of the order, Brother Edmund Rice, who agreed to lend her one of his brothers for a while. When he first arrived, the convent annalist remarked, "he had to whistle and shout to secure silence" in the schoolroom. But he soon took full command and gradually over the next several months he handed it over to the sisters. By the time that he ceased coming to Gardiner Street, Sister Hennessy had achieved the "perfect order" she wanted. To the disciplinary system of the Christian Brothers, she added her own curriculum, with religious education at the center, and modified the Bell and Lancastrian system to suit her own tastes. The product was a comprehensive system of Catholic education for poor females that became the model on which many other convent schools of various orders in Ireland and England were based.[50] Within two years of their formation, Hennessy assessed the effect of her schools on Irish Catholic children:

> Experience proves our system to excel any other; the children are induced to love their lessons by the attractive manner in which they are given, and religion is a basis of every part of their education. The mind is formed to a sense of piety which does not abandon them.[51]

The effect that the Gardiner Street schools had on their young pupils was repeated in convents throughout the country over the course of the nineteenth century. Priests and bishops praised the schools for the products they turned out. In 1839, Father William Walsh, a parish priest in Kingstown, County Dublin, wrote a letter to the Dublin archdiocesan office to ask if it was true that the Sisters of Charity were considering coming to the town. He and the other priests in the town could hardly contain their excitement, so strong was their belief that only a convent school would be able to counteract the effects of a Protestant proselytizing campaign.[52] And in 1864, John MacEvilly, bishop of Galway, told leaders of the Sisters of Charity that he was much in favor of schools conducted by women religious.[53] Several of his parish priests had told him that they could "easily distinguish the convent children from others by their humble and modest demeanour."[54]

Convent pupils were encouraged not only to learn their new lessons but also to teach them to others at home. By 1860, the Sisters of Charity convent in Clarenbridge was able to report that the use of the rosary in their area had become a general devotional practice. This had not always been the case. "Some years ago," the annalist observed, "the people thought it quite enough in the evenings of Lent, but now it is said daily throughout the year nearly in every house. The children in school did a great deal for Our Lady's glory in this way." The children also did a great deal for mass attendance in this rural area. The annalist who praised the schoolchildren for increasing the frequency with which the rosary was said also lauded them for seeing to it that their parents attended mass on Sundays. She complained that parents often had some "trivial cause" for not attending. Consequently, the children, on the authority of the nuns, were instructed to tell their parents that they were compelled to go. Apparently the message was delivered, for the nuns reported that adult mass attendance began to rise shortly after.[55] Children, then, were an indispensable means of persuading the larger community of Irish Catholics to accept the new code of religious behavior.

The effect that convents had in spreading post-Tridentine Catholicism was impressive, to say the least. In Dublin by the 1860s, orthodox religious practice and the role of women religious in fostering it were the norm. During that decade, for example, the Gardiner Street Sisters of Charity recorded the story of a seventy-year-old Catholic woman who "had no religion her whole life." She came to the convent for the first time because she had "begun to go to mass like other people." A parish priest then discovered her total lack of religious training and sent her to the nearest convent for instruction.[56] At St. Vincent's Hospital, where their successes in advancing the new religious code were routinely recorded, the sisters occasionally had to report a surprising failure. One patient, a middle-class, nominally Catholic man about forty years old, steadfastly refused to approach the sacraments while in the hospital. He was a curious anomaly, and the sisters knew it: "There was skepticism in every feature of his face—in tone, manner, and expression. . . . [He was a man] who seemed to have formed himself on the type of a former century and another country rather than express what is usually met with here."[57]

The religious impact of the work of women religious is perhaps best illustrated by an account of the founding of the Sisters of Charity community in County Sligo. When the sisters arrived at Benada in 1862, they found the neighborhood in a state of "neglect of every Christian duty." They attended the parish chapel and saw that few adults and no children came to church, and "only two or three persons approached the Holy Communion on the first Sunday of the month." After just two years of work, the sisters reported that men, women, and children, who had previously appeared indifferent about performing the essential duties of their religion, now crowded into the convent school for instruction. On Sundays and holy days, the sisters led those attending church services in hymn singing and in the recitation of the rosary. Where two years earlier the chapel was nearly empty, it was now full, and seventy or eighty people were receiving the Eucharist weekly.[58] It is no wonder that Cardinal Paul Cullen came to believe by the 1860s that women religious were "the best support to religion."[59]

Constructing the New Irish Catholic Culture

When the Brigidine Order was founded in 1807 by Bishop Daniel Delany with the help of his friend Judith Wogan-Browne, it was done with the idea that the sisters would be a crucial part of the great task of social reform that Delany saw ahead. According to community records, Delany told the sisters that when he first came from France to the diocese of Kildare and Leighlin as a parish priest early in the 1780s, "there was more sin committed on the Sunday than during the entire week, that day being spent by the greater number of the people at public dances, card-playing, cockfighting, and drinking." Delany decided to try to put an end to the "Sunday abuses," hoping especially to influence the parish children. In the chapel at Tullow, he formed a Sunday school and a children's choir. He himself taught the children hymns to sing, while he engaged "some pious persons" of the parish to teach them prayers and simple religious principles.

In fact, the Sunday school was soon expanded to fill the entire day. The children arrived early in the morning and sang hymns before mass in both Latin and English. Singing was followed by readings from the meditations of the great English Catholic Reformation leader, Richard Challoner. Meditations were followed by the first session of Sunday school classes and then by the celebration of mass at noon. At two o'clock, classes resumed until four. The day ended with vespers, and the children left the chapel at five. Soon the numbers of children attending increased, as "many of their own accord began to withdraw from those public amusements" that had previously entertained them on Sundays, and they spent the day instead in religious classes. It was not long, Delaney reported, before

> even the married people began to attend them. . . . Every class went on increasing, and in a short time such numbers attended that the Sunday was spent in a most edifying manner. The profane amusements were abandoned and the whole face of the parish was changed.[60]

Within a few years, however, this ambitious program of behavior modification faltered. The "pious persons" whom Delaney had engaged to run the program did not long remain involved. According to the Brigidine annalist, "the greater part of them did not continue. Some were married and taken up with the care of families. Others left the parish, more died, and many fell away."[61] It was at this point that Delany decided that what was needed to accomplish his goals was an order of women religious. He had learned of the new order founded by Nano Nagle in Cork city, and he appealed to the motherhouse to make a foundation in Tullow. But because of a shortage of sisters at the time, the Presentation Order decided to refuse Delany's request. Consequently, with the help and advice of Judith Wogan-Browne, he decided to set up the Brigidines.[62] These women were able to achieve much of what Delany had envisioned but was unable to do alone. Just one year after the order was founded, the sisters recorded their assessment of the impact their community had made:

> In a short time the people became greatly edified with the persevering, pious conduct of the sisters, and many were led to piety by their example and instructions. The Sunday schools were more frequented, and the children of the convent school became remarkable for their sense of religion, their mildness and general good conduct, and particularly their fear of sin.[63]

This story of the foundation of the Brigidine sisters in Tullow illustrates the dual nature of the impact of the women's orders on Irish society. Religious women not only helped to transform devotional attitudes and practices in Catholic Ireland but also helped to build an Irish Catholic community with new and clearly articulated standards of social behavior. Encouraging the rural population to plant flowers in their yards where dung heaps had once been and training girls to adopt a humble and modest demeanor represented a new dimension of influence which the elite Catholic classes exercised over the "lower orders." The Presentation Sisters of Castleisland, County Kerry, had behavior modification in mind when they opened a convent and schools there during the 1840s. They believed that "it was impossible but that the habits of industry and an improvement of manners, so much wanted by these poor children, should be soon introduced among them."[64]

When the Sisters of Charity opened their convent in the seaside town of Tramore during the 1860s, they considered the girls there to be in sore need of their attention. The town was a popular resort, and the nuns thought the young people too much influenced by their contact with wealthy tourists. According to the sisters, the Tramore girls were too "fond of amusement and dress and were totally wanting in that modest and reserved manner which carefully brought up Catholic girls usually possess."[65] Needless to say, the Tramore nuns moved quickly and decisively to erase the former conduct of the young girls and to replace it with their version of appropriate behavior.

If the young did not escape the transforming power of the nuns, neither did their elders. When three sisters from the South Presentation convent in Cork began that order's second community in the city in 1799, they immediately opened a school for the many poor adults in the neighborhood, "whom they found stupid and ignorant, and many amongst them, who were unfortunately the victims of crime, were speedily reformed."[66] So confident were these women of their ability to reform and "improve" the behavior and manners of the Irish people that they themselves hurried needy friends and relatives into convent-run institutions. One Carmelite nun arranged to have an old friend of hers, who was reportedly living in "sin and misery," admitted to the Donnybrook Magdalen asylum. "I have no doubt," observed Sister Catherine Callaghan, "but [that] the motherly eye, the intelligence, firmness, and sweetness of the Sisters of Charity would not be long without bringing her round."[67]

Adult habits were also thought to be molded by the reading material women religious made available through their lending libraries. This material typically consisted of devotional literature, temperance magazines, and periodicals such as *Catholic Fireside*, which depicted model Catholic life.[68] According to women religious, convent-operated lending libraries discouraged the reading of "pernicious books" and promoted the reading of texts designed to inspire sober attitudes and industrious habits.[69] The reformation of one Clonmel man, "greatly given to intoxication," was reportedly the result of his contact with the nuns. According to his daughter, who read to him in the evenings from books she borrowed from the lending library of the Sisters of Charity convent, this man was "entirely transformed." The sisters steadfastly believed that because of the books made available to him, he became "altogether domestic and continued sober to his dying day."[70]

The nuns also encouraged a new work ethic among the poor. The Monaghan reformatory run by the Sisters of St. Louis was famous for its attitude toward work. According to a report of one inspector of reformatory and industrial schools, "the great principle inculcated in this school is that labour is a duty and that it is an obligation to be constantly occupied."[71] Not only did they preach the beneficial effects of regular work but also they put their beliefs into practical form through the development of small-scale employment schemes. The many convent-run enterprises that sprang up around the country, such as bakeries, laundries, linen schools, woolen factories, and needlework industries, were all aimed at enabling the people to labor for their support rather than having to resort to the common custom of begging.[72] When the Sisters of Charity convent in Benada began to manufacture linen during the 1860s, they believed that the factory would enable

> poor women, who would otherwise spend much time in idleness, with all its vicious consequences, to earn wherewith to supply some of the pressing wants of their families. And such as have not families, to escape by this little addition to their means the poorhouse or beggary.[73]

Perhaps the most significant impact women religious made on social attitudes and behavior was through their sponsorship of the Sodality of the Children of Mary.[74] This society, which appeared in Ireland as early as 1842 in the Ursuline convent in Cork, was promoted as the "highest privilege" to which an Irish Catholic girl could aspire.[75] While sodalities were formed in elite boarding schools and poor schools alike, the code of behavior demanded was the same across the board. According to the rules of the Ursuline sodality in Cork, "the members of the congregation are chosen amongst those who in the schools are most remarkable for piety, regularity, and good conduct." Girls submitted their own names for election to the sodality, and convent superiors made the decision on their admission three months later. Girls who were chosen as members were expected to be "the mainspring and, as it were, the soul and leaders of their companions."[76] There was a period of probation during which the girls were observed in order to determine whether they could fulfill the expectations. If any members were found "frequenting disedifying companions," for example, or exhibiting such faults as "want of reverence" or "disobedience to superiors," they were expelled. In 1875, the governing council of the Children of Mary at the Brigidine convent in Tullow expelled several members who gave "great disedification by speaking in the church and even during mass."[77] During regularly scheduled meetings, the girls listened to lectures delivered by nuns and priests on the importance of prayer and the sacraments and on the necessity for "proper" and "edifying" behavior.[78] For the Children of Mary at the Cork Ursuline convent, that meant obeying such commands as "to be resolved to labour to acquire the spirit of charity and meekness" and "to avoid with particular care all faults which tend to diminish respect for or dependence on [convent] superiors."[79] Their privileged positions were displayed to the public by the blue ribbons and badges they donned whenever they attended processions, funerals, or other community functions.[80]

It is not surprising, given the distinction and honor accorded to a girl accepted into the sodality, that considerable numbers of them applied for admission. At the prestigious Ursuline convent school in Blackrock, 75 percent of the total number of girls attending the school between 1842 and 1852 became Children of Mary.[81] In 1862, the Sisters of Charity at Clonmel began the Children of Mary for the girls attending their poor schools, and 25 percent of the total student body joined in the first two years.[82] These percentages, multiplied by the hundreds of thousands of girls who went through the convent schools between 1840 and the later decades of the nineteenth century, are an indication that, judged by numbers alone, the twin messages of social virtue and religious sanctity were widely disseminated among Irish girls.

Evidence suggests that the messages were received. Nuns' expectations of transforming Children of Mary into virtuous and devout Catholics seem to have been more than satisfied. When Eliza Whelan died in 1872, the annals of the Children of Mary at the Brigidine convent in Tullow recorded that on her death she was awarded the society's highest honor, the so-called Crown of Mary. She had earned this distinction by having never deviated from the code of behavior expected of members in her eleven years as a Child of Mary. According to the annals, she had lived a life of constant sanctity and had displayed the desired virtues of "meekness" and "patience in suffering."[83] The Sisters of Charity kept an unusually detailed account of their girls. The Harold's Cross community in particular was gratified by the behavior of their many sodality members. Reportedly, these model young women, who were "all of the poorer class," were kind and caring individuals who did not speak "uncharitably" of one another and showed kindness to one another, as well as to the poor. If one was sick, the rest provided and cared for her and did her washing, cleaning, and cooking. When one of their poorer members could not afford to take three days off from her job to attend the yearly retreat, those who were a little better off contributed toward making up for her lost wages so that she could attend.

One popular story in this convent's memory concerned a young woman saved from what the sisters were sure would have been a disastrous marriage because she had placed her obligations as a Child of Mary above a romantic excursion to the countryside. The story went as follows. In 1881, one of their older sodality girls agreed to marry a young man named Joe Brady. Not long afterward, however, the man broke off the engagement because, according to the convent annalist, his fiancée would not go on a picnic to Powerscourt, County Dublin, with him and his friends, as she refused to neglect her Sunday sodality obligations. She was upset for a while, but just one year later, when Joe Brady was arrested for the murders of Cavendish and Burke in Phoenix Park, the sisters remarked that she no longer doubted that she had made the right decision.[84] In Tramore, the behavior of the girls whom the Sisters of Charity had at first found "too fond of amusement and dress" was transformed by the effects of this sodality. Through regular attendance at Sunday meetings and the annual retreat, "piety and fervour" were instilled, and according to both the sisters and the parish priests the "modest demeanour" now in evidence, which stood in "stark contrast to their former levity," was universally remarked upon and praised.[85]

In country convents in the west, where nuns found traditional patterns of behavior more difficult to eradicate, the effect of the sodality on young rural females was perhaps even more impressive. When the Clarenbridge Sisters of Charity first organized the Children of Mary for the girls in their neighborhood, they were unable to enroll many members because of popular customs that directly violated the code of behavior promoted by the nuns. According to the convent annals, the country girls in the vicinity of Clarenbridge were unable to attend Sunday meetings because of "the customs of the people," some of which were "occasions of evil and therefore cannot be tolerated in those who claim the happy privilege of being the special children of Mary." The annalist continued:

> What they call matchmaking, for instance, is not unusually carried on at fairs. The young girl's parents or friends bringing her to meet the proposed bridegroom with his friends, one party invites the other into a tent or a public house to treat them. . . . All this is of course considered quite at variance with the decorum required in the Children of Mary.[86]

The Sisters of Charity of Benada, County Sligo, also met with the same difficulties when they began their sodality in 1865. At its commencement, the sisters reported that members were not very numerous because of the "selfish obstacles" parents threw in the way of joining. Specifically, the sisters complained of the traditional Sunday entertainments "from which they [the girls] either cannot or will not be exonerated, even on Sundays, by those to whom they owe submission."[87]

While the sisters first believed the traditional custom of Sunday fairs in the Clarenbridge area to be so deep-rooted that progress was impossible, in fact, it was not many years before they reported a revolution in girls' Sunday habits. According to the nuns, there was a steady and significant increase in the number of girls who abandoned the fairs and attended religious meetings at the convent. This was reportedly the result of the influence of several girls who joined in the first years and who had been willing to meet the demands of the sodality. Because they were acting against community norms, these early members formed a tight-knit and self-supportive group. They evangelized the other girls and young women in the area, "trying to draw others" into the sodality and more generally into practicing the new customs encouraged by the religious women.[88] Twenty years after its troubled beginning, the Clarenbridge community reported that the sodality had become a great success. Most of the girls of the area were involved, and more than a hundred members regularly attended meetings. The fairs and other once-popular Sunday gatherings had declined and been replaced by the orthodox religious practices encouraged by the increasingly numerous and visible Catholic institutions. Twenty years after the Sisters of Charity had despaired of instilling their concept of Catholic female virtue in the girls of Clarenbridge, they could fairly claim that the Sodality of the Children of Mary was responsible in "great measure" for solidifying "the spirit of piety and innocence of the young girls."[89]

The influence of the sodality on the lives of Irish women extended beyond their native Ireland, for Irish nuns believed that membership in the Children of Mary was a perfect preparation for emigration. Membership in the sodality was thought to be foolproof insurance against the many dangers encountered by single emigrant women, especially estrangement from Irish Catholic social values and mores. One religious woman who directed the Clarenbridge Children of Mary maintained that this sodality above all others proved itself wondrously able to prepare Irish emigrant women "to face the temptations to be encountered" in life away from Ireland.[90] They were guided before they left to be devout, chaste, and obedient Catholic girls, and after they arrived in their new surroundings, they continued to be coached by the nuns. Young sodality women who emigrated were encouraged to maintain regular contact with the nuns back home in Ireland. One community reported that, "when the girls go to America or elsewhere seeking employment," they kept up a regular correspondence with the sisters. According to the Sisters of Charity at Harold's Cross, they "invariably" did "good in the different places they are stationed."[91] Children of Mary who had settled themselves in jobs in America were often able to secure jobs for other members of their former sodality who were emigrating.

But even more important in the mind of the Irish sisters was the way Children of Mary preserved Irish Catholic religious and moral values among the emigrant population. One Child of Mary, formerly a member of the Harold's Cross Sisters of Charity sodality in Dublin, provides a perfect illustration of the influence of this sodality in supporting Catholic practice among emigrant Irish Catholics. This particular young woman settled in America at the end of the nineteenth century and found employment in a factory in New York. When she first arrived, none of the other Catholics employed there attended mass because the nearest Catholic church was four miles away, a distance they considered too far to travel. According to the story, this woman persuaded the other Catholics to make the long journey and in so doing was responsible for seeing to it that they all fulfilled their "Sunday duty."[92]

As significant as the Sodality of the Children of Mary was in molding Irish girls and instilling in them a new standard of normative behavior, perhaps the greatest impact of the sodality was in its role as a feeder system for the convents. Overwhelmingly, recruits to Irish convents came directly from sodalities around the country. The Sodality of the Children of Mary was in essence the training ground for future religious women. Children of Mary adopted patterns of behavior similar to those of religious women whenever they met together. For instance, the Brigidine Sisters of Tullow required that girls coming to and going from the weekly sodality meetings adopt a code of silence when encountering one another on the walk to the convent.[93]

The effect of the spread of this sodality on the increase in vocations is not to be underestimated. It is certainly no accident that the beginning of the sharp increase in the number of religious women during the 1860s closely coincided with the establishment of the sodality in convents around the country. From the first years, how frequently Children of Mary entered religious orders was noticeable. The Brigidine Sisters rejoiced over the regularity with which their sodality girls took themselves off to convents around the country.[94] The Ursuline convent in Cork, later Blackrock, expressed similar pride in its results. During the first 10 years (1842–1852) of the Ursuline sodality, 22 of the 84 convent girls (or 26 percent) who enrolled in the sodality entered religious orders. During the second decade (1853–1862), 139 convent pupils were enrolled as members, and 30 (or 22 percent) of these became nuns. The trend continued in later decades: between 1863 and 1872, 118 young women joined, and 28 (or 24 percent) of them entered convents. In fact, so great was the number of Ursuline students who took religious vows that the annalist was prompted to remark that modern Irish convents had reemerged staffed with Ursuline Children of Mary.[95]

If the convents in Ireland were filled with sodality girls from convent boarding schools like that of the Ursulines, missionary convents outside Ireland were popular destinations for the many poorer Irish girls educated by orders such as the Sisters of Charity and the Presentation Sisters.[96] In places like Australia and the United States, wealth and status were not required to become a choir sister. As a result, many women chose to emigrate and enter religious life abroad rather than remain in Ireland and serve as lay sisters.

The Sisters of Charity motherhouse in Dublin in particular trained large numbers of poor young women for the missions by means of the Children of Mary. After the first 25 years of the sodality's existence in Harold's Cross, Dublin, there were 1,647 members on the books. The annalist was pleased not only by the popularity of the society but also by the fact that "vocations to religious life have wonderfully developed" from within the membership. Of the first 1,647 members, for example, 370 (22 percent) joined religious orders in countries all over the world, including Ireland, England, Scotland, France, Belgium, Norway, India, the United States, Mexico, Australia, and New Zealand.[97] By 1900, 2,279 young women had joined the sodality, and 534 (23 percent) of them had entered convents.[98] The Presentation convent in George's Hill, Dublin, which operated a large orphanage, reported similar success. Established in 1862, this convent's sodality produced many "useful members" of religious communities throughout the world. The Ursuline and Incarnate Word convents in America in particular were staffed by women raised and educated by the George's Hill Presentation nuns and trained to the religious life within the context of this vanguard sodality.[99]

It is clear that within fifty years of the Cork magistrate's decision not to prosecute the errant Presentation Sisters for violating the penal laws, his inability to conceive of any large-scale impact resulting from the gathering together of religious women proved singularly shortsighted. Other members of the Protestant minority were more alert. One Protestant woman complained bitterly to both Archbishop Murray and the *Comet* in 1831 of the creeping influence of the

Sisters of Charity. Her concern was not so much with the religious impact of the order but, rather, with the effect that their work was having on the Protestant community. It was her opinion that, in "oppress[ing]" the Catholic people "into better manners," the Sisters were the cause of increasing unemployment of Protestant women in the city of Dublin and, consequently, at the root of growing hostility between the Protestant and Catholic communities.[100] What this woman was able to appreciate was the fact that the work of women religious was more than just religious work. Home visitation as well as convent-run schools, asylums, industries, training institutions, and employment services had a much broader impact than merely changing devotional practices. Women religious were not only crucial in transforming religious practice but also central to the transformation of Irish Catholic culture and identity.

By the 1830s, women religious were well on their way to establishing themselves as the leading female molders and reproducers of the developing modern Irish Catholic culture. The first convent-run institutions had proven their worth and were rapidly duplicated by the many new convents and orders that began to emerge in the following decades. Gradually, these women came to exert a powerful influence over the people of Ireland. Consequently, they became vital components of the social and religious structure that supported the increasingly dominant Irish Catholic culture, and they used their authority to effect changes in both the religious attitudes and the normative behavior of the larger Irish Catholic population. Though the Cork magistrate may not have seen the writing on the wall, the transformation of Irish Catholic culture was to have enormous consequences for the religious, social, and political development of Ireland. And central to this process were women religious.

SEVEN

Bishops, Priests, and Nuns

IMOTHY MURPHY, BISHOP OF CLOYNE, wrote to Michael Slattery, arch-bishop of Cashel, in 1851 complaining of what he believed was a serious problem in his diocese. As we have already seen, Angelina Gould was professed in the Presentation convent at Doneraile in 1829, bringing with her a fortune of approximately £60,000, which, from her profession until her death forty years later, she used to found a dozen convents in the dioceses of Cloyne and Ross.[1] It was not until the early 1850s, however, that this woman came to be seen as a problem in the eyes of the church. At her profession Gould had appointed two clergymen of the diocese of Cloyne as the sole trustees of her property, one of whom was the chaplain of the Doneraile convent where she was professed and an intimate friend, Father Morgan O'Brien.[2] Murphy pointed out to Slattery that because of this arrangement "the bishop was excluded from all and any voice, whether potential or optative, in the management or dispensation of her property." Moreover, "the absolute dominion and power claimed" by her clerical trustees was, according to Murphy, "directly in conflict with the recognized canonical rights of a bishop in his diocese."[3] Those rights which Murphy felt had been abrogated were set out at the Council of Trent almost three hundred years earlier, and of particular importance here was the right of the bishop to sanction "in the first place" the building of all monasteries and convents. The problem in Cloyne was that because Gould had not designated the bishop as a trustee, the decision about where to build a convent, as well as the choice of the order, was a power that legally belonged to two priests and not to the bishop. For twenty years, Gould and her trustees had been founding convents and asking for "the bishop's sanction in *the second place*."[4] In other words, for twenty years the bishops of Cloyne had been acting as something of a rubber stamp to the decisions made by Gould and her clerical friends. Murphy's outrage was clear. In closing his letter to Slattery in 1851, he declared disgustedly: "[I]n all this the bishop in his own diocese must be an humble and often a disappointed suppli-ant from *two* of his own clergymen while dispensing the religious bequest of a professed nun!!!"[5] Although according to Murphy, two of his predecessors in Cloyne, Bishops Coppinger and Crotty, had complained of the absence of con-trol over Gould's money, the existing evidence does not support this conten-tion. On the contrary, neither Coppinger nor Crotty appears to have objected to the arrangement, while Coppinger, a cousin of both the foundress Nano Nagle and Angelina Gould, promoted the new Presentation Order while at the same time playing a supporting role to its strong female leadership.[6]

This "problem" in the diocese of Cloyne was brought to the attention of Archbishop Paul Cullen, who at this time was beginning to promote increased episcopal control over the burgeoning conventual movement as part of the on-going drive to transform the Irish church. In the following year, Cullen negoti-ated a settlement that allowed the bishop of Cloyne to claim the right to be-come a permanent trustee.[7] An important feature of the development of Irish women's orders is illuminated by this account of the controversy surrounding one of the great Irish foundresses. Prior to the middle of the nineteenth century, family and local interests were of paramount importance to the clergy and hier-archy of the unreformed Irish church. In this atmosphere, individual bishops and clergymen were more interested in assisting and supporting the women who ran the new orders than in controlling them. The example of Coppinger's willing-ness to allow his cousin Gould and her trustees so much power in decisions about where to found convents illustrates this point.

With the growth of a strong national Irish Catholic church, this situation changed. The successful establishment of women's orders and the increasing visibility and impact of their work made them a prominent part of the Irish church and therefore subject, as were all other church personnel and institutions, to the effects of reforming bishops. Furthermore, by the middle of the century the prevalence of wealthy women like Gould was becoming much rarer. The reli-gious authority of the early foundresses had been intensified by the authority they could claim as members of a wealthy Catholic elite. But later, as both con-vent leaders and rank-and-file members were gradually drawn from less wealthy and influential segments of society, their authority was weakened vis-à-vis the male hierarchy.

Increasing episcopal control led to conflict between the convents and the hierarchy. Eventually, the degree of autonomy possessed by the women's orders in their formative years declined. Orders whose early leaders had exhibited a great deal of independent spirit were slowly brought under stricter control. In this process, orders like the Mercy Sisters, which were organized in a way that facilitated this extension of episcopal authority, came to be dominated by the bishops during the great postfamine period of expansion.

Contesting Clerical Authority

In the eighteenth and nineteenth centuries, women's religious orders and con-gregations in Ireland, like women's orders throughout the rest of the world, were subject to male governance. A general management model was established at the Council of Trent, and religious communities had followed that model ever since. Briefly, all religious orders and congregations were subject to the authority of a male superior, though there were several different arrangements possible. Religious orders associated with male orders—for example the Carmelites, Poor Clares, and Dominicans—were traditionally governed by the male wing of the order. The superior who oversaw the male houses also supervised female ones. This traditional arrangement was particularly prevalent at the beginning of the period of this study. As part of the process of increasing episcopal control to be discussed here, some of these communities came under the jurisdiction of diocesan bishops. This came about most often as the result of conflicts within the order or as a means of reforming particular lax communities. Again, the move for reform usually originated within the communities themselves.[8]

The modern, centralized women's congregations like the Irish Sisters of Charity and the Holy Faith sisters were under the jurisdiction only of the bishop of the diocese in which the motherhouse was located. While it behooved each convent of the order to establish a working relationship with the local bishop (benefits, especially financial ones, could accrue to those on friendly terms with the local hierarchy), convents in centralized orders required the authority of the mother general and not that of the bishop in order to act on many matters of importance. The most significant of these was the domain of financial affairs. Nonetheless, centralized congregations were still subject to the bishop of the diocese in many important matters. They still needed the local bishop's permission to engage in charitable enterprises, for example, and to open schools. The diocesan bishop was also responsible for assigning priests to act as chaplains and confessors.

Finally, in modern, decentralized orders and in congregations that were not affiliated to a male order, such as the Presentation Sisters and the Sisters of Mercy, each house was under the direct jurisdiction of the local bishop. The Mercy constitutions, for example, stated that all convents in the congregation "shall be always subject to the authority and jurisdiction of the diocesan bishop, and the sisters shall respect and obey him as their principal superior after the Holy See."[9] If the bishop was too busy to oversee the convents in his diocese, the rule stipulated that he would appoint a priest to act as superior in his place. According to the constitutions, the superior, whether the bishop himself or a proxy, exercised a considerable degree of control over the community. He was charged with approving all women to be admitted or dismissed, with overseeing the financial accounts of the convent, and with attending to all "weighty matters" put before him by the mother superior. Finally, the Mercy constitution stipulated that "the superior shall visit the convent every year . . . to examine whether the rule and constitutions be exactly observed, the obligations of the institute be duly fulfilled, and whether the sisters live in perfect harmony, union, and charity."[10]

While the degree of control that bishops and their clerical representatives could exercise over convents was quite considerable in theory, in practice it varied depending on time and place. Before 1850, few bishops exercised their obligation and right to oversee the convents in their dioceses. Even after 1850, when the reform movement entered its most intense phase, there were a few bishops who never developed a policy of interfering in women's religious establishments. Yet, as episcopal control was gradually increased, it was often contested, especially if it was thought excessive.

Women religious, especially those in leadership positions within the community, developed a set of strategies designed to moderate or deflect the effects of such interference and to allow them to maintain as much control as they could over their communities. These strategies ranged in earnestness from subtle manipulation of the clergy in matters of small importance to open defiance of episcopal directives in matters that threatened the integrity of the community. As a consequence, when episcopal control was intensified beginning in the 1830s as part of the reform movement, nuns, priests, and bishops coexisted in considerable tension and conflict.

The female leaders of the prefamine years were fairly aggressive in their dealings with the clergy and hierarchy. Except for leaders of financially troubled convents (who tended to be very obsequious in their communications with the hierarchy), mother superiors liked to tell priests and bishops exactly what they expected of them in a bold and forthright style. When, according to the rules, events took place that required episcopal participation or supervision, convent mothers typically made the arrangements and then dictated, with assurances of respect and obedience, these arrangements to their male superiors. Diocesan archives are filled with letters like the one from Sister Mary McKeown of the Presentation convent in Maynooth, County Kildare, to Dean John Hamilton, male superior and confessor to the community: "I come to beg as a particular favour that you will take the earliest train after your mass tomorrow as I am very anxious to see you for confession, but you will be able to return to Dublin on Tuesday morning."[11]

The foundress and general superior of the Loreto Order, Mother Teresa Ball, regularly made the arrangements for the required attendance of prelates at receptions and professions and then informed them of what had been done after the fact. In one letter to Hamilton, she indicated that the receptions and professions had been arranged, that Archbishop Murray was to say mass for the event, that he (Hamilton) was invited to come, and that she had arranged for another priest to pick him up and take him to Rathfarnham at 7:30 on the morning of 21 December.[12] To judge by the fact that there was almost no negative reaction on the part of bishops or male superiors to this practice, it appears to have been widely accepted by the hierarchy.

Sometimes bishops would not or could not be told what to do. In these cases, convent leaders resorted to subtle (and sometimes not so subtle) manipulation. Priests and prelates alike were manipulated, generally in order to achieve one of several things. First, women religious used this tactic to modify the decisions or views of the bishop or male superior so that their decisions conformed to the wishes of the convent.

In 1802, Mother Mary Francis Tobin successfully persuaded the bishop of Cork to have a beloved advisor and confessor, Reverend Jeremiah Collins, returned to the South Presentation convent. A year earlier, in anger over the fact that Collins had sided with the nuns (and consequently against the bishop) in a major convent dispute, Bishop Moylan had had the priest transferred to a parish outside the city. Despite the difficulties of travel and the expense of food and lodging for both himself and his horse, Collins continued to come regularly to the convent. Finally, Tobin launched a determined campaign to get the priest back. Tobin addressed a long and persuasive letter to Moylan that informed him that the community was on the verge of collapse. Tobin explained that to carry on steadily in an institute like theirs, where there was so much labor, "requires the spiritual helps of a regular daily mass, the frequent use of the sacraments, [and] the zealous, prudent direction of a confessor such as he [Collins] has proved himself to be." Furthermore, their spirit was currently flagging; zeal was desperately needed and this could only be had, according to Tobin, through the means of daily mass and Jeremiah Collins. Tobin added that the parent house of the Presentation Order was in danger of "fall[ing] to the ground," and should this happen, she assured the bishop that the entire institute would fail.[13] Moylan responded to Tobin's assessment (which included the implication that it would be his fault if the institute collapsed) by granting her request, and Collins returned as confessor to the community, where he remained until his death in 1829.[14]

Women religious also engaged in manipulation when they wished to defy the wishes of a male superior directly. In December 1846, for example, Walter Meyler, a member of Archbishop Murray's council and acting superior of the Poor Clare convent in Harold's Cross, County Dublin, was forced to rescind an order he had given the community. Meyler discovered that the orphans under the care of the sisters were not going to confession because, as the prioress of the community had informed him, the community's confessor was not liked by the children and most of them refused to confess to him. Meyler told the nuns that since the children had been away from the sacrament for too long, they must confess to the priest regardless of their inclinations. The prioress decided to resist his order. She informed him that in so serious a situation she had had to lay the matter before the archbishop. Meyler, upon learning that the archbishop was involved, "immediately acquiesced."[15] What she failed to tell him was that the community had had no response from Archbishop Murray. The prioress knew that Meyler would not intervene if he learned that Murray was involved, and so she led Meyler to believe that he was, when, in fact, he had only been formally notified of the situation. The prioress used the archbishop's higher authority to deflect Meyler's directive. Consequently, the Poor Clares were able to achieve their immediate goal of refusing the services of their confessor.

Women religious also manipulated episcopal authority in order to achieve clearly identified community objectives. Understanding completely what kind of pressure could be brought to bear by members of the hierarchy upon all members of the church, both male and female, women religious often attempted to use that authority for their own purposes. Not surprisingly, money was a frequent motivating factor. When charitable legacies were being divided up, for example, women religious regularly appealed to their local bishops to persuade them to use their influence upon the trustees in order to secure some of the funds for their enterprises.[16]

Money for charitable works—or rather the lack of it—was a continual source of insecurity for the Sisters of Charity in Cork city. Because this community had been in serious conflict with the bishop since they came to the city, they had not benefited financially from the distribution of certain funds such as legacies, which the bishop had at his disposal. Because the convent was part of a centralized order, it was able to survive with financial support from the motherhouse in Dublin, but it did not thrive in the same way that the Presentation or Mercy convents in the city did. Shortly after the death of Bishop Murphy, however, the community wasted no time in ingratiating itself with the new bishop with an eye to bettering their position in the city. In a letter to Mary Aikenhead, the foundress and general superior of the order, the rectress of the Cork community described her community's efforts in this regard. Mother Mary de Chantal Coleman told Aikenhead that when the new bishop paid his first visit to the convent, she asked him to have his name inserted, instead of the late bishop's, as a trustee for the funds of the house. When he replied that he saw no need for this, as he thought that the current trustees were sufficient, Coleman responded that "we wished for the bishop of the place" to be a trustee. She informed Aikenhead that she could see that this acknowledgment of episcopal importance "pleased [him] and it is to be done."[17] She then immediately proceeded to discuss with him a problem which troubled the community. While Bishop Murphy was alive and a trustee, they had never received the rents from several houses they owned. The new bishop assured her that "there was no doubt of our succeeding in getting them,"[18] and it was not long before they did. Though certainly it was not their only motivation, one reason why this community sought better relations with the new bishop was to get him to work on their behalf.

Sometimes it was necessary to use other tactics to get things done efficiently. One of these was to consult the bishop after decisions had been taken and plans already made. This enabled communities to take action in a timely manner, especially when bishops neglected to respond to requests as promptly as women religious wished. In 1807, for instance, a neighbor of the Presentation convent in George's Hill, Dublin, informed the community that he was selling his property to a distillery. The sisters were reportedly "distressed" at the "nuisance" of having another distillery in the neighborhood, and since time was of the essence, they decided that they would buy the property themselves. It was only after the decision to make the purchase was made and the money was raised that permission was requested of the bishop.[19]

This tactic was not used only by the Presentation Order. Two weeks after the Sisters of Charity arrived in Waterford city to make a new foundation there, they began their work among the Catholic population. Teaching and home visitation duties were assigned to the sisters and to several laywomen friends of the community, and the job of soliciting money from the wealthier Catholics was begun. After all the preparations were completed and the work commenced, the new community wrote a letter to the bishop of the diocese seeking his permission.[20] So pervasive was this way of doing business with their male superior that permission to execute their plans came to be viewed almost as a rubber stamp by women's communities in the prefamine period. This is well illustrated by a postscript to a letter written to the male superior by Reverend Mother Magdalen Rafferty of the Presentation convent in Richmond, County Dublin: "I almost forgot to ask permission to have the retreat early. A good priest from All Hallows will give it before he leaves for the country."[21] And so he did.

It was in the attempt to control their spiritual life that women religious were probably most adamant about negotiating with their male superiors and prepared to use every tactic they could think of to get what they wanted. Indispensable in women's communities were the chaplain and confessor. These priests had considerable influence over the spiritual life of the convent, and in order to determine the quality of that life, mother superiors, feeling it their responsibility and their right, attempted to exert as much control as they could over their selection.

The attributes most desired, which convent mothers attempted to ensure in their priests, were religious zeal and accommodation to the needs of the community. Several well-respected nineteenth-century chaplains were described by convent annalists as possessing "ardent zeal" and "saintly" dispositions, as being examples of "living sanctity," and as serving the community with "strict exactness to every duty."[22] Furthermore, the priests who were most valued were those who respected and complied with the rules of the women's communities. One particular favorite was Father Horgan, chaplain to the South Presentation community in Cork city for thirty-two years: "Winter and summer found him undeviatingly at the foot of the altar at seven o'clock, the hour appointed by the holy rule for mass. And when on a few occasions illness obliged him to be absent, he was most exact in securing a priest to supply his place."[23]

In contrast, clergymen who did not devote themselves exclusively to the spiritual needs of the women or, even worse, who attempted to change or deviate from the duties as prescribed in the rules were not long tolerated by convent mothers. Communities of women expended a great deal of time and energy in ridding themselves of advisors whom they found unacceptable and in replacing them with those who were. The South Presentation community encountered unresolvable problems with one parish priest who was acting as chaplain in 1835. According to convent records, because "the many engagements and parochial duties of Archdeacon O'Keeffe [were] a hindrance to the attention essential for him to give to our affairs," the community asked for a visitation from the bishop, who agreed to give them a new chaplain, their close friend Father Theobald Mathew.[24]

In 1841, the William Street Poor Clare convent in Dublin had one of their confessors removed from his post. The prioress informed Archbishop Murray that the priest in question, Reverend Murphy, would not do: "Our sisters are not satisfied with him as confessor. . . . If you please to inform Rev. Mr. Murphy." She concluded by telling Murray that "Rev. Mr. Quin of Westland Row has been mentioned [as a replacement] if Your Reverence would approve of it."[25]

Between 1845 and 1847 the superior of the Carmelite community in Blackrock, County Dublin, Sister Gertrude White, was also busy appealing to the archbishop in order to rid herself of an unsuitable chaplain. The chief complaint against Henry O'Shea was that he was willing neither to provide a mass at the desired hour of seven o'clock in the morning nor to furnish services on the many holy days set aside for special devotional practices. Upon discovering this defect, White immediately attempted to have him removed and to name his replacement. She told the archbishop that "if Doctor Ennis," who was acting in Murray's place as male superior of the convent, "cannot supply us with a clergyman that will say mass at the community hour and give sufficient time and the holy benediction, there are two clergymen that I think would be happy to come as chaplain."[26] White's attempt to secure one of her own candidates was not successful at this point and the hierarchy's appointee remained in the position. But in 1847, after two years of unreliable and unacceptable spiritual service, White dismissed O'Shea on her own authority and found another chaplain to serve the convent.[27] O'Shea declined to acknowledge White's dismissal, and with the archbishop's knowledge he refused to leave the convent. After five months without an income, however, O'Shea begged Murray to give him a post elsewhere, and after a prolonged but determined struggle the Blackrock community was finally free of him.[28] Although White had already engaged another chaplain in his place, the bishop still had the right to formally appoint one. Before this was done, White suggested to the bishop a candidate of her own who "would attend here if your Lordship approves."[29] To judge by the fact that no further correspondence took place over this issue, it is likely that White got the appointment she wanted.

Manipulating episcopal appointments of chaplains and confessors, though fairly effective, was not foolproof. Irish convents therefore developed a regular and widespread custom of inviting their clergymen friends to visit and minister to their spiritual needs. Encouraging visiting clerics to call on them and even to stay in the convent was a means of ensuring their access to priests of their own choosing. In exchange for the convent's hospitality, these men provided the community with masses and confession. Clergymen and religious women also took this opportunity to socialize and visit with special friends and relatives.[30] Reverend Mother Ignatius Taylor, part of a family with many religious members, including William Walsh, archbishop of Dublin, regularly entertained visiting clerical relatives at the Presentation convent in George's Hill, Dublin, during the 1840s and 1850s. Among the most frequent guests was her cousin, the abbot of Mount Melleray, who, it was said, "always visited her when in Dublin and said mass for the community," as did "many other fathers of his monastery."[31]

The Mercy convent in Baggot Street, Dublin, was particularly adept at utilizing the services of visiting priests. After a long disagreement with the Dublin hierarchy, during which the community refused to use the services of the diocesan-appointed chaplain, the head of the community, Mother Vincent Whitty, wrote to one of her opponents at the archbishop's house, explaining (after she had been asked) how it was possible for the convent to do without the chaplain's services: "I did not need [to] engage a priest to say mass, for on account of the [business] with Dublin of bishops and clergy from the numerous localities where our convents are established, we have frequently 2, 3, and even 4 masses on one day."[32]

During the 1820s, the Sisters of Charity convent in Cork city made use of a visiting priest from the neighborhood to fulfill their spiritual needs. For several years after its foundation this community had been without a chaplain because Bishop John Murphy had refused to appoint one. His resistance was an act of pique in response to Mary Aikenhead's refusal to relinquish centralized control over the Cork community or its financial resources. In lieu of a chaplain, the sisters were expected to hear mass at the nearby cathedral. As a rule, this was a mandate generally disliked within communities of religious women, who preferred having a private mass within their convent at times convenient to their own daily routines. In addition to the loss of control over their own schedules which attending the cathedral entailed, the Cork community was also critical of the irregularity of the masses there, which were often canceled at the last moment. The sisters were angered by the bishop's action, and in response they befriended a young priest in the parish, Father Crowe, whom they began to invite to the convent to say mass. Within a short time, Father Crowe became their "de facto chaplain," filling that post for two years, without any formal permission of the bishop, in exchange for the convent's hospitality.[33]

Because priests were a necessary and important element in the spiritual life of the convent, mother superiors attempted to exert as much control as they could over their selection and their performance in order to maximize the quality of that life. The appointment of chaplains and confessors ultimately rested with the hierarchy, however, and when convents were unable to influence the choice to the degree that they wished, they resorted to entertaining reverend friends and relatives in exchange for masses, confessions, and spiritual advice and guidance. This was a powerful weapon. In utilizing visiting clergymen in this way, mother superiors not only augmented the richness of their community's spiritual life but also undermined episcopal authority by circumventing the services of regularly appointed advisors if the need or desire arose.

Leaders of women's communities in the prefamine period were cognizant of the limits of the authority of their male superiors, and when strategies like those already mentioned failed to quell unwarranted priestly or episcopal power, they were prepared to challenge and confront their authority. The justification for doing so rested on their right to defend the well-being of their communities. Sister Gertrude White, superior of the Carmelite community at Warrenmount in Blackrock, County Dublin, for several decades during the first half of the nineteenth century, was particularly outspoken in her attempts to defend her community. During the 1820s, she was involved in a controversy with the clergymen of the parish, who attempted to claim the convent chapel as a parish church. The clergymen appealed to the Dublin hierarchy to help the priests to secure a formal agreement with the convent to use the chapel. The attempt ended in failure, however, for the Carmelites refused to acquiesce in such an arrangement. In a letter to Archbishop Murray (who in mediating the dispute asked the convent to share the chapel with the parish clergy), White defended her decision to oppose the plan by saying that, while she had

> the most sincere desire to comply in every way possible to the least intimation of your Lordship's wish, [there was] an *entire impossibility* of discharging our religious duties as we are bound to do while the convent chapel is subject in any way to the interference of the clergymen of the parish.

She also stated that her community did not wish her to agree to such a proposal. According to White, "we cannot sacrifice our quiet and tranquility . . . in order to please or convenience others. . . . It is evident, my Lord, that the clergymen of the parish wish to have everything according to *their wish*."[34] Religious women were careful to differentiate between the warranted and unwarranted exercise of authority by priests and bishops. The power of the bishops was restrained by the understanding that a bishop did not have the right to order a woman to do something that she felt was against her religious duty as a nun or a convent leader. Given this fact, the reverend mother of this community felt able to refuse compliance with the solution proposed by Murray and the parish priests.

Consciousness of the limits and the hazards of male authority was perhaps most artfully stated in a letter written in 1795 by Mother M. Francis Tobin to Teresa Mullaly, foundress of the Presentation convent in George's Hill, Dublin. Mullaly, a laywoman, was trying to increase the number of hours that the sisters were permitted to teach in the schools. Those hours were regulated by the congregation's rules, and Tobin, as spiritual head of the new order, had already refused to entertain the idea of any alteration. In response Mullaly had written to Francis Moylan, bishop of Cork, in an attempt to persuade him to authorize the increase. According to Mullaly, Moylan indicated that he could make the necessary changes. Tobin responded with determined and uncompromising opposition. She allowed that technically a bishop might be able

> to regulate the hours of the day that would be convenient to the children to attend, [but] not additional hours. . . . My dear friend, if every bishop or person that had to do with our institute looked on themselves as authorised to change our constitutions according to each one's zeal, against the will of its members, surely none of us could know at our profession what it was we were obliging ourselves to. Consequently, there would be no use in serving a noviceship, nor in reading and studying our rules during it, if it was not by them we were to live after our vows, and if such was to be the case, I would look on our state not as that of religious but a slavery. And though I know there are few religious orders which have not made some little changes of either taking from or adding to the manner their constitutions have been first formed in, I also know that such changes were the result of chapters held by the religious of the order and not by the wishes or directions of others.[35]

Besides stating clearly the limits of episcopal authority, Tobin also expressed her cautious attitude toward episcopal power in general in an effort to convince Mullaly of the wisdom of keeping control of the community in the congregation's hands:

> Though His Holiness left the forming of our constitutions to the bishops as being [the] best judges of what would answer best in this kingdom, yet he very wisely cautioned them . . . and I can tell you that so much power being left in the hands of the bishops over our institute *was a thing really disapproved* by Father Laurence Callanan, OSF, and other wise heads in Cork.[36]

It was perhaps because of this attitude toward bishops that the early Presentation mothers were steeled to oppose Moylan in order to push through a major alteration of their order. In 1800, the members of the South Presentation convent, with the support of the four other Presentation communities, decided to establish themselves as a religious order within the church rather than remain a religious congregation. This community had had a very difficult time establishing itself in Cork city, where wealthy and prominent women who aspired to the religious life regularly chose the Ursuline convent, which offered its members greater religious status within the church. The physical workload of the typical Presentation sister was also rumored to be far too taxing for most gentlewomen to endure. Consequently, competition for novices, which was in essence a struggle for survival, led the second generation of Presentation leaders to make this modification. While the change meant that these women would increase their status within the church, in accepting increased status the community had to accept the constraint of enclosure that accompanied the privilege. The action taken by the community, then, was a rejection of Nano Nagle's pioneering vision, and for this reason Moylan forcefully opposed it.

Though in the beginning Moylan had not supported Nagle's plan for an unenclosed congregation of women that would continue its philanthropic work within the city (the community believed that he opposed the formation of any new community that would compete with his sister's Ursuline order), since then he had come to support her vision very strongly. Consequently, when Nagle's successors informed him of their decision, he was enraged. A battle ensued in which Moylan decided to use "the full extent of his authority to force" the Presentation Sisters to remain an unenclosed congregation. After having given the sisters "some days to consider well the momentous move we were about to make, and having threatened us with his displeasure did we depart from his views," Moylan met with the community and "asked them in a peremptory manner had they resolved upon relinquishing the project of turning their congregation into a religious order." Mother Angela Collins responded that they had considered Moylan's position, that "they had consulted God by constant prayer," but "still [they would] observe enclosure."

On learning that the sisters would oppose him, Moylan became "much displeased" and "poured forth on them many reproaches." The annalist painted the final scene of this dramatic encounter: "After uttering in as charitable a manner as could be done, the severe threatenings of his wrath as superior (the nuns on their knees all the while), he forbade them to approach the Holy Communion until they yielded to his authority and to his wishes." The Presentation community, however, did not yield. After three weeks without communion, Moylan met with the sisters and "enquired if there had been any change wrought in their feelings or sentiments." The nuns responded that there had been none. In order to defend the interests of their community, these women absolutely refused to accede to episcopal power, which they believed they had the right to challenge. Moylan, "without relenting his former severity," gave way and, according to the annalist, "after some jealous reproaches he withdrew the rigorous command."[37]

The relationship between nuns and their male superiors during the years before the famine was, in sum, a complex one. Though by the rules women religious appeared to have been placed in a hopelessly subservient role to the male members of the church, in practice, convent leaders, who were conscious of the drawbacks of episcopal power, developed a set of effective techniques by which they were able to evade and even contest episcopal authority and control while enhancing their own. The priests who were charged with overseeing these communities were often aware of the inconsistency. One ventured to express his perception of the real state of relations between nuns and their male superiors in a pithy letter to Archbishop Paul Cullen in 1854: "Although after *their* fashion they will do nothing but as they will be told, still, they know how to manage so as to be told what they wish."[38]

Increasing Episcopal Control

By the mid-nineteenth century, the reform of the Irish Catholic church was well underway and, as we shall see, would eventually have serious consequences for the women's orders. In the prefamine, prereform period, individual bishops and priests had not been in a position—nor did they desire—to exert monolithic control over the wealthy and articulate female leaders who were having such a pronounced effect on the revitalization of the Catholic church and the shaping of a devout populace. As previously noted, the fact that the early bishops did not oppose the arrangements Mother Gould made for the disbursement of her inheritance is a clear indication of their lack of concern with control. Moreover, most of the early foundresses were women from the upper echelons of Irish society, and their authority within the church was relatively greater than in later years, when women of less wealthy and influential backgrounds had to contend with a more powerful and authoritarian hierarchy. With the development of a strong, national Irish Catholic church, the relationship between the women's orders, whose leaders were increasingly drawn from less prosperous classes, and their bishops changed. As the hierarchy began to control and regularize all aspects of the church, they focused their attention on this new Catholic institution. The power struggles that ensued both at the level of the individual convent and at the diocesan level demonstrate this process of increasing episcopal control, as well as the loss of power and control experienced by the women's orders. Ultimately, these contests over the claims of female authority within the church led to a serious loss of autonomy for the women's orders.

The maneuvering and manipulation practiced by the swelling ranks of women religious did not go unnoticed by the male members of the church. By the middle decades of the nineteenth century, these women were increasingly made to answer for their attempts at independent action. For example, in 1849 a leader of the Presentation convent at Richmond, County Dublin, was called on the carpet by Dean John Hamilton, the community's male superior. He was angered that the community had gone to court without his permission in order to settle a controversy over a required sewer construction project. In fact, the community had written to him on several occasions, informing him of the plans and requesting his permission. Not receiving a reply, the Richmond community followed a customary and, indeed, routine procedure practiced by convents all over the country of assuming that episcopal silence meant permission. Consequently, the Richmond community, acting on its own behalf, went to court, only to be rebuked by Hamilton. His position thus challenged the customary meaning of silence. The community responded firmly to the challenge. The spokesperson for the Richmond community, Mother M. Rorke, informed Hamilton:

> It appears you forget we were visited twice by the board of health commissioners. . . . Rev[erend] Mother and we all thought you would excuse us if, in the state of uncertainty we were in after having written so often to you without getting a reply, we let the thing be brought before a magistrate.

Though Rorke and her community were angered by Hamilton's position in this affair, their actions were nonetheless constrained by the fight. They would no longer be able to assume the sort of customary lack of interest in convent affairs that had allowed women to act on their own authority unless they heard otherwise. Henceforth, the Richmond community would not act on any matter until they had heard from their male superior. "I beg your forgiveness," said Rorke. "I will know better what you mean by silence for the future."[39]

The process of increasing episcopal control evoked the most controversy over the issue of the convent chaplaincy. As we have seen, during the early days of the conventual movement, convent leaders were fairly successful in their attempt to choose their chaplains and confessors. By midcentury, however, the bishops were challenging this custom. The chaplaincy controversies that resulted appear to have been virtually universal and were a very important arena in which power struggles for the control of the convents were carried out.

The most famous dispute took place in the first Mercy convent in Baggot Street. Throughout the 1840s, this convent was engaged in a battle with the Dublin hierarchy over the right to choose its chaplain. The Baggot Street sisters wanted to associate their chaplaincy with either the Carmelite or the Augustinian fathers. They believed, as did most women religious, that regulars, or priests who were members of religious orders, were more zealous, more dependable, and less demanding in terms of salary than diocesan priests. Furthermore, because the regulars were not associated with the diocesan-based male governance of the women's orders and were therefore not directly involved in relationships of power and control with the women (indeed, they themselves were subject to many similar constraints vis-à-vis the diocesan clergy and hierarchy), they were also more willing to meet the demands of the women than were secular priests. The Dublin hierarchy, however, decided to assert its authority over the women's orders by preventing an alliance between the convent and the regulars, which it feared could pose a challenge to diocesan authority. Consequently, the hierarchy refused to acquiesce in the convent's choice.

Frustrated by their loss of control, the Baggot Street nuns responded by pleading poverty and refusing to pay the bishop's choice the standard rate for a diocesan chaplain. The consequence of this resistance by the convent was that the hierarchy was not able to provide reputable priests as chaplains because only priests who could find no other employment would agree to work for the meager salary the nuns offered. The result was a string of eccentric, incompetent, and mentally unbalanced chaplains. The Reverend Colgan, for example, was hardly a priest whom nuns would long tolerate. Mother Vincent Whitty, then superior of the community, commented on his demonstrated incompetence: "When giving communion, he became so ill and nervous that he told one of the sisters he should rest awhile" and ended the mass.[40] Whitty informed the priest that they would dispense with his services for a few days, but when he returned to the altar, he was no better. "He trembles so," Whitty complained, "that the B[lessed] S[acrament] touches the nose and chin before he can command his hand to place it in the mouth. Altogether, he seems as if he were likely to get an attack of paralysis."[41] To demands by the hierarchy that they increase the chaplain's salary in order to attract priests of better character, the sisters responded that they would do so only if the choice of chaplain was theirs to make.[42]

News of the controversy spread throughout the country through the vast network of convent contacts and because the Mercy mothers contacted every influential cleric they could think of to ask for support. In May 1851, the hierarchy was forced to call a meeting to resolve the issue. The bishop in council refused the convent's request for a regular priest and upheld its decision to appoint a diocesan priest to the post. But because the hierarchy had not the right to force the convent to pay an acceptable salary (it still refused to do so), the hierarchy had to assume the responsibility of seeing to it that its appointees were priests in good standing. The controversy ended in the summer of 1851 with the appointment of a newly ordained diocesan priest to the Baggot Street chaplaincy. The hierarchy had asserted its right to make this appointment, and that right was henceforth accepted by the convent.[43]

The conventual movement experienced increasing control at the diocesan level as well. This was accomplished primarily by the increasing frequency and rigor of episcopal visitations. The half-dozen convents in the diocese of Elphin, for example, were not visited by a bishop until Laurence Gillooly took over the job in 1858. Gillooly's predecessor, George Plunkett Browne, died without ever once having made a visitation. "The old bishops acted similarly," one convent annalist noted. "They felt things were going on right and needed no interference." Gillooly, however, felt differently and began to "interfere" on a regular basis.[44]

In 1854, just three years after the bitter controversy with the Mercy Order, the Dublin hierarchy, now led by Paul Cullen, began to exert greater control over all of the convents in that diocese by means of a comprehensive, documented visitation. Though regular visitations by the bishop were a stated requirement in the constitutions of all the women's orders, in practice they had been used only as a means of settling intractable community disputes. Consequently, as in the case of the convents in Elphin, if things were going well, visitations were often not made at all. This new, diocese-wide visitation was something entirely different. Rather than assuring the well-being of the individual convent, this visitation, like parish visitations, which were also on the increase, was an explicit statement and a clear representation of episcopal authority. As such, its aim was to assess the entire conventual movement itself in order to firmly establish hierarchical control over it. The visitation included a thorough examination of the convent and an interview with each member of the community.

Information was elicited and recorded about the identity of the convent's confessors and chaplain, the lengths of their tenure and their salaries, and the convent's financial affairs. Cullen now wanted a detailed record of all the priests who had regular contact with the convent and of convent income and its sources.[45]

The demand to have fuller knowledge of a convent's financial affairs touched a particularly sensitive nerve, for like control over the choice of attending clergymen, fiscal control was a primary instrument and measure of the autonomy of these communities. Women's orders in Ireland during the eighteenth and nineteenth centuries were self-supporting institutions whose leaders, of necessity, had to be diligent and effective money managers. They were required to divulge their general financial position only to the bishop who exercised authority over them, and they rarely did so unless requested. Never did they share their fiscal business with anyone else. It has been suggested by at least one historian that women's orders were vulnerable to financial victimization by grasping and unscrupulous priests and bishops.[46] Although the occasional convent was sometimes swindled out of its funds in just this way, these incidents were the exception rather than the rule and usually the result of weak leadership. By and large, women religious in the prefamine period maintained tight and efficient control over their money. Furthermore, they realized that this control was central to their ability to direct their institutions and their lives. They knew the value to themselves and their communities of financial autonomy and expressed that awareness in many ways.

Perhaps the way that most alarmed their contemporaries was the frequency with which convents entered the courts to sue for money they felt was rightfully theirs. The majority of convents in this study were involved in lawsuits at one time or another, most of which were efforts to retain control over disputed dowries or other convent property. As a general rule, priests and bishops were alarmed at the alacrity with which nuns resorted to courts of law. They made their displeasure known, but to no avail. This was an area of their lives that women religious defended quite persistently. Financial autonomy, then, was a principal means by which Irish women's religious orders were able to create and preserve a sense of independence within the larger church.

Given this fact, Cullen's diocese-wide visitation of 1854, as well as the even more comprehensive and intrusive one of 1869 (the year of the first Vatican council), was a particular challenge to women's communities. In the process of closer scrutiny, women religious were required to share the details of their fiscal management with the bishops. In so doing, they were made aware both of their accountability to the male hierarchy and of the loss of personal control which sharing that knowledge entailed. By the later decades of the century, bursars of rich and poor communities alike were sending regular financial reports to their bishops, whereas fifty years earlier only struggling convents in attempts to secure monetary assistance had been required to humble themselves in this way.

By the 1860s, challenging episcopal control was becoming increasingly futile. This can be seen in the response of the Irish bishops to a general meeting of the mother superiors of all the Mercy convents in Ireland and England called by the Kinsale and Limerick convents in March 1864. Within twenty years after the death of Catherine McAuley, the Mercy Sisters had become the most popular women's order in Ireland and were spreading at an amazing rate. A serious problem had developed because of this almost uncontrollable growth, however, and some of the old founding mothers began to call for meetings to deal with it. As early as 1847, just six years after McAuley's death, a move was made to centralize the congregation in order to address the problem, and throughout the 1850s Mercy leaders continued to attempt to organize.[47] The problem that so urgently needed addressing was the disunity that was becoming apparent in the order. Some of the founding mothers believed that the growing influence of the bishops threatened the cohesiveness and the spirit of the order itself.[48] It was also thought that because of what had come to be called "private" or "individual interpretation" of its rule, the work that the Mercy Order did and the definition of what it meant to be a Mercy nun differed from one diocese to the next. It appeared to many sisters at the time that the bishops were actually redefining the meaning of the Mercy Order by encouraging individual reverend mothers to take up work that was not in the original Mercy mission.

The controversial pension day school was a good example of this. Although the order had been founded for the care and education of poor girls and women, in many towns the Mercy Sisters were encouraged by the bishops to run pay schools for the middle classes, which many in the order considered a breach of the Mercy mission.[49] In an effort to reassert the sisters' control over the direction of their order, the Limerick convent called this meeting.[50]

Sixty-three convents received invitations. Of these, forty-eight did not attend. Fourteen excused themselves for reasons of old age, sickness, or difficulty in traveling. Seven convents refused to come because the Baggot Street motherhouse was not supportive of this meeting. Without the participation of the first house and spiritual head of the congregation, many Mercy mothers would not take part.[51] Ten Mercy mothers were unable to participate expressly because the bishop refused them permission to do so. Nine convents gave no reason at all for not attending, though veiled comments like "M[ary] Francis of Kinsale . . . can explain why I cannot act as I should wish" lead one to believe that some of them may have been prevented from coming by their bishops.[52] If we eliminate those unable or unwilling to attend, then the bishops refused permission to at least ten of twenty-seven convents invited, and the number may actually have been higher since we do not know if all sixty-three convents asked permission from their bishops to attend.

Several reasons were given by the bishops for their opposition to the meeting, all of which demonstrate the centrality of the issue of episcopal control. John Derry, bishop of Clonfert, refused the Mercy superior of the Ballinasloe convent permission to attend because he did not know precisely what subjects would come under discussion.[53] John MacHale, archbishop of Tuam, who prevented all the Mercy convents in his diocese from attending, objected to the meeting for two reasons. First, he believed that the Mercy leaders who called the meeting did not have the authority to do so without having first consulted the bishops. He reportedly said to one of the Mercy superiors that "he was shocked and scandalized at the idea of nuns having a meeting" without "first having consulted their bishops and making known to them the object of their meeting and consultation." In fact, he made it clear that he would "excommunicate any nun in his diocese who would go to the meeting."[54] MacHale's second objection demonstrates in and of itself the phenomenon of increasing episcopal domination. According to one of the Mercy mothers, "he saw no necessity for any change," and therefore no change was necessary.[55]

Thomas Grant, bishop of Southwark, forbade the two convents in his English diocese from participating because it appeared to him that this meeting, an attempt by several of the remaining founding mothers to clearly define and codify the purpose of their order, would threaten the rights of bishops under the present constitutions. In his letter refusing permission for the Mercy leaders in his diocese to attend, he went to the very heart of the issue. After reading the proposed agenda of the meeting, he observed that if the goal of the meeting "had regarded only the method of doing certain things," for example, how the sisters should dress or conduct certain ceremonies, he "should not be afraid of concurring with other bishops" in allowing the sisters to make these changes on their own behalf. But the agenda also included a proposal to publish the decisions taken at the meeting as a guide to be adopted by all Mercy convents. It was this part of the agenda that disturbed the bishop so. Grant saw "this compilation as defining the meaning of the holy rule itself, and this could not be done even by a meeting of the bishops of the dioceses in which you have houses."[56] Although he was certainly right that a meeting of bishops could not define the Mercy rule, this letter begs the central issue, which was that individual bishops were practically doing this very thing. It is not surprising, then, that Bishop Grant should be alarmed at a Mercy meeting aimed at redefining the order, for such a meeting threatened his own unacknowledged right to define the rule.

The tension that surrounded the 1864 meeting was not just between convents and bishops. The situation was more complex. In the first place, although there were no ecclesiastics who were as outspoken in their support as MacHale was in his opposition, not all bishops opposed the meeting. But of greater importance was the role that women themselves played in undermining the goals of the meeting. The fact that Baggot Street refused to attend came as a great blow to the organizers. The Baggot Street community, however, was led by a very different type of woman than the mothers who waged that long struggle with the Dublin hierarchy discussed earlier. The present superior, Sister Mary of Mercy Norriss, had been in power in the community since shortly after the battle with Archbishop Murray had ended. In 1864, she declined to be involved in the Mercy meeting because, as she declared, "I have always had a holy horror of a 'meeting of women.'"[57] Because of the failure of the Baggot Street community to take the leadership on this very important issue or, indeed, even to consider the complaints of the old mothers, the initiatives of the 1850s and the 1860s repeatedly failed, and competing visions of the order and its organization consequently emerged within the congregation itself.

One of those competing visions came from a Mercy superior in the Sligo town convent, Mother Joseph Jones. She suggested a plan for the reorganization of the order that conflicted with that contemplated by the Limerick community. In 1859, Jones had received a letter from the superior of the Queenstown convent consulting her about "the necessity of some united action and legislation for the establishment of a central authority to secure uniformity of customs and unanimity of views" among the Sisters of Mercy.[58] Jones, whose sister was a prominent superior of the centralized Irish Sisters of Charity, and whose brother Father Daniel Jones was friend and chief advisor to that congregation, consulted both of them for advice on how best to secure a central government like that of the Sisters of Charity:

> He [Fr. Daniel Jones] and my sister, Mother M. Justinian, one of the superiors of the Irish Sisters of Charity, gave me every help and encouragement to undertake the work and procured for me, by special permission, the loan of their own rules in guiding me in putting my work into systematic form.[59]

Jones, in addition to providing his sister with a copy of the Jesuit rule, also carefully examined the constitutions of the Mercy Order. After he had done so, he informed his sister that centralization of the entire Mercy Order was impossible because its constitutions stipulated, as mentioned earlier in this chapter, that all Mercy convents were "subject to the authority and jurisdiction of the diocesan bishop."[60] He did suggest, however, that centralization "could be carried out in each diocese . . . provided the several chapters and communities agreed to it and the bishop approved of it and was willing to carry it out."[61]

Jones decided, beginning in 1860, to work for centralization in the Elphin diocese. She raised the matter with the new bishop, Laurence Gillooly, who was taking much more interest in the affairs of the convents in his charge than had any of his predecessors. According to Jones,

> the bishop entered into the proposed details seriously but seemed cautious and wary about the undertaking. . . . He said and admitted the necessity of it . . . yet until circumstances compelled him to it, he made no move to carry out the programme decided on until 1870, upwards to ten years subsequently.[62]

In January 1871, the Mercy convents in the diocese of Elphin were united into one centralized congregation headed by the motherhouse in Sligo; Jones became the first diocesan general superior. Important here is the fact that the move was initiated by a Mercy leader with intimate connections with the most prominent centralized Irish order of the time. She apparently decided that, barring the possibility of centralization of the entire order, she would settle for centralization of the Mercy convents within her own diocese under her leadership. It is less clear, however, what her plans were for encouraging centralization of the Mercy convents in other Irish dioceses. When the call was issued by the Limerick community in 1864, Jones does not appear to have wanted to participate. The superiors of the other Mercy convents in the Elphin dioceses, however, felt different. Opposed to a merger with Jones, they preferred instead to attend the general Mercy meeting in Limerick. Yet when the heads of the Roscommon and Athlone communities applied for permission to attend the Limerick meeting, Gillooly refused to grant it. "When I have time," he remarked, "I intend to draw up regulations myself."[63]

The important point to be made here is that several different tensions were in play. It is certainly true that, regardless of Jones's disinclination to participate in the Limerick initiative, Gillooly was ultimately responsible for preventing the other two Mercy convents in his diocese from attending the 1864 meeting. Hence, for Gillooly, as for the other bishops, this meeting proved a litmus test of the rights of women religious to control their own orders. As his language clearly demonstrates, Gillooly came down on the side of episcopal rights. But Gillooly's decision to unify the Mercy convents in his own diocese (and, as a consequence, to forbid the Roscommon and Athlone convents from attending the Mercy meeting in Limerick) was not taken on his own initiative. Rather, the determination to do so was the direct result of the persuasion of a Mercy mother herself. Furthermore, that Mercy leader chose to act on behalf of only the Mercy convents in her own small corner of the world. Thus, at the same time that she was responsible for centralizing the convents within her diocese, Jones helped to prevent the larger Mercy congregation from becoming a centralized order. Consequently, her parochial vision promoted the order's continued subservience to local bishops, thus decreasing its autonomy within the church.

One could reasonably argue, however, that Jones's vision was the only practicable one. The Mercy rule, with McAuley's concurrence, had placed its houses in a vulnerable position with regard to episcopal power. While she lived, her influence and supervision were enough to act as a shield against hierarchical domination, which after all was not that strong in the prefamine years. After her death, bishops increasingly manipulated the convents in their dioceses until it was sometimes difficult to know exactly what the Mercy Order stood for. In order to remedy this situation in her own diocesan world, which was all, she was convinced, that could ever be controlled, Jones worked to establish her system of centralization. Significantly, all the Mercy convents were eventually organized on the basis of her plan, thus perhaps vindicating her actions. Nonetheless, if there ever was a time when the Mercy Order might have stood up to the bishops, it was during the 1860s, and Jones did not lend her authority to the task.[64]

The fifteen Mercy mothers who did attend the 1864 meeting produced the famous *Mercy Guide*, an attempt to codify the meaning of the order. But the meeting was unable to do anything effective to stem the power of the bishops. Whereas the Presentation Sisters in the early part of the century believed that they had the right to fight episcopal ambitions when they interfered with the good of the order, individual Mercy mothers by the second half of the century did not feel themselves either willing or able to do so. Hence, the great majority did not come or feel themselves bound by the goals of those who did. It is only fair, of course, to suggest that if the first house of the order had been willing to take a leadership position and challenge the bishops, as had the South Presentation convent, Mercy mothers in many convents might have been inspired to take a stand. But as we have seen, the resistance of the Baggot Street community had been quelled by 1850, and the leadership that emerged in the postfamine period was no longer inclined to confront the bishops. Although there were still some Mercy women who were cognizant of the threat that episcopal power posed for the cohesiveness of their order, their attempt to gain more control came at the very time when the bishops were successfully asserting their authority over the conventual movement.

With the successful establishment of the orders and the reassertion of episcopal authority by the mid–nineteenth century, then, this new, female-led church institution was gradually brought under the firm control of the bishops. The outspoken and assertive character of the early leaders stands in stark contrast to the convent leaders of the later decades of the century, who lacked the elevated class status of the founding women. A certain slavish mentality crept into the convents, and a qualitative assessment of their records shows a much greater concern with episcopal approval and with popularity than had ever existed previously. Thus, in 1866, the Presentation nuns of the George's Hill convent in Dublin remarked with pride and delight that on his return from Rome after receiving his cardinal's hat, the George's Hill community was the first convent Paul Cardinal Cullen visited. It was the next part of the story that really filled the community with pride, however, for on that visit Cullen reportedly declared that the George's Hill community were "the finest nuns in the world."[65]

If the convents began to accept the idea that being pleasing to the bishops was a goal of religious life, the bishops developed an air of possession about the convents. Bishop John Murphy of Cork, for example, became notorious for his possessive and controlling attitude toward the women's orders. Both the Mercy Sisters and the Sisters of Charity mentioned that by the time of his death in 1847 he referred to the religious women in his diocese as "his nuns."[66]

Of course, not all convents or all religious women responded to increasing episcopal control or, indeed, felt that control in the same way or at the same time. There are many examples of communities, especially centralized ones, that sought to exercise their autonomy in the face of increasing hierarchical pressure. Fights between bishops and reverend mothers, for example, did not stop altogether. Several very serious struggles occurred long after Cullen and MacHale had died.[67] Still, by the later decades of the century, these instances became rarer.

By 1850, the women's orders, once a novel and semiautonomous element in a poorly organized and laxly disciplined Irish Catholic church, had become an integral part of that institution. The newly centralized church hierarchy, which was demanding tighter control over all aspects of church life, began to check and regulate this large and influential group of women. Having done so, the church was in a position to fully exploit the explosive growth of the conventual movement, which occurred during the last half of the century.

EIGHT

Conclusion

$\mathcal{T}$ HIS BOOK SET OUT to examine, more closely and more fully than has been done before, the reemergence of women's religious orders in Ireland after 1770. A number of important questions have been posed, and the answers leave us with a very different understanding of the significance of the religious life for women in the nineteenth century. In considering the question of the initiative or the responsibility for the emergence and spread of the new orders in Ireland, the assertion that reforming bishops and priests initiated and managed the modern conventual movement appears to be faulty. From the late eighteenth century on, Irish women, responding to new opportunities for religious expression, formed new religious orders and branch houses of these orders largely on their own initiative. They typically sought support from individual members of the clergy and hierarchy who were either related to the women by ties of kinship or long-standing family friendship or who were known to be sympathetic to women's religious organizations. Though biographies of bishops, histories of individual Irish dioceses, and general Catholic histories routinely credit bishops and priests with providing the motive force behind the spread of convents throughout the country, an examination of the actual ways in which the orders and early convents came into being demonstrates the centrality of women in the development of the conventual movement.

Given that women themselves generated the momentum that led to the rapid expansion of female congregations and orders during the period 1770–1850, the next question addressed was why they should have wanted to found and join these orders. Popular explanations have revolved around the changing social and cultural conditions of postfamine Ireland. Severe demographic changes (which included the virtual disappearance of an entire section of the population), the emergence of a new dominant model of inheritance that precluded the division of property among all children, an unprecedented increase in emigration, and a

marked decrease in the incidence of marriage created social conditions that encouraged and even privileged celibacy. These social imperatives corresponded
perfectly with religious ones. At a time when neither Irish men nor Irish women
had unimpeded recourse to the married life, the reemerging Catholic church
absorbed armies of women and men in its complex mission of social, political,
and religious change.

A close inspection of the lives of women religious, however, makes clear
that these explanations, important as they are, fail to explain fully the reemergence of women's orders. The focus on social and demographic conditions in
the postfamine period ignores the reality that the new congregations had been
formed and had already spread to all areas of the country before the famine. What,
then, is the explanation? The development of women's orders in the nineteenth
century did, indeed, reflect larger changes in the social and economic structure
of Irish society, the most important of which, in terms of the emergence of the
modern conventual movement, was the growth of the socially and politically
ascendant Catholic middle class during the eighteenth and early nineteenth centuries. It was women from this class who filled the new convents, bringing with
them the goals and the responsibilities of their class. Furthermore, these women
made personal, individual choices to join the movement. Their ability to make
these choices and their reasons for doing so tell us much about women religious
and the society in which they lived. While it is certainly possible to argue that,
in the particular context of nineteenth-century Catholic Ireland, women's choices
were limited, still, for their own set of reasons they did create this especially
popular option.

One compelling reason why women made the choice to enter religion was
the nature of that life itself. Communal life was both a spiritual and a material
experience that many women found highly desirable. Of central importance were
relationships of spiritual and personal intimacy that were at the very heart of
religious life. Every community attempted to define and regulate these relationships, for when they were successful, women's communal life had the potential
to be an immensely satisfying experience.

Irish women also joined convents with the hope of effecting social and religious change. In this respect, they undoubtedly achieved a great deal. The re-
organized church that emerged during the nineteenth century was intimately
involved, for better or worse, with its people. This was true not only in Ireland
but also throughout most of Europe. During this century, the Roman Catholic
church, divorced since the French Revolution from its alliance with the ruling
elite, put on a caring face. In all the Catholic countries of Europe, the church
developed large-scale institutions for the care of the sick, the poor, and the destitute, as well as an extensive system of popular education.

A principal goal of this book has been to challenge the notion that the male
leaders of the nineteenth-century Catholic church encouraged female religious
orders in order to facilitate its change in direction toward an emphasis on education and social services. Rather, it was the desire and the ability of women to
create socially active religious orders that made this change possible. Women's
formative work in educational and charitable enterprises helped to create the

"caring" path that the church was able to follow. In the specific case of Ireland, the development of women's religious orders should not be seen as a consequence of the transformation of the Catholic church and Irish Catholic society, but rather as central to the construction of the new, devout, modern Irish Catholic culture.

With the help of women religious, then, the Irish church moved a long way from the state of decay that Nano Nagle decried in the 1750s when she saw "the pulpits deserted and the voices silent which should have thundered aloud with all their energy."[1] Noticeable changes were apparent by the 1820s and 1830s, when a new generation of reforming bishops were appointed. These men, of whom Cardinal Cullen was the most powerful, began regular parish and convent visitations in their dioceses and organized retreats and theological meetings. The objective was to raise the morale and professional competence of Irish priests, to reform and centralize the hierarchical leadership, and to create an influential Irish church firmly attached to Rome. The result was a politically conservative, religiously aggressive, and highly centralized and bureaucratized church.

The women's orders were greatly affected by this transformation. Because of their successful establishment and spread, and because of their significant impact on both the church and society by the middle of the nineteenth century, the women's orders had grown to be a major institution within that church. When the new reforming bishops began to check, control, and regularize church personnel, they focused their attention on this new Catholic institution, as well as on unruly and uncouth parish clergy. Yet the episcopal move to exert control provoked a considerable degree of tension between the burgeoning conventual movement and the hierarchy. Women religious, though they were always careful to acknowledge episcopal authority, were also quick to defend their own. Because of this, relationships between convent leaders and their male superiors were often strained, and many orders were involved in significant power struggles with the hierarchy. These struggles, though they persisted during the entire period of this study, appear to have been most intense and widespread between 1830 and 1860. The same decades that witnessed the transformation of the Irish church also witnessed the peak of the conflict between nuns and bishops.

The efforts of the hierarchy to gain control over the movement were not in vain. Nowhere does this conclusion seem more warranted than with respect to the character of convent leaders in the later decades of the nineteenth century. Earlier women, like Nano Nagle, Teresa Ball, and Mother Vincent Whitty (the Mercy leader involved in the long chaplaincy dispute with Archbishop Murray), had often boldly stood up for themselves and their communities, cognizant of episcopal power but not afraid to confront it. Convent leaders late in the century appear on the whole to have been women of less wealth and very different character.

Admittedly, earlier bishops, taken as a group, were not the force that they became by the 1860s, but later leaders of women's orders appear to have been more obsequious and, sadly, more resigned to submit to male authority. I do not want to suggest that social class determines a type of personal behavior, but class privilege did give some women a voice that the nineteenth-century Irish gender system would not have provided them. Class was crucial, as it always has been, to the ability of women religious to determine the terms of their lives and their work. If depictions of women religious as humble, subservient, and powerless fit at all, they fit the women religious of the years after 1870 or 1880.

Of course, this is a subjective assessment, but it results from a close analysis of the personal documents and correspondence of these women. There were also exceptions. Margaret Aylward, a wealthy woman from a prominent Waterford family, remained a singularly opinionated and outspoken woman until her death in 1889, once prompting a bishop of Ossory to come to Dublin to engage in a face-to-face fight with Holy Faith leaders.[2] And surely the most independent and daring religious woman of the nineteenth century, the famous Nun of Kenmare, Mother Mary Francis Clare (Margaret Cusack), born a Protestant, was involved in a raging dispute with several members of the Irish hierarchy. But if these women stand out as exceptions during the postfamine years, they would not have stood out during the earlier period, and that is precisely the point.

By midcentury, it was clear that the nuns were rendering extremely valuable service. Convent education was instilling into Catholic Irish women those much desired virtues of meekness, patience, modesty, and piety. During the postfamine period, new generations of women religious emerged from those schools. Models of virtue, they were of a decidedly different temperament than those independently wealthy women (some of whom were widows, some born Protestant) who were founders of the orders during the prefamine years. By 1850, these commanding, early leaders were besieged on all fronts. At the same time that the hierarchy pressed for greater supervision and control from above, a new model of Catholic womanhood, which prized docility above most other qualities, was overwhelming them from below. Victims of their own success, it was perhaps only to be expected that the relative independence that early leaders of Irish convents fought to maintain during the prereform period was lost with the devotional revolution. It was a loss that some convent leaders at the time regretted very deeply and that some still mourn today.[3] The irony is that as the creators and enforcers of a new, modern, Irish Catholic ideology that idealized meek and docile women, Irish nuns themselves helped to create the very conditions that ultimately robbed them of their autonomy.

Appendix

List of institutions managed by convents in this study, in operation by 1870

Brigidine Sisters, Tullow
  Convent school (for all classes of children)
  Orphanage (children boarded out to nurses)
  Convent day school ("pay" school, established at request of wealthier Catholics)
  Boarding school

Presentation Sisters, Douglas Street, Cork (South Presentation convent)
  Almshouse (for the aged)
  Convent school (girls)
  Convent school (boys)

Presentation Sisters, George's Hill, Dublin
  Convent school
  Orphanage

Presentation Sisters, Kilkenny
  Convent school
  Lace school

Sisters of Charity (1882: 23 convents)
  Benada Abbey Convent
    Linen school and factory
    Convent school

Clarenbridge Convent, Clarenbridge, Co. Galway
   Convent school
   Lace school (1853–1862)
Clonmel Convent, Clonmel, Co. Tipperary
   Convent school
   Convent day school
Cork Convent
   Magdalen asylum
   Convent infant school
   Convent school
   St. Patrick's Hospital
Donnybrook Convent, Dublin
   Magdalen asylum, formerly Townsend Street Asylum
   Convent school
Gardiner Street Convent, Dublin
   Widows' home
   Convent school
   St. Martin's Orphanage
Harold's Cross Convent, Dublin
   Night school for adults
   Convent primary school
Kilkenny Convent
   Industrial school, linen making
Sandymount Convent, Co. Dublin
   Convent school
   Convent day school
   Industrial school
St. Vincent's Convent, Dublin
   St. Vincent's Hospital
   House of convalescence
Stanhope Street Convent
   Refuge for destitute females of good character, formerly lay-operated
      Ash Street
   House of refuge convent school
   Convent day school
Tramore Convent
   Convent school
Waterford Convent
   Infant school
   St. Martin's Orphanage, formerly Trinitarian Orphanage
   Night school
North William Street Convent
   Orphanage, taken over by Poor Clare Sisters in 1827
   Convent school, taken over by Poor Clare Sisters in 1827

Sisters of the Holy Faith, Glasnevin
    Convent school
    Orphanage

Sisters of Mercy
    Athlone Convent
        House of Mercy laundry
        Lace school
    Sligo Convent
        Orphanage/industrial school
        Laundry
        Farm/training school
        Convent school
        Convent day school
    Mercy Convent, Baggot Street, Dublin
        House of Mercy
        Convent school
        Training college
    Mercy Convent, Limerick
        House of Mercy
        Infant school
        Orphanage
        Lace school (for "indentured" orphans)

Sisters of Our Lady of Charity of Refuge, Drumcondra, Dublin
    Magdalen asylum, formerly Asylum of St. Mary Magdalen
    High Park Reformatory

St. Louis Sisters, Monaghan
    Spark's Lake Reformatory School
    Boarding school
    Industrial school

Ursuline Sisters, Blackrock, Co. Cork
    Boarding school
    Day school

ABBREVIATIONS

Archives cited in this work are referred to by the abbreviations listed below. Full details of the source material used appear in the bibliography.

Convent Archives

B/B	Brigidine Generalate, Blackrock, Co. Dublin
COR/HP	Our Lady of Charity of Refuge Convent, High Park, Drumcondra, Dublin
HF/G	Holy Faith Generalate, Glasnevin, Dublin
M/A	Mercy Diocesan Generalate (Elphin), Athlone
M/B	Mercy Convent, Baggot Street, Dublin
M/C	Mercy Convent, Cork
M/Cf	Mercy Diocesan Generalate (Dublin), Carysfort
M/L	Mercy Convent, Limerick
P/C	South Presentation Convent, Cork
P/GH	Presentation Convent, George's Hill, Dublin
P/F	Presentation Convent, Fermoy
P/K	Presentation Convent, Kilkenny
P/Y	Presentation Convent, Youghal
St.L/M	Sisters of St. Louis Generalate, Monaghan
SOC/M	Sisters of Charity Generalate, Milltown, Dublin
U/C	Ursuline Convent, Blackrock, Co. Cork

Diocesan Archives

CAA	Cashel Archdiocesan Archives (on microfilm, NLI)
DDA	Dublin Diocesan Archives

EDA   Elphin Diocesan Archives
KDA   Kerry Diocesan Archives

Other Archives

NLI   National Library of Ireland

NOTES

Chapter 1

1. Emmet Larkin, "The Devotional Revolution in Ireland, 1850–1875," *American Historical Review*, 77 (1972): 625–52; David Miller, "Irish Catholicism and the Great Famine," *Journal of Social History*, 9 (1975): 81–98; Desmond Keenan, *The Catholic Church in Nineteenth-Century Ireland: A Sociological Study* (Dublin, 1983); Sean Connolly, *Priests and People in Pre-Famine Ireland, 1780–1845* (Dublin, 1982); Patrick Corish, *The Irish Catholic Experience: A Historical Survey* (Dublin, 1985); Kevin Whelan, "The Catholic Church in County Tipperary, 1700–1900," in William Nolan and Thomas G. McGrath, eds., *Tipperary: History and Society* (Dublin, 1985); Whelan, "The Regional Impact of Irish Catholicism, 1700–1850," in W. J. Smyth and Kevin Whelan, eds., *Common Ground* (Cork, 1988); Whelan, "The Catholic Community in Eighteenth-Century County Wexford," in Thomas P. Power and Kevin Whelan, eds., *Endurance and Emergence: Catholics in Ireland in the Eighteenth Century* (Dublin, 1990).

2. Connolly, *Priests and People*, pp. 6–9.

3. Maureen Wall, *The Penal Laws* (Dundalk, 1961), pp. 15–19, 36–37; Connolly, *Priests and People*, pp. 60–61. Ireland is divided into four ecclesiastical provinces or archdioceses: Armagh, Dublin, Cashel, and Tuam. The four archdioceses are in turn divided into a total of twenty-six episcopal dioceses. Each of the four archbishops heads not only the archdiocese but also the diocese in which his see is located. Consequently, there are twenty-two bishops and four archbishops in the country.

4. Connolly, *Priests and People*, pp. 65–70.

5. Larkin, "The Devotional Revolution," pp. 625–52.

6. For a recent discussion of the devotional revolution debate, see John Newsinger, "The Catholic Church in Nineteenth-Century Ireland," *European History Quarterly*, 25 (1995): 247–67.

7. See especially, Miller, "Irish Catholicism and the Great Famine," pp. 81–98, and Keenan, *The Catholic Church in Nineteenth-Century Ireland*.

8. Connolly, *Priests and People*; Whelan, "The Catholic Church in County Tipperary," "The Regional Impact of Irish Catholicism," and "The Catholic Community in Eighteenth-Century County Wexford."

9. Louis M. Cullen, "Catholic Social Classes under the Penal Laws," in Power and Whelan, *Endurance and Emergence*, pp. 57–62; Maureen Wall, "The Rise of a Catholic Middle Class in Eighteenth-Century Ireland," *Irish Historical Studies* 11 (1958–59): 91–115.

10. Whelan, "Regional Impact of Irish Catholicism."

11. Connolly, *Priests and People*, pp. 22–23.

12. Joseph Lee, *The Modernisation of Irish Society, 1848–1918* (Dublin, 1973), pp. 1–3.

13. Ibid., p. 271.

14. Throughout this work I refer to groups of religious women who, though technically distinct, are treated as similar entities in the popular consciousness. Like most individuals working in this area, I have chosen to refer to these two different types of religious women as if there were no such distinction. For the record, however, there were two canonically valid forms of religious organization for women in the nineteenth-century Catholic church. First, there was the religious *order*. Women in these communities took solemn, lifelong vows, were committed to strict enclosure within their convents, and received the title of *nun*. There was also a newer form of organization known as the *congregation*. Women in congregations took simple, less binding vows, worked outside the convent, and went by the title of *sister*. In all but the most arcane of circumstances, "order" and "congregation," "nun" and "sister" were used interchangeably. Given this fact, I have chosen to do the same.

15. The only way in which women were able to continue living together in religious communities throughout the period between about 1550 and 1750 was by stealth and subterfuge. At this they became quite adept. Women religious, dressed in sober, black gowns and living in ordinary-looking dwellings, masqueraded as spinsters running boarding schools and boarding houses. Elizabeth Barnewell, for example, organized a secret conventual establishment during the reign of Elizabeth I. Honoria Burke became a professed Dominican in Ireland at the same time. She and several other women lived together until the winter of 1653, when some of Cromwell's men raided their establishment, beat and stripped the women, and turned them out of doors to die near Burrishoole, Co. Mayo. For more information on the religious life of women during the years 1550–1750, see Mrs. Thomas (Helena) Concannon, *Irish Nuns in Penal Days* (London, 1931).

16. These establishments included two Poor Clare communities, one each in Galway and Dublin (in 1753, a second Dublin community brought the number of houses up to three); four Dominican convents in Galway, Dublin, Drogheda, and Waterford; four Carmelite communities in Galway, Loughrea, Cork, and Dublin; and finally, two Augustinian establishments in Galway and Dublin.

17. Richard W. Southern, *Western Society and the Church in the Middle Ages* (New York, 1970), pp. 310–31; Anthony Fahey, "Female Asceticism in the Catholic Church: A Case-Study of Nuns in Ireland in the Nineteenth Century" (Ph.D. Dissertation, University of Illinois at Urbana, 1981), pp. 19–23.

18. Eileen Power, *Medieval English Nunneries, c. 1275 to 1535* (Cambridge, 1922), pp. 341–50. Women who joined the Dominicans, for example, took solemn, lifelong vows and lived in perpetual seclusion within the convent cloister. This degree of containment obviously prevented female Dominicans from adopting the order's social mission because they were unable to leave the convent.

19. Concannon, *Irish Nuns*, pp. 22–25.

20. Power, *Medieval English Nunneries*, pp. 345–93; Caroline Walker Bynum, *Holy Feast and Holy Fast: The Religious Significance of Food to Medieval Women* (Berkeley, 1987),

pp. 13–22. Bynum stresses the fact that after the Cluniac reform new forms of religious life for women appeared in addition to the new monastic arrangements. These included not only the tertiary and Beguine movements but also mystical, prophetic, and heretical movements.

21. After getting out of a German prison, Ward took her case to Rome, where she was exonerated by the pope, who then provided her with enough protection to ensure the order's survival. Its main English convent was the Micklegate Bar convent in York, where several of the foundresses of Irish orders served their novitiates during the early nineteenth century.

22. Fahey, "Female Asceticism," pp. 31–46; Mary Ewens, *The Role of the Nun in Nineteenth-Century America* (New York, 1978), p. 20.

23. T. J. Walsh, *Nano Nagle and the Presentation Sisters* (Monasterevan, Co. Kildare, 1980, first published 1959), pp. 36–100.

24. Corish, *Irish Catholic Experience*, p. 203.

25. Charles Vane, ed., *Memoirs and Correspondence of Viscount Castlereagh* (4 Vols., London, 1848–49), 4:99. This percentage is derived from Vane's figures for nuns and priests, which are 122 and 1,850, respectively.

26. These percentages are derived from census figures cited in Fahey, "Female Asceticism," p. 57. The 1851 census tables of occupation listed 2,500 secular and regular priests. The 1901 tables listed 3,436 priests and 1,159 brothers.

27. Caitriona Clear, *Nuns in Nineteenth-Century Ireland* (Dublin, 1987), pp. 48–53.

28. This information is derived from Concannon, *Irish Nuns*; *Annals of the Dominican Convent of St. Mary's, Cabra, with Some Account of Its Origin, 1647–1912.* (Dublin, 1912); and Walsh, *Nano Nagle.* The twelve convents of the Dominicans, Poor Clares, Carmelites, and Augustinians were now augmented by the Ursuline convent and five Presentation communities.

29. Clear, *Nuns*, p. 36.

30. Ibid., p. 37; Fahey, "Female Asceticism," pp. 68–76.

31. The best examples of this sort of rural convent were the Sisters of Charity convents of Clarenbridge in County Galway, funded in large part by the Kilcornan family, and the Benada community in County Sligo, funded by the Jones family.

32. Clear, *Nuns*, p. 37.

33. Clear, *Nuns*.

34. Fahey, "Female Asceticism."

35. Anthony Fahey, "Nuns in the Catholic Church in Ireland in the Nineteenth Century," in Mary Cullen, ed., *Girls Don't Do Honours: Irish Women in Education in the 19th and 20th Centuries* (Dublin, 1987).

36. Maria Luddy, *Women and Philanthropy in Nineteenth-Century Ireland* (Cambridge, England, 1995).

37. Clear, *Nuns*, p. 35.

38. The assumption of powerlessness has, I think, been caused by two factors. First, these scholars have relied too heavily on ideological notions of women's place in social and cultural hierarchies and not looked closely enough at these women's own voices to assess whether ideology reflected reality or whether it, in fact, masked what these women were actually doing. Second, they have also relied too heavily on secondary source material, which for a number of reasons is highly unreliable. Much of the published material for a study of nuns, such as the biographies of the great foundresses or centenary celebrations of the major orders, is hagiographical in nature and therefore provides a highly distorted version of the history of the modern conventual movement. The

remainder, including general Catholic histories, has mostly been written by men. The voices of women religious are seldom if ever heard. Reading and "hearing" those voices result in a considerably different understanding of the meaning of the religious life for women.

39. Larkin, "Devotional Revolution," p. 644.

40. Peadar MacSuibhne, *Paul Cullen and His Contemporaries* (5 vols., Naas, 1961–77), 4:50.

41. Larkin, "Devotional Revolution," pp. 625, 639–48. Though for the past ten or fifteen years historians have rightly disputed Larkin's thesis that Paul Cullen was single-handedly responsible for the striking transformation of devotional practice and religious behavior in Ireland, he was nonetheless a very powerful and effective church leader who achieved a degree of centralization and modernization only dreamed of by earlier re-forming bishops. For a very thoughtful analysis of the debate over the concept of a devotional revolution, see S. J. Connolly, *Religion and Society in Nineteenth-Century Ireland* (Dundalk, 1985), especially chapter 4, "A Devotional Revolution?"

42. Their prominent role has been diminishing only in the past decade or so as the number of Irish women entering convents has declined precipitously. The drop in the number of novices means that the vast institutional structure supported by these women will not be maintained. Throughout Ireland, the orders are wrestling with this cataclysmic trend, and many are being forced to close some of their convents, reduce their workforce at institutions like convent-owned hospitals, and curtail many of their other concerns. The public response to this recent contraction, as well as to the overall dilemma facing these women today, only confirms the notion that these women have occupied a position of considerable authority. On the one hand, many educated, urban Irish women have welcomed the decline of the women's orders and have become in-creasingly critical of the influential role that nuns have played in all areas of their lives. On the other hand, many other people mourn the loss of this part of their social and cultural heritage. As a case in point, early in 1988 the Mercy convent in Elphin, Co. Sligo, which had been in existence for well over a hundred years, was closed owing to the fact that there had been no new novices in the diocese of Elphin for several years. The townspeople were shocked and saddened at the closure and begged the Mercy generalate at Athlone to reopen the community. After an initial negative response, the parishioners of Elphin circulated a petition to try to persuade the Mercy Sisters to re-consider. To the order's very real concern that there were no young women to sustain the community, the people responded that they needed a convent in the town and that they would rather have old nuns than no nuns at all. Consequently, on 11 October 1988, the Mercy Sisters reopened the house at Elphin when three elderly sisters agreed to move back and carry on that most important of Irish religious and social traditions.

43. This was the British government's position in 1850 when a parliamentary bill was proposed to enforce the inspection of convents.

44. See Ewens, *The Role of the Nun*, for a good general discussion of the Protestant view of Roman Catholic convents during the nineteenth century.

45. Witness a letter, incomplete, unsigned, and undated, written by several women at the turn of the nineteenth century, who, in professing their desire to live in a com-munity of charitable women, also stated clearly that they did not choose this style of life for lack of suitors. Each could have married if she had wished. See "Letters and Docu-ments from 1800," Presentation Convent, Kilkenny (hereafter cited as P/K).

46. See, for example, Official Annals, vol. 5, 1870–76, Benada Convent, Sisters of Charity Generalate, Milltown, Dublin (hereafter cited as SOC/M) pp. 268–69.

47. See, for example, Mary Carbery, *The Farm by Lough Gur: The Story of Mary*

Fogarty (1937; reprint, Cork, 1973); Kate O'Brien, *The Ante-Room* (London, 1934), "Aunt Mary in the Parlour," *University Review* 3 (1963), no. 3, pp. 3–9, *The Flower of May* (London, 1953), *The Land of Spices* (London, 1941), and *Presentation Parlour* (London, 1963); Peig Sayers, *Peig* (1974; reprint, Dublin, 1983).

48. Harry Levin, ed., *The Portable James Joyce* (1947; rev. ed., 1985), p. 437.

49. Clear, *Nuns*, pp. 157–67; Fahey, "Nuns in the Catholic Church," pp. 28–30. Clear, for example, situates religious women within the context of women workers, arguing that although they were not progressive women, they are still worthy of study because they are our foremothers and were exploited like all other women workers. Fahey, by contrast, believes that nuns laid the foundation for modern feminism (a notion Clear finds inconceivable), as if only women who can somehow be connected to feminism are worthy of study.

50. For a very interesting discussion of women, property, and sexual dependence, see Gerda Lerner, *The Creation of Patriarchy* (New York, 1986).

Chapter 2

1. Annals of the Presentation Convent, Youghal, 1869, Presentation Convent, Youghal (hereafter cited as P/Y).

2. Annals of Presentation Convent, Fermoy, Presentation Convent, Fermoy (hereafter cited as P/F); Sermon preached by John McCarthy, Bishop of Cloyne, at the Funeral Mass for Mother Gould, P/F.

3. "Convents of Presentation Order from its Foundation in the year 1777 to the year 1841," (hereafter List of Presentation Foundations to 1841), File box marked "Very Old Documents," folder marked "Information about Convents and Nuns," P/C; Annals, 1869, P/Y.

4. Morgan O'Brien to Dean John Hamilton, 5 Aug. 1830, File 35/2, Folder Priests, Hamilton Papers, Dublin Diocesan Archives (hereafter cited as DDA); Mother Magdalen Gould to Dean John Hamilton, 21 May 1835, File 35/5, Folder Nuns, Hamilton Papers, DDA.

5. Walsh, *Nano Nagle*, pp. 62–63, 118–19. William Coppinger was an outspoken advocate for the Presentation Order, addressing charitable institutions in order to gain public support for the work of the sisters, especially in the 1790s, when the congregation almost failed.

6. See, for example, Larkin, "Devotional Revolution," pp. 639–45; Fahey, "Female Asceticism," pp. 1–2, 160–62.

7. For the best example of recent literature that credits the hierarchy with initiation and management of the conventual movement, see Caitriona Clear, "The Limits of Female Autonomy: Nuns in Nineteenth-Century Ireland," in Maria Luddy and Cliona Murphy, eds., *Women Surviving: Studies in Irish Women's History in the Nineteenth and Twentieth Centuries* (Dublin, 1990), pp. 27–32. This assumption also informs almost every discussion of convents found in the general body of literature concerning the nineteenth-century Irish Catholic church. See, as just one example, Keenan, *The Catholic Church*, p. 147: "About 1812 Archbishop Murray took steps toward founding the Irish Sisters of Charity by sending Mother Mary Aikenhead to the Bar convent, York."

8. This erroneous assumption is found in Whelan, "The Regional Impact of Irish Catholicism," p. 269.

9. Annals, p. 12, P/C; Annals of the Ursuline Convent, Cork, 1775–1825, Ursuline Convent, Blackrock (hereafter cited as U/C).

10. Annals, p. 12, P/C. The Ursuline Order, founded in Italy by Angela Merici

in 1535, was originally an uncloistered community of women dedicated to the education of females. The order thrived in France, led by the great Ursuline convent in Paris. It became an enclosed order in 1612 owing to pressure from the archbishop of Paris. Although the teaching of poor children was never expressly forbidden, the Ursuline Order came to specialize in the education of social elites.

11. Ibid.

12. Ibid., pp. 1–5; Walsh, *Nano Nagle*, pp. 38–44, 56–61.

13. Annals, p. 19, U/C.

14. Annals, pp. 12–13, P/C; Annals, p. 19, U/C.

15. Walsh, *Nano Nagle*, p. 61.

16. Annals, Obituary of Bishop Francis Moylan, 1815, P/C.

17. Ibid., pp. 16–17, 20.

18. Ibid., p. 18; Annals, pp. 54–55, U/C.

19. Annals, 1775, P/C.

20. Ibid. The Ursulines were aware of Francis Moylan's special liking for their establishment. When he left Cork in 1775 and went to Killarney as bishop of Kerry, the Ursuline annalist noted the great loss they suffered with his departure. See also Annals, especially p. 44, U/C.

21. Annals, 1775, U/C.

22. When first established in 1775, the name of Nagle's new Irish congregation was the Institute of the Charitable Instruction of the Sacred Heart of Jesus. In the course of presenting the constitutions to Propaganda Fide for approval by the pope, the congregation was given its final name, the Presentation of the Blessed Virgin Mary.

23. Biographical works on bishops routinely count among their accomplishments the founding of religious congregations of women or their branch convents, just as they count the number of churches built during their tenure. These sorts of works are responsible for the greatest distortion of the role that women themselves have played. See, for example, William Meagher, *Notices of the Life and Character of His Grace Most Rev. Daniel Murray, Late Archbishop of Dublin* (Dublin, 1853).

24. Mary Aikenhead's father, David, was an Anglican doctor and her mother, Mary Stackpole, was a Catholic. The Aikenhead children were raised in the Church of Ireland, but because of close association with the Stackpoles, Mary Aikenhead was drawn to Catholicism and converted in 1802 at age 15.

25. A Member of the Congregation of the Irish Sisters of Charity. *The Life and Work of Mary Aikenhead, Foundress of the Congregation of Irish Sisters of Charity, 1787–1858* (London, 1925), pp. 10–14.

26. Official Annals, Vol. 1, pp. 7–12, SOC/M. Anna Maria O'Brien was a lifelong and intimate friend of Murray and was with him in his study before mass on the morning that he suffered his fatal seizure in 1852.

27. Annals of the Congregation of the Religious Sisters of Charity, Founded in Ireland in 1815, p. 10, SOC/M.

28. Official Annals, Vol. 1, p. 8, SOC/M; Member, *Mary Aikenhead*, pp. 14–19. Aikenhead's father had died in 1801, and her mother was unwell. Because Mary was the only adult child, the care of family affairs was her responsibility.

29. There is some conflict over the date. The Official Annals, Vol. 1, pp. 8–9, states that Murray first suggested bringing the French Sisters of Charity to Ireland in 1810, while he suggested that Aikenhead head the foundation in 1811. The earlier document, Annals of the Congregation, p. 10, states that both occurred in 1811. See also Official Annals, Vol. 1, pp. 12–14, SOC/M.

30. Official Annals, Vol. 1, p. 42, SOC/M. There is a discrepancy in the annals

about the rule sent. In one place it is stated that Murray sent the constitutions of the French order, but later in the annals it is said that Mary Aikenhead never received the constitutions, only a description of the rule and the agreement, or *Projet d'Accord*.

31. Archbishop Daniel Murray to Mrs. Coyney, 13 April 1814, 1/B/6, SOC/M.

32. Official Annals, Vol. 1, pp. 41–43, 58, SOC/M.

33. Archbishop Daniel Murray to Mrs. Coyney, 13 April 1814, 1/B/6, SOC/M.

34. Archbishop Daniel Murray to Mary Aikenhead and Alicia Walsh, 31 Dec. 1814, copy in Official Annals, Vol. 1, 1814, SOC/M.

35. Archbishop Daniel Murray to Mary Aikenhead and Alicia Walsh, 6 Feb. 1815, File 1/B/8, SOC/M.

36. On women's philanthropic activities in Ireland during the nineteenth century, see Luddy, *Women and Philanthropy*.

37. Mother M. Clare Moore to Sr. M. C. Augustine Moore, 28 Aug. 1844, file marked "Letters of Mother M. Clare Moore to Sister M. Clare Augustine Moore, 1844," M/B.

38. Sr. M. A. Doyle to Sr. M. C. Augustine Moore, 17 Nov. [?], file marked "Correspondence," M/B.

39. Sr. M. A. Doyle to Sr. M. C. Augustine Moore, undated, Correspondence, M/B.

40. Mother M. Clare Moore to Sr. M. Clare Augustine Moore, 23 Aug. 1844, Letters of Mother M. Clare Moore, M/B.

41. Memoir of M. Clare Augustine Moore, quoted in typescript account, "Baggot Street as a Charitable Institution of Secular Ladies," 1827–31, M/B.

42. Quoted in ibid.

43. Memoir of Mother M. Clare Augustine Moore, quoted in ibid.

44. Annals of the Sisters of Mercy, Carlow, July 1829, quoted in ibid. The Carlow annalist had this to say of one priest who objected to McAuley on the grounds of depleting available recruits and funds for charitable work: "Strange it did not occur to him that there is and, so far as we know, ever will be more sorrow and misery in this poor world than charity and mercy in all their human embodiments will ever be able to relieve."

45. Story told by Mother Warde, who was present when the letter was delivered, quoted in ibid.

46. Ibid.

47. Ibid.

48. Mother M. Clare Moore to Sr. M. C. Augustine Moore, 23 Aug. 1844, Letters of Mother M. Clare Moore, M/B. At the height of the furor over the new charitable institution in July 1829, Kelly came to see McAuley with the intention of intimidating her. According to Mother Moore, he "led Rev. Mother through the house, telling her to select a room or two for herself, as it was the archbishop's wish to give the house to the Sisters of Charity." Murray later told McAuley that he had never intended to take over her institute (a controversial right over Catholic charities which Irish bishops claimed to possess), nor had he authorized Kelly to harass her, but that Kelly had undertaken this action on his own initiative.

49. Quoted in "Baggot Street," M/B.

50. Ibid.

51. Ibid.

52. Sr. M. A. Doyle to Sr. M. C. Augustine Moore, undated, Correspondence, M/B; "Baggot Street," M/B. McAuley's property included £30,000 in the Bank of Ireland, £600 per annum in perpetuity, the home in which she was raised (Coolock

House), jewels, and several life insurance policies.

53. "Sketch of Mrs. Ellen Woodlock's Life," file box marked "Monaghan Box," Sisters of St. Louis Generalate, Monaghan (hereafter cited as St.L/M).

54. John Lentaigne to Mrs. Ellen Woodlock, 21 June 1859, file marked "Founders' Letters and Early Documents," St.L/M. It is interesting to note that the down payment for the brewery was provided by Charles Bianconi, who is Kevin Whelan's "classic case" of the rising Catholic middleman—the emerging Catholic entrepreneur who became "the hinges in the social system, the brokers who articulated and transferred opinion up and down the social ladder," and who were a vital element in the growth of Catholic power in the nineteenth century. See Whelan, "Catholic Church in Tipperary," p. 217.

55. Ibid.

56. Sr. Miriam Commins, "Our Charism: The Irish Dimension," Pamphlet, St.L/M.

57. Mrs. H. A. Lloyd to Bishop Charles McNally, [?] Jan. 1859, Monaghan Box, St.L/M.

58. Commins, "Our Charism," St.L/M.

59. John Lentaigne to Mrs. Woodlock, 21 June 1859, Monaghan Box, St.L/M.

60. Mrs. H. A. Lloyd to Rev. Mother Priscilla Beale, 22 Jan. 1861, Monaghan Box, St.L/M.

61. Annals of the Brigidine Convent, Tullow, 1807–14, Brigidine Generalate, Blackrock (hereafter cited as B/B). In 1808 Delaney also established a monastery for men, the Order of St. Patrick, or the Patrician Brothers. Although I am not aware of the extent to which Delaney dominated this male community, it is clear from the Brigidine annals that he determined the site of their monastery, required that the brothers share the garden with the sisters, and wished that both communities along with the parishioners would constitute "but one interest."

62. Ibid., 1807.

63. Ibid., 1814; Margaret Gibbons, *Glimpses of Catholic Ireland in the Eighteenth Century* (Dublin, 1932), pp. 15–27. Information on the intimacy of the relationship between Wogan-Browne and Delaney was supplied by the superior general of the Brigidine Order in 1988.

64. Annals, Tullow convent, 1824–1836, B/B. It was not until 1836, when Judith Wogan-Browne was an elderly and infirm woman, unable any longer to dominate the order, that a boarding school was finally begun.

65. Annals, 3 Sept. 1798, P/C; List of Presentation Foundations to 1841, file marked "Very Old Documents," and folder marked "Information about Convents and Nuns," P/C.

66. Annals, 3 Sept. 1798, P/C. The story of the foundation in the annals makes it clear that Hussey was expected to assist financially in the foundation.

67. "Free Schools for Catholics, 1792–1820," in "Special List, 170C," Calendar of the Cashel Archdiocesan Archives (microfilm, National Library of Ireland, hereafter cited as NLI); Dr. Patrick Everard to Archbishop Thomas Bray, 4 Nov. 1815, 1815/10, Cashel Archdiocesan Archives (hereafter cited as CAA) (microfilm, NLI); "Records and Memories of One Hundred Years, 1817–1917," Presentation Convent, Thurles.

68. Annals of the Sisters of Charity, Stanhope Street, 1815 and 1816, SOC/M; Annals of the Congregation, 1817, SOC/M. In both of these sources, it is remarked that Troy was too busy to take much notice of the new order, but several years after it was established, he began to become more involved. It is interesting to note that in the first annals kept by the young congregation, known as "Mother Clifford's Annals," Mother Clifford made no mention of the death of Archbishop Troy, a fact significant

by its omission. Rarely did a convent fail to note the death of a clergyman associated in any way with the convent, and when the convent annalist did fail to mention it, it was usually because of tension between them. Torn between the duty to honor an ecclesiastical superior and unwillingness to lie about a conflictual relationship, the sisters often opted in such cases for silence.

69. Official Annals, Vol. 5, Benada Convent, 1875, SOC/M.

70. Overall, 61 percent of the foundations made by these three orders prior to the famine were initiated and paid for by women and 14 percent by bishops and priests. At this time, I have not been able to discover the origins of the remaining 25 percent of the convents. But even in the unlikely event that the remaining convents were all initiated by bishops and priests, the proportion would only reach 39 percent of all convents. This information was derived from the following sources: List of Presentation Foundations to 1841, file marked "Very Old Documents," and folder marked "Information about Convents and Nuns," P/C; Annals of the Mercy Convent, Limerick, "Foundation, 1837," M/L; William Hutch, *Nano Nagle: Her Life, Her Labours, and Their Fruits* (Dublin, 1875); Mary Josephine Gately, *The Sisters of Mercy: Historical Sketches, 1831–1931* (New York, 1931); Annals of the Congregation, SOC/M.

71. Annals, 1809, P/C; Walsh, *Nano Nagle*, pp. 154, 192.

72. Annals, 1828, 1829, P/C.

73. This anecdote, part of the Presentation tradition, was provided by Sr. Rosario, archivist, P/C.

74. John Murphy to Daniel Murray, 24 Oct. 1824, File 30/8, folder Irish Bishops, Murray Papers, DDA.

75. Rev. P. Murphy to Daniel Murray, 20 May 1847, File 32/3, folder Ordinary, Murray Papers, DDA.

76. Annals, 1799, P/C; Letter, undated and unsigned, from North Presentation convent to superioress of South Presentation convent relating details of the foundation in the North parish, in file marked "Very Old Documents," and folder marked "Information about Convents and Nuns," P/C.

77. Official Annals, Vol. 4, Benada convent, 1864–70, SOC/M.

78. Annals, Tullow Convent, 1850, B/B.

79. Annals, P/C; List of Presentation Foundations to 1841, file marked "Very Old Documents," and folder marked "Information about Convents and Nuns," P/C; Annals of the Mercy Convent, Cork, Mercy Convent, Cork (hereafter M/C); Gately, *Sisters of Mercy*, pp. 3–93; P. Murphy to Daniel Murray, 20 May 1847, File 32/3, folder Ordinary, Murray Papers, DDA; Official Annals, Vols. 1–3, SOC/M.

80. Annals, 1826, 1832, 1835, 1836, 1846, P/C.

81. Ibid., 1846.

82. "Pastoral Address to the Catholic Clergy and Laity," File 30/7, folder Pastorals, Murray Papers, DDA; "Testimonials" on the Miracle of Mrs. Mary Stuart, 15 Aug. 1823, File 30/7, folder Pastorals, Murray Papers, DDA; Sr. M. F. de Sales Stuart to Daniel Murray, 23 June 1831, File 31/2, folder Ordinary, Murray Papers, DDA; John Kingston, "The Carmelite Nuns in Dublin, 1644–1829," *Reportorium Novum*, 3 (1964): 358–59.

83. Sr. M. Aloysia Eleanor Arthur to Reverend Mother Ball, undated, File 33/3, folder undated Nuns, Murray Papers, DDA.

84. Sr. Aloysius to Mother M. X. Finnegan, 29 April 1897, file box marked "Founders' Letters and Early Documents," St.L/M.

85. Sr. Mary M. L. Rorke to Archdeacon John Hamilton, undated, File 37/7, folder undated Nuns, Hamilton Papers, DDA.

86. Mother M. de Chantal Coleman to Mary Aikenhead, 23 Dec. 1846, 1/B/

100, SOC/M.

87. Bishop William Walsh to Dean John Hamilton, 13 Feb. 1845, File 36/7, folder Non-Irish Bishops, Hamilton Papers, DDA.

88. Official Annals, Vol. 1, 1823, SOC/M.

89. Annals, 1836, Presentation Sisters, George's Hill, Dublin (henceforth P/GH).

90. Official Annals, Vol. 3, 1857, SOC/M. The annals also note that the reverend mother of the Montreal community had been in the noviceship at York with Aikenhead. It is reasonable to speculate that Mother Aikenhead did not wish to compete with this particular woman's community. The bonds of friendship and loyalty that developed in the noviceship of women's orders were very strong, and in this case they may have influenced her decision to refuse the bishop. Aikenhead does not seem to have had the same scruples when it came to competing with the Sisters of Mercy.

Chapter 3

1. Annals, 1869, Presentation Convent, Youghal (henceforth P/Y).

2. Ibid.

3. See, for example, Joseph Lee, "Women and the Church since the Famine," in Margaret MacCurtain and Donncha O. Corrain, eds., *Women in Irish Society: The Historical Dimension* (Dublin, 1978), pp. 37–45; Robert E. Kennedy Jr., *The Irish: Emigration, Marriage, and Fertility* (Berkeley, 1973), pp. 139–72; Janet Nolan, *Ourselves Alone: Women's Emigration from Ireland, 1885–1920* (Lexington, Kentucky, 1989), pp. 9–42; Fahey, "Female Asceticism," pp. 59–64.

4. This is not a new explanation for the popularity of religious life for women. The popularity of the religious life in medieval Europe is also often attributed to family strategies meant to support surplus or unwanted women. See, for example, Bynum, *Holy Feast and Holy Fast*, pp. 18–30. Bynum also dismisses an explanation of medieval women's religious organization that rests solely on demographic considerations.

5. See, for example, 12 Aug. 1839 and 9 Sept. 1839, C. A. O'Callaghan to Dean John Hamilton, File 36/2, folder Ordinary, Hamilton Papers, DDA. In these letters, Miss O'Callaghan, who wanted "very badly" to join a convent, sought out Hamilton's help in gaining admittance to the Dominican convent at Drogheda because her parents were against the idea of her becoming a nun.

6. On the class and regional background of the reemergence of Catholicism, see Whelan, "Catholic Church in County Tipperary," "Catholic Community in Eighteenth-Century County Wexford," and, especially, "Regional Impact of Irish Catholicism," pp. 258–274.

7. W. R. Greg, *Literary and Social Judgments* (London, 1869), p. 314.

8. Luddy, *Women and Philanthropy*.

9. Sheila Jeffreys, *The Spinster and Her Enemies: Feminism and Sexuality, 1880–1930* (London, 1985), pp. 86–88.

10. For the interconnection between religious fervor and the spread of charitable institutions in Ireland, see Luddy, *Women and Philanthropy*.

11. F. K. Prochaska, *Women and Philanthropy in Nineteenth-Century England* (Oxford, 1980), pp. 8–11.

12. The role of "good works" was, in fact, a central issue of contention during the Reformation. At the Council of Trent in the sixteenth century, the Roman church reaffirmed the power of good works to ensure one a place in heaven after the concept had been denounced by Martin Luther in his Ninety-five Theses.

13. Prochaska, *Women and Philanthropy*, p. 11.

14. Quoted in Prochaska, *Women and Philanthropy*, p. 9.

15. Women's preponderant position in the financial support of the philanthropic movement in England is well covered in ibid., pp. 10–18.

16. Luddy, *Women and Philanthropy*, Appendix 10, "The contribution of women in financial terms to selected charitable societies," p. 506.

17. Official Annals, Vol. 6, Harold's Cross Convent, 1879, SOC/M. Though this example and Luddy's figures on a selected number of charitable societies are very interesting, they are based on a very small number of organizations. In the convents studied in my own work, which include the first foundations and motherhouses of the major Irish orders, there were many male financial supporters. Until a definitive study is done similar to Prochaska's, I hesitate to suggest that women were the main contributors to the philanthropic system. Certainly, however, there is no doubt that their support was very considerable. My own assessment, albeit a qualitative one, of the female portion of the funding of convent charities might perhaps be in the range of 35 to 50 percent. This support of the work of the convents is not to be confused with support for the convents themselves, which were supported, in the main, by the women members and their families.

18. Quoted in Prochaska, *Women and Philanthropy*, p. 13.

19. For an excellent discussion of the meaning and impact of benevolent work in the United States, see Lori D. Ginzberg, *Women and the Work of Benevolence: Morality, Politics, and Class in the Nineteenth-Century United States* (New Haven, 1990).

20. Walsh, *Nano Nagle*, pp. 23–43; Whelan, "Regional Impact of Irish Catholicism," p. 268.

21. Member, *Mary Aikenhead*, pp. 1–9. The Stackpoles were noted at the time for refusing to adopt that "slavish spirit" that the majority of Catholics thought prudent during the Penal Law period, believing rather that "they had every right to walk through life with an erect posture and a heavenward face."

22. Information provided by Sister Rosario, Archivist at the South Presentation Convent, Cork.

23. Annals, P/Y; Annals, M/C.

24. "Sketch of Mrs. Ellen Woodlock's Life," Monaghan Box, St.L/M.

25. See, for example, comments on the acceptance to profession of Sister Copperthwaite in the Chapter Book, 18 Mar. 1817, P/GH.

26. Chapter Book, Jan. 1810, P/GH.

27. Lord Clifford to Archbishop Daniel Murray, 1 May 1841, File 31/8, folder Ordinary, Murray Papers, DDA.

28. Sister I. M. Cater to Archbishop Daniel Murray, [?], File 33/12, folder undated Nuns, Murray Papers, DDA. Although it appears that women were admitted to convents without dowries on a fairly regular basis so long as there were enough women entering who brought more than the minimum required, knowledge of individual dowry arrangements were generally suppressed within religious communities. This was done primarily to reduce any possible tension that might result from widespread discussion of who brought how much with them. Specifically, it was meant to avert the possibility that wealthier women might attempt to dominate those not so well endowed and, therefore, disrupt the smooth functioning of the community. Consequently, convents aimed to deemphasize what was an essential feature of their financial survival in order to facilitate the functioning of the community at the social level. Therefore, dowry information is not always readily available in convent archives. This attitude of sensitivity to

the communal aspects of convent life has sometimes meant that dowry information from earlier centuries is kept private and in the possession of the community bursar rather than released to the community archivist. More often it has meant that information on the exact amounts of money women contributed was not systematically recorded but rather it "disappeared" in general statistics of yearly income.

29. By way of comparison, K. H. Connell reported that, during the 1880s, Cork farming families who paid rents of £30 to £40 per year were providing their daughters with dowries of £300 to £400 with which they could enter a convent, be educated, or marry. See Connell, "Peasant Marriage in Ireland: Its Structure and Development since the Famine," *Economic History Review* 14 (1961–62): 504.

30. Clear, *Nuns*, pp. 87–89.

31. Ibid., p. 107.

32. See, for example, Novitiate Account Book, Mercy Diocesan Generalate (Elphin), Athlone (hereafter cited as M/A). Women in the Mercy convents in the diocese of Elphin were not required to provide a dowry by 1900, granted that they were either "trained" teachers or nurses. During one ten-year period 1908–18, eleven of thirty-four women accepted into the Mercy novitiate in Sligo were trained teachers and nurses and were admitted without dowries.

33. Sophia McCormick to Archbishop Daniel Murray, 10 Dec. 1846, File 32/2, folder Nuns, Murray Papers, DDA.

34. Official Annals, Vol. 2, 1850, SOC/M.

35. Joseph Brophy to Archbishop Daniel Murray, 2 Jan. 1850, File 32/6, folder Ordinary, Murray Papers, DDA.

36. Chapter Book, 10 May 1824, P/GH.

37. See, for example, "Testimony of Mother Mary Vincent Harnett," 1860, Cullen Papers, DDA.

38. Ibid.

39. Mary Francis Tobin to Teresa Mullaly, 28 Feb. 1795, file marked "Correspondence," P/C.

40. "Education Packet," file marked "Baggot Street Convent," M/B.

41. Official Annals, Vol. 2, Cork Convent, 1837, SOC/M.

42. Annals, p. 6, P/C.

43. Ibid., pp. 1–4. These annals were begun by Mother Leahy shortly after her entrance into the community in 1832. Evidence for the story of Nano Nagle and the foundation of the Presentation Order, which Leahy did not herself witness, was provided by "the verbal information procured from the Mothers Mary Angela Collins, Mary Francis Tobin, Mary Monica Collins, Mary Clare Callaghan, and all the Religious who saw the commencement of this Foundation."

44. Ibid., p. 5.

45. Ibid., p. 4; Walsh, *Nano Nagle*, pp. 46–48.

46. Annals, p. 7, P/C.

47. Nano Nagle to Miss Fitzsimons, 17 July 1769, cited in Walsh, *Nano Nagle*, pp. 344–83.

48. Annals, p. 7, P/C.

49. That they did not prosecute her is consistent with the fact that enforcement of the Penal Code began to be relaxed at about this time. The Ascendancy may also have allowed the schools to operate because of the belief that the introduction of middle-class morals to the wider Catholic population would create a more peace-loving and governable Irish population.

50. Annals, pp. 11–12, P/C.

51. Mary Francis Tobin to Teresa Mullaly, 28 Feb. 1795, Correspondence, P/C.

52. Archbishop Daniel Murray to Mrs. Lucy Clifford, 24 March 1847, 1/B/35, SOC/M.

53. Annals, 1809, P/C.

54. Annals, 1869, P/Y.

55. Annals, P/F.

56. Quoted in "Baggot Street," M/B. Emphasis added.

57. See Registers of Professions at the convents under study for the exact percentages of lay sisters in any given community. The largest proportion of lay sisters that I encountered was that of the Mercy convents in the diocese of Elphin. During the period 1840–1914, a total of 272 women joined the half-dozen convents in the diocese. Of that number, 104, or 38 percent, were lay sisters.

58. Clear, *Nuns*, pp. 91–99.

59. For a discussion of the many justifications made by nineteenth-century religious orders for the institution of domestic sisters, see ibid., pp. 91–99.

60. Bishop Clancy to Archbishop Daniel Murray, 20 Sept. [?], File 32/1, folder Foreign Bishops, Murray Papers, DDA.

61. "Form of Declaration for Lay Sister," 1872, Novitiate Box 23, M/A.

62. Mother de Chantal Coleman to Mary Aikenhead, 30 Mar. 1847, 1/B/101, SOC/M.

63. See, for example, the story of the path to becoming a lay sister in the Annals, 1857, P/C, and also the story of Brigid Buhmur's path to lay sisterhood in the Annals of the Children of Mary, 1876, Tullow convent, B/B. Although Clear (*Nuns*, p. 94) has suggested that lay sisters replaced servants in the convent, I have not found this to be the case, certainly not as a general rule.

64. Mother de Chantal Coleman to Mary Aikenhead, 1 Dec. 1845, 1/B/89, SOC/M.

65. Official Annals, Vol. 2, 1844, SOC/M.

66. Ibid., Stanhope Street Convent, 1852, SOC/M.

67. The rigid class stratification among Roman Catholics that was such a prominent feature of the nineteenth century has been nicely described by K. H. Connell in "Catholicism and Marriage in the Century After the Famine," *Irish Peasant Society: Four Historical Essays* (Oxford, 1968).

68. Mary Francis Tobin to Teresa Mullaly, 28 Feb. 1795, Correspondence, P/C.

69. Catherine McAuley, "The Mercy Ideal," M/B.

Chapter 4

1. See, for example, Sr. Mary Joseph Lloyd to Archdeacon John Hamilton, 23 Dec. 1835, File 35/5, folder Nuns, Hamilton Papers, DDA. This religious woman had lived in several convents and finally settled in that of Youghal. In describing her "good fortune" in having been directed to Mother Gould's community, she declared the convent "the most amiable, zealous, and best united community" that she knew.

2. Annals, 1869, P/Y.

3. See, for example, Clear, *Nuns*, pp. 155–56.

4. Sister Mary Magdalen de Pazzi Leahy, Manuscript Collection of Her Writings, P/C.

5. Notebook of Sister M. Magdalen de Pazzi Leahy, 23 Aug. 1843, section titled "Duties of the Novices," P/C.

6. "Summary of Constitutions," HF/G. Many congregations have either deleted

or papered over the rules pertaining to the examination of conscience with the superior because the practice was banned by papal decree in 1894. For information on this custom, it is necessary to consult individual orders' constitutions and rule books written or printed before 1894.

7. Notebook of Sister M. Magdalen de Pazzi Leahy, 23 Aug. 1843, Duties of the Novices, P/C.

8. Sister M. Magdalen de Pazzi Leahy, "Customs Book," P/C.

9. Manuscript entitled "Composition written in 1861 concerning Sr. Mary Teresa Paul Higgins, Mistress of Novices who trained Mother Mary Catherine McAuley," P/GH.

10. "Summary of Constitutions," HF/G.

11. Notebook of Sr. M. Magdalen de Pazzi Leahy, 23 Aug. 1843, Duties of the Novices, P/C.

12. Mary Ann Donovan, *Sisterhood as Power: The Past and Passion of Ecclesial Women* (New York, 1989), pp. 5–23.

13. Official Annals, Vol. 6, 1876, SOC/M; Official Annals, Vol. 2, 1851, Obituary of Sister Segrave, SOC/M.

14. Annals, Community, Deeds of Great Nuns, M. M. B. Carroll, P/GH.

15. Annals, 1826, P/C.

16. Mother Mary Francis Tobin to Mother Joseph McLoughlin, 9 May 1802, Correspondence, P/C.

17. Letter from Mother Genevieve Beale to Sisters at Branch Houses on Occasion of Eve of St. Louis Day, 1874, "Monaghan Booklet," B7, St.L/M.

18. Annals of the Congregation, 1858, SOC/M.

19. See, for example, Alicia Brown to Margaret Byrne, 22 May 1834, File 35/4, folder Ordinary, Hamilton Papers, DDA.

20. Official Annals, Vol. 2, 1854, SOC/M.

21. Caitriona Clear, "Nuns in Ireland, 1850–1900: Female Religious in the Economy and Society" (M.A. thesis, University College, Galway, 1984), p. 265: "It must be concluded, therefore, that convents did not, could not, realize their potential as effective and co-ordinated networks of women workers in this era. Their chance to do so was severely limited, not only by ecclesiastical authority, and curtailments of nuns' freedom of movement, but also by the demands which were made upon convents to found other convents in Ireland and abroad. Furthermore, the state of life in which the work was carried out forged what was primarily a religious, as opposed to a sexual, identity. The sense of being an essential part of a crusade . . . retarded the development of a woman-centred perspective, and invested bishops and priests, helmsmen of this path-finding journey, with greater moral authority than ever."

22. Summary of the Constitutions, *Rules of the Congregation of the Religious Sisters of Charity* (Dublin, 1941).

23. Rule 17, *Rules of the Sisters of Charity*.

24. Contrary to popular opinion, women often joined convents against the wishes of their families. Though this appears to have been more frequent during the prefamine period, it was also often the case during the postfamine years. One mother, who reluctantly gave permission for her three daughters to join the Loreto Order, penned an angry letter to the archbishop of Dublin when the youngest joined and was sent on a mission to Cadiz. She had agreed to her last daughter's entering religion only on condition that she would not be sent on a mission abroad. When the Loreto sisters reneged on their agreement, she begged Daniel Murray to help her to get her daughter sent home. "I have already lost two daughters in the Loretto [*sic*] order," she lamented. "I seek to

have the child I now write about brought home. . . . I appeal as a widow seeking the comfort of a lost child." Mary Eliza Rorke to Archbishop Daniel Murray, 4 Feb. 1852, File 32/8, folder Ordinary, Murray Papers, DDA.

25. List of Professions, Vol. 1, U/C.

26. Ibid.

27. Register of Professions and Deaths, P/C.

28. Book of Professions, P/GH.

29. Life Stories of Baggot Street Entrants, M/Cf.

30. Clear, *Nuns*, pp. 80–83.

31. List of Professions, Vol. 1, U/C.

32. Register of Professions and Deaths, P/C.

33. Book of Professions, P/GH.

34. Life Stories of Baggot Street Entrants, M/Cf.

35. Annals, Tullow Convent, 1808, B/B.

36. Annals, Community, Deeds of Great Mothers, M. M. Columba Brophy, P/GH.

37. Manuscript notebook titled, "Sketch of S. M. Stanislaus Kehoe's Life Written by Herself," St. L/M.

38. See, for example, Official Annals, "Benefactors and Benefactresses," M. M. Clare Doyle, SOC/M; Official Annals, Stanhope Street Convent, Vol. 6, Obituaries, p. 33, SOC/M.

39. Ibid., Vol. 2, Obituary of Sister Segrave, 1851, SOC/M.

40. Ibid., Vol. 1, 1813–14, SOC/M.

41. Ibid., Vol. 2, 1854, SOC/M.

42. D'Alton Papers, 20.954, 20.955(i), 20.957, 20.958(i), NLI.

43. Eliza M. Xavier D'Alton to Mrs. John D'Alton, 26 Jan. 1851, 31 Jan. 1851, 20.954; Eliza M. Xavier D'Alton to John D'Alton, undated, 1 Aug. 1851, 20.954; Eliza Sr. M. Margaret D'Alton to Mr. and Mrs. John D'Alton, Easter Sunday [?], 25 Dec. [?], 20.955(i); Eliza Sr. M. Margaret D'Alton to John D'Alton, 28 Sept. [?], 16 Feb. [?], 24 July [?], 5 June [?], 4 Sept. [?], Easter Monday [?], 3 Jan. 1865, 20.955(ii), D'Alton Papers, NLI.

44. Eliza D'Alton to Mrs. D'Alton, 26 Jan. 1851, 31 Jan. 1851, 5 Feb. 1851, 12 July 1851, 20.954, D'Alton Papers, NLI.

45. Eliza Sr. M. Margaret D'Alton to John D'Alton, 6 Mar. 1859, 4 Sept. [?], 24 July [?], Easter Sunday [?], 20.955(i); Eliza Sr. M. Margaret D'Alton to Mrs. John D'Alton, 12 July 1851, 20.954, D'Alton Papers, NLI.

46. Annals, Section titled "Benefactors and Benefactresses," P/GH.

47. Chapter Book, 1810, 1880, P/GH.

48. Sr. Aloysius to Mother M. Francis Xavier Finnegan, July 1892, St.L/M.

49. Eliza Sr. M. Margaret D'Alton to Mrs. John D'Alton, Easter Sunday [?], 20.954, D'Alton Papers, NLI (emphasis in the original).

50. Mother M. Francis Xavier Finnegan to [?], undated, Notebook of Draft Letters of Mother Finnegan, St.L/M.

51. See, for example, Eliza D'Alton to Mr. and Mrs. John D'Alton, [?], 20.954, D'Alton Papers, NLI.

52. Letitia More-O'Ferrall to Bishop James Doyle, 25 Sept. 1825, 21.758, NLI.

53. Composition Written in 1861 concerning Sr. Mary Teresa Paul Higgins, 1861, P/GH.

54. Ellen Bodenham to Mary Aikenhead, [?] 1826, reproduced in Official Annals, Vol. 2, 1836, SOC/M.

55. Official Annals, Vol. 2, 1836, SOC/M.

56. Ellen Bodenham to Mary Aikenhead, [?] 1826, reproduced in Official Annals, Vol. 2, 1836, SOC/M.

57. Official Annals, Vol. 2, 1836, SOC/M. Aikenhead wrote to Robert St. Leger asking him to explain his remarks. In response, St. Leger retracted his disparaging remarks, though he assured her he had not intended to offend ladies like Aikenhead.

58. It is not clear how many women were asked to leave and how many left of their own accord in support of Bodenham. After a failed attempt to begin a new order with Aylward in the years immediately following this incident, Bodenham went on to live in several other congregations of religious women on the continent but never took religious vows.

59. Official annals, Vol. 1, pp. 306–11, 314–23, SOC/M.

60. Anna Maria Leix to Mother Rafferty, [?] 1848, File 37/1, folder Nuns, Hamilton Papers, DDA.

61. Annals, section titled "Community," Sister Mary Augustin Aylmer, P/GH.

62. Sister Mary M. Rorke to Archbishop Daniel Murray, 12 Sept. [?], File 33/3, folder undated Nuns, Murray Papers, DDA.

63. Official Annals, Vol. 3, 1859, SOC/M.

64. Eliza Sister J. Xavier D'Alton to John D'Alton, 1 Aug. [?], D'Alton Papers, 20.954, NLI.

65. Annals, 1842, P/C.

66. Professions, Vol. 1, U/C; Register of Professions and Deaths, P/C; Book of Professions, P/GH; Register of Postulants and Novices, P/K; Alphabetical Catalogue, SOC/M; Baggot Street Entrants, M/Cf.

67. See, for example, the foundation of the Presentation convent in Kilkenny, Annals, 1800, P/K.

68. Manuscript Account of the Life of Mother de Chantal Wilmerding, file marked "Letters," folder marked "Information about Converts and Nuns," P/C.

69. Professions, Vol. 1, U/C; Register of Professions and Deaths, P/C; Book of Professions, P/GH; Register of Postulants and Novices, P/K; Alphabetical Catalogue, SOC/M; Baggot Street Entrants, M/Cf; Clear, *Nuns*, pp. 80–83.

70. Sister Mary Rorke to Archdeacon John Hamilton, [?], File 37/7, folder undated Nuns, Hamilton Papers, DDA.

71. Notebook of Sister M. Magdalen de Pazzi Leahy, 23 Aug. 1843, Duties of the Novices, P/C.

72. Annals, 1838, P/C.

73. See, for example, Sister Mary of Jesus to Sister M. Francis Allingham, 1889, AA/F/04, no. 7, HF/G.

74. Annals, 1818, P/C.

75. Ibid., 1825; Annals, 1825, U/C.

76. Annals, 1826, P/C.

77. Ibid., 1834; Annals, section entitled "Remarkable Events," 1834, P/GH.

78. Annals of the Congregation, 1841, SOC/M.

79. Annals, Remarkable Events, 1855, P/GH.

80. Throughout the nineteenth century, it was a normal practice to send ailing sisters to other convents for a change of air, a practice considered standard medical treatment at the time. Frequently, women's orders made seaside foundations expressly in order to meet the pressing health needs of their sisters. For a particularly instructive example of a convent that, for several decades, sent sisters to other convents for change of air before finally purchasing a seaside house to be used specifically for rest and resto-

ration of health, see Chapter Book, 1875–1913, P/GH.

81. Annals, 1803, P/C.

82. Ibid., 1822.

83. Annals, Remarkable Events, 1860, P/GH.

84. Ibid.

85. Ibid., 1867.

86. Ibid., 1855.

87. Ibid.

88. Ibid., 1867.

89. Life Stories of Entrants to Baggot Street Convent, M/Cf.

90. Annals, Remarkable Events, 1831–1900, P/GH.

91. I was struck by the importance of convent visiting in the lives of these women while I lunched with the community of the Sisters of Charity of Refuge at High Park, Drumcondra, during a research visit to that convent. The mother superior there asked me in what other convents I was working. When I mentioned the George's Hill Presentation archives, she informed me that High Park has a special regard for the George's Hill community because they gave the Charity of Refuge sisters hospitality in the past. Later, when looking through the George's Hill records, I learned that hospitality had been given on numerous occasions more than one hundred years earlier yet the hospitality was still remembered and valued by the High Park community in the 1980s.

92. To my knowledge, however, no one has done any work on the visiting or correspondence networks of secular women similar to what has been done for either English or American women. Consequently, it is not really known to what extent Irish women traveled around the country.

93. Official Annals, Vol. 7, 1886, SOC/M.

94. See for example, Judith C. Brown, *Immodest Acts: The Life of a Lesbian Nun in Renaissance Italy* (New York, 1986); Rosemary Curb and Nancy Manahan, eds., *Lesbian Nuns: Breaking Silence* (Tallahassee, 1985); Janice Raymond, *A Passion for Friends: Toward a Philosophy of Female Affection* (Boston, 1986).

95. For arguments on both sides of this ongoing debate, see, for example, Adrienne Rich, "Compulsory Heterosexuality and Lesbian Existence," *Signs: Journal of Women in Culture and Society*, 5 (1980): 631–60; Anne Ferguson, "Patriarchy, Sexual Identity, and the Sexual Revolution," *Signs* (Autumn 1981): 158–66; John Boswell, "Revolutions, Universals, and Sexual Categories," in Martin Duberman, Martha Vicinus, and George Chauncey Jr., eds. *Hidden from History: Reclaiming the Gay and Lesbian Past* (New York, 1989).

96. John Boswell, review of Judith Brown, *Immodest Acts*, in *New Republic*, 194 (1986): 36.

97. Raymond, *A Passion for Friends*, pp. 76–82.

98. John Boswell, *Christianity, Social Tolerance, and Homosexuality* (Chicago, 1980), pp. 159–220.

99. Ibid.; Aelred of Rievaulx, *Spiritual Friendship*, translated by Mary Eugenia Laker (Kalamazoo, Michigan, 1977).

100. Quoted in Raymond, *A Passion for Friends*, p. 87.

101. Boswell, *Christianity*, pp. 221–22.

102. Notebook of Sr. M. Francis Allingham, 1864–76, AA/F/04, HF/G.

103. Boswell, *Christianity*, pp. 91–241; Brown, *Immodest Acts*, pp. 3–41.

104. Quoted in Brown, *Immodest Acts*, p. 8.

105. For a discussion of the meaning and the use of the term "unnatural" to describe sexual practices between persons of the same sex, see Boswell, *Christianity*,

pp. 149–51, 303–32; and Brown, *Immodest Acts*, pp. 6–20.

106. Raymond, *A Passion for Friends*, p. 91.

107. Particular Examen of Mary McPhillips (Sr. Gonzaga), Monaghan Box, St.L/M.

108. Official Annals, Vol. 7, Kilkenny Convent, 1882, SOC/M.

109. *Rules and Constitutions of the Institute of the Religious Called The Sisters of Mercy* (Pittsburgh, 1852), p. 20.

110. Composition Written in 1861 concerning Sr. Mary Teresa Paul Higgins, P/GH.

111. Particular Examen of Mary McPhillips, Monaghan Box, St.L/M.

112. Ibid.

113. Mother M. F. Tobin to Mother M. Joseph McLoughlin, 9 May 1802, Correspondence, P/C. For several decades the Thurles Ursuline convent remained plagued by problems. The local community failed to send its daughters to the school, and rifts within the convent made it a very unstable environment for women to begin their religious lives. It was not until well into the second half of the century that the community recovered from this controversy.

114. Intense homoemotional relationships between women have been shown to have been a common and accepted part of the friendships of educated middle-class women throughout the nineteenth century in England and America and may perhaps be a context in which women's friendships within the convent were accepted and admired. However, in the absence of any research on this subject for Irish women, and given the very great difference in religious culture between Ireland and England or the United States, I would hesitate to claim the prevalence of loving women's friendships outside Ireland as a basis for acceptance of the kind of loving friendships that I am about to discuss. There are certainly examples of Irish women who spent their lives with other women, but these were Anglo-Irish women and not Catholic Irish women. See for example, Gifford Lewis, *Eva Gore-Booth and Esther Roper: A Biography* (London, 1988).

115. Annals of the Congregation, 1875, SOC/M.

116. Annals, pp. 12–13, P/C; Annals, p. 19, U/C.

117. Annals, 1809, P/C.

118. Official Annals, Vol. 2, 1825, SOC/M.

119. Ibid., Stanhope Street convent, 1841.

120. Annals of the Congregation, 1825, SOC/M.

121. Notebook of Sr. Mary Francis Allingham, 1864–76, AA/F/04, HF/G.

122. Particular Examen of Mary McPhillips, St.L/M.

123. Spiritual Exercise Book of Sister Gonzaga, 1886, St.L/M.

124. Ibid.

125. Ibid.

126. List of Entrants, St.L/M.

127. Archbishop William J. Walsh to Mother A. Vickers, [?], 1890, AV/C/10, HF/G.

128. Account of the Life of Ada Allingham, AA/F/04, no. 7, HF/G.

129. John Steiner to Mother Magdalen, 29 Nov. 1908, JS/BC/09, HF/G.

130. This information was provided by the Superior General of the Holy Faith Order, 1988.

131. Notebook of Sr. M. Francis Allingham, 1864–76, AA/F/04, HF/G. Although Allingham never mentions Aylward's name in the diary, circumstantial evidence already presented has led me to surmise that her particular attachment was to Margaret Aylward.

132. Ibid.

133. Notebook of Sr. M. Francis Allingham, 1864–76, 31 Dec. 1875, AA/F/04, HF/G.

134. Reasons for Dismissal, Constitutions of the Religious Sisters of Charity, SOC/M. One reason stated for automatic dismissal from the congregation was engaging in "unnatural relations" with another individual. In this early version of the constitutions, "unnatural" relations—specifically, sexual relations between women—was considered to be the same as forming particular attachments with other women.

Chapter 5

1. Sister Mary J. P. Bigger to Mrs. Mary Frances Tobin, 21 Aug. 1802, file marked "Letters," P/GH.

2. See, for examples of convents acting in the capacity of landlords, Sister Mary Andrew to Archbishop Daniel Murray, 20 Sept. 1849, File 32/5, folder Ordinary, Murray Papers, DDA; Mother de Chantal Coleman to Mary Aikenhead, 11 Dec. 1847, 1/B/104, SOC/M; Annals, Vols. 1–4, SOC/M; Bequest of Father Lawrence Callanan, Annals, 1818, P/C; Will of Ellen Kelleher, 24 June 1823, file marked "Agreements of a Legal Nature," P/C.

3. Francis Grene to Archbishop Murray, 24 Feb. 1843, File 32/1, folder Ordinary, Murray Papers, DDA.

4. Annals, 20 Aug. 1840, P/C.

5. Nicholas Murphy to Dean John Hamilton, 12 Dec. 1850, File 37/3, folder Ordinary, Hamilton Papers, DDA.

6. "The Late Reverend Mother Mary Genevieve," poem written by "a native of Aughananamy" in honor of Mother Genevieve Beale, 20 Apr. 1878, St.L/M.

7. Father John Quicky to Mrs. Mary Clare Callaghan, 10 June 1813, Letters, P/C.

8. Official Annals., Vol. 3, Clarenbridge Convent, 1858–64.

9. Official Annals, Vol. 4, Clarenbridge Convent, 1864, SOC/M.

10. See, for example, Notebook of Draft Letters of Mother Mary Xavier Finnegan, 22 Dec. 1885, Character for Mr. John Dooley, St.L/M.

11. Florence Callanan to Archbishop Daniel Murray, 16 Apr. 1849, File 32/5, folder Ordinary, Murray Papers, DDA.

12. "Prospectus of an Institution Intended to be Established in Stephen's Green, Dublin, by the Sisters of Charity," File 37/7, folder undated Nuns, Hamilton Papers, DDA.

13. Robert More-O'Ferrall, Peter Purcell, et al., to Mother Cecilia Marmion, 5 Nov. 1844, File 32/1, folder Nuns, Murray Papers, DDA.

14. See Official Annals, Vols. 1–3, Visitation Records, SOC/M. This conservative estimate should also counterbalance the effects of counting one individual more than once owing to multiple illnesses in the course of one year.

15. None of the Presentation convents studied kept any figures of the numbers of individuals they served in this way.

16. This figure was derived from the manuscript notebook entitled "Names of the Sick visited by the Sisters from September 1838 to April 1847," M/L. The sisters on the sick mission of this community visited a total of 5,799 persons in an eight-and-one-half-year period, or approximately 700 per year on average.

17. Clear, *Nuns*, pp. 40–42.

18. Ibid., p. 104.

19. See Ibid., pp. 159–60, for a brief discussion of the unreliability of the Catholic directories for statistics and general information about nuns.

20. Joseph Robins, *The Lost Children: A Study of Charity Children in Ireland, 1700–1900* (Dublin, 1980), p. 13.

21. Ibid., p. 297. This number was smaller than the number of children in Irish prisons, which, in 1861, was almost 7,500.

22. The four girls' reformatories were operated by the Mercy Sisters in Limerick, the Sisters of Our Lady of Charity of Refuge in Drumcondra, Dublin, the St. Louis Sisters in Monaghan, and the Mercy Sisters in Goldenbridge, Dublin.

23. Robins, *Lost Children*, p. 303.

24. Ibid., p. 305.

25. Clear, *Nuns*, p. 108; Robins, *Lost Children*, p. 304–5. Unlike the small impact made by the reformatory schools, the number of destitute children this program kept out of the workhouse was very significant. For example, in 1899 there were 8,422 children enrolled in the training school program and just 5,988 children in workhouses.

26. Helen Burke, *The People and the Poor Law in 19th-Century Ireland* (Littlehampton, England, 1987), pp. 4–5. The other five Dublin hospitals in existence in 1834 were the Jervis Street Charitable Infirmary (founded in 1718), Dr. Steven's Hospital (1720), Royal Hospital for Incurables (1744), Rotunda Hospital (1745), and St. Patrick's Hospital (1745).

27. Ibid., p. 6.

28. Ibid., pp. 162–63.

29. Clear, *Nuns*, p. 107.

30. Ibid., pp. 104, 109.

31. Fahey, "Female Asceticism," p. 96; Connolly, *Priests and People*, p. 81. Connolly points out that in 1825 the great majority of Catholic children were being educated in institutions known as hedge schools. Attendance was erratic, and the quality of education provided in these schools varied considerably. They are not considered to have raised literacy rates among the Catholic population. With the expansion of the national school system and the expanding educational resources of the Catholic church, the hedge school system disappeared.

32. Connolly, *Priests and People*, p. 81; Fahey, "Female Asceticism," p. 96.

33. Connolly, *Priests and People*, p. 81.

34. Clear, *Nuns*, p. 107; Fahey, "Female Asceticism," p. 96.

35. Fahey, "Female Asceticism," p. 96.

36. Ibid., pp. 97–98.

37. Ibid., p. 81.

38. "Resolution of the Irish Bishops," 9 May 1862, M/Cf.

39. Fahey, "Nuns in the Catholic Church," p. 24.

40. [?] to Dean John Hamilton, 20 June 1851, File 37/3, folder Ordinary, Hamilton Papers, DDA.

41. For a very good account of the Magdalen asylums, see Maria Luddy, "Prostitution and Rescue Work in Nineteenth-Century Ireland," in Maria Luddy and Cliona Murphy, eds., *Women Surviving: Studies in Irish Women's History in the 19th and 20th Centuries* (Dublin, 1990), pp. 51–84.

42. Official Annals, Vols. 4–5, Donnybrook Convent, 1864–76, SOC/M.

43. Ibid., Vol. 4, Donnybrook Convent, 1864–70, Story of Mary Hanlon.

44. Father William Walsh to Dean John Hamilton, 19 Feb. 1839, File 36/2, folder

Priests, Hamilton Papers, DDA.

45. Prospectus titled "Ulster Reformatory School for Catholic Girls, Monaghan," August 1859, file marked "Monaghan," St.L/M.

46. "Report of Mr. Fagan, Inspector of Reformatory Schools," 1903, File Monaghan, St.L./M.

47. Ibid.

48. Their efforts sometimes failed, however. When one Mary O'Brien left the Monaghan institution, the sisters there tried to persuade her to leave the country, but without success. Reverend Mother Mary Xavier Finnegan recorded that she had "offered to pay her passage to America, but she has refused to go, saying wherever they sent her, she would return to her mother." In despair, Mother Finnegan declared that they would have to trust to God that Mary O'Brien would not come to harm. "Even that the mother be bad herself she can scarcely have the heart to give up her child to a life of wickedness." Mother Mary Xavier Finnegan to Father Daniel, 21 Mar. 1882, "Notebook of Draft Letters of Mother M. X. Finnegan," St.L/M.

49. For example, shortly after midcentury, a Catholic employee of a railway company died, leaving his Protestant wife a widow with ten children. The man's employer collected some money for the family's support, but it proved to be too little. Consequently, the woman was forced to find alternate means of providing for her children. Relatives took a set of three-year-old twins, the Christian Brothers took four boys, and the Sisters of Charity in Stanhope Street, Dublin, took three girls. The woman herself kept one infant child. According to the Stanhope Street records, the children in the Catholic institutions became Catholics and the mother also elected to convert. The result was an amicable relationship between the mother and the institutions that raised her children, with whom she was able to keep in close contact. This incident, to judge from the existing evidence in many convents, appears to have been quite a common occurrence. Official Annals, Vol. 5, Stanhope Street convent, 1871, SOC/M.

50. Sister Mary Joseph Augustine to Dean John Hamilton, [?], File 37/7, folder undated Nuns, Hamilton Papers, DDA. A guardian who had been named for the children came one Christmas and asked to take the children away with him for a visit. The nuns allowed the guardian, "being a very trustworthy person," to do so, but the children were not returned. When the Carmelites sent someone to bring them back to the orphanage, they learned that the man had sent them to their mother and that she would "never let them return."

51. The older boy was sent to the Brown Street Orphanage and was eventually returned to his mother.

52. Typescript account titled "Trial of Margaret Aylward," HF/G; Margaret Gibbons, *Life of Margaret Aylward* (Dublin, 1928), pp. 149–78; Jacinta Prunty, "Margaret Louisa Aylward," in Mary Cullen and Maria Luddy, eds., *Women, Power and Consciousness in Nineteenth-Century Ireland* (Dublin, 1995), pp. 55–88.

53. "The Court of Queen's Bench in Re: Mary Mathews, an Infant, The Queen v. Miss Margaret Aylward," *The Freeman's Journal*, 7 June 1860, in "Trial of Margaret Aylward," HF/G.

54. See, for example, *Morning News*, 4 Jan. 1861, quoted in Gibbons, *Margaret Aylward*, p. 164.

55. Quoted in Gibbons, *Margaret Aylward*, p. 169.

56. *The Freeman's Journal*, 17 Jan. 1861, copy in "Trial of Margaret Aylward," HF/G.

57. Gibbons, *Margaret Aylward*, pp. 179–80.

58. *Morning News*, 4 Jan. 1861, quoted in Gibbons, *Margaret Aylward*, pp. 164–65.

Chapter 6

1. Annals, 1800, P/C.

2. On the characteristics of popular Catholicism before the famine, see Connolly, *Priests and People.*

3. Whelan, "Catholic Church in County Tipperary," "Regional Impact of Irish Catholicism," and "Catholic Community in Eighteenth-Century County Wexford."

4. For a discussion of whether these prefamine rural religious practices and traditional customs are accurately labeled "non-Christian" or "pre-Christian" or pagan survivals (a language that many scholars have used in the past decade), see Michael P. Carroll, "Rethinking Popular Catholicism in Pre-Famine Ireland," *Journal for the Scientific Study of Religion,* 34 (1995): 354–65.

5. See, for example, Sean Connolly, *Priests and People,* pp. 276–77; Desmond Mooney, "Popular Religion and Clerical Influence in Pre-Famine Meath," in R. V. Comerford, Mary Cullen, Jacqueline R. Hill, and Colm Lennon, eds., *Religion, Conflict, and Coexistence in Ireland: Essays Presented to Monsignor Patrick J. Corish* (Dublin, 1990), pp. 217–18.

6. Connolly, *Priests and People,* p. 276.

7. Official Annals, Vol. 2, 1851, SOC/M.

8. See the entire collection of letters from Eliza D'Alton to Mr. and Mrs. John D'Alton, D'Alton Papers, 20.954 and 20.955, especially Eliza (Sister Mary Margaret) D'Alton to John D'Alton, Easter Monday, [?], 25 April [?], 5 Jan. [?], 16 Jan. [?], 23 Jan. 1855, Feast of the Purification, [?], Feast of Corpus Christi, [?], D'Alton Papers, 20.955, NLI.

9. Sister Mary Margaret D'Alton to John D'Alton, 23 Jan. 1855, D'Alton Papers, 20.955, NLI.

10. Sister Mary Margaret D'Alton to John D'Alton, Feast of Corpus Christi, [?], D'Alton Papers, 20.955, NLI.

11. Sister Mary Margaret D'Alton to John D'Alton, Feast of the Purification, [?], 20.955, D'Alton Papers, NLI.

12. Official Annals, Vol. 4, Benada Convent, 1864–70, SOC/M.

13. Ibid., Vol. 3, Benada Convent, 1858–64.

14. Ibid.

15. Ibid., Vol. 3, Clonmel Convent, 1864.

16. Ibid., Vol. 7, Ballaghadereen Convent, 1882–88.

17. Ibid., Vol. 3, Clonmel Convent, 1864.

18. Ibid.

19. Ibid., Vol. 1, 1816, 1825; Annals, 1842, P/C.

20. Annals, Remarkable Events, 1886, P/GH.

21. See, for example, Official Annals, Vol. 3, Clarenbridge Convent, 1858–64, SOC/M. In speaking of the success of the new devotion of the Perpetual Lamp in honor of the Blessed Virgin Mary, this community attributed its success to the fact that the society had begun to enroll members: "They [the people] do look upon it as a great honor to themselves when their names are registered in any of the convent books."

22. Register of the Immaculate Heart of Mary, 1840–68, U/C.

23. Official Annals, Vol. 5, Donnybrook Convent, 1870–76, SOC/M.

24. Ibid., Vol. 4, Harold's Cross Convent, 1864–70.

25. Ibid., Vol. 6, Clarenbridge Convent, 1876–82.

26. Ibid.

27. Ibid.

28. Ibid.

29. James S. Donnelly Jr., "Patterns, Magical Healing, and the Decline of Traditional Popular Religion in Ireland, 1700–1850," unpublished paper delivered at McGill University, Montreal, November 10, 1988, p. 1.

30. Ibid., pp. 1–21.

31. Tom Inglis, *Moral Monopoly: The Catholic Church in Modern Irish Society* (Dublin, 1987), pp. 14–32.

32. Annals, Benefactors and Benefactresses, Rev. Dr. Nicholson, P/GH.

33. Annals of the Congregation, 1844, SOC/M.

34. Inglis, *Moral Monopoly*, pp. 14–32.

35. Official Annals, Vol. 4, Benada Convent, 1864–70, SOC/M.

36. Ibid.

37. Ibid.

38. Ibid., Vol. 5, 1870–76.

39. Ibid., Vol. 3, Clonmel Convent, 1863.

40. Ibid., Vol. 7, Cork Convent, 1886.

41. Ibid., Vol. 4, Clarenbridge Convent, 1864–70.

42. Ibid.

43. Burke, *The People and the Poor Law*, p. 6.

44. Official Annals, Vol. 3, St. Vincent's Hospital, 1864, Soc/M.

45. Ibid.

46. Women's religious orders mobilized over the issue of Catholic children's enrollment in "Bird's Nest" institutions and were determined to counteract the effects in a massive way through their expanding network of Catholic institutions. But the Catholic response does not always appear to have been a defensive one. Evidence of purposeful conversion of Protestants exists in every convent studied and in every institution the nuns operated, though only in celebrated fights over "orphans," such as the Mary Mathews case, was the Catholic community openly charged with proselytism. Though schools that enticed the Catholic poor to enroll their children as Protestants in exchange for material benefits seem to have been the most serious type of proselytism practiced by Protestant societies, methods of Catholic proselytism were more diffuse and more widespread. Given the weight and authority of the Catholic church by the second half of the nineteenth century, I would also argue that the Catholics were considerably more effective. For some examples of the more subtle variety of proselytism, see ibid., Vol. 3, 1864; ibid., Vol. 4, Clarenbridge Convent; ibid., Vol. 6, Waterford Convent; and Sister Mary Peter Byrne to Dean John Hamilton, [?], File 37/7, folder undated Nuns, Hamilton Papers, DDA.

47. Sister Mary Doyle to Mrs. Teresa Mullally, 7 July 1794, Correspondence, P/C.

48. Annals, 1829, P/C.

49. Official Annals, Vol. 4, Clonmel Convent, 1864–70, SOC/M.

50. Annals of the Congregation, 1828–30, SOC/M.

51. Ibid., 1830.

52. Father William Walsh to Dean John Hamilton, 19 Feb. 1839, File 36/2, folder Priests, Hamilton Papers, DDA.

53. Official Annals, Vol. 4, Clarenbridge Convent, 1864, SOC/M.

54. Ibid.

55. Ibid., Vol. 3, Clarenbridge Convent, 1858–64, section titled "Devotions."

56. Ibid., Vol. 4, Upper Gardiner Street Convent, 1864–70.

57. Ibid., Vol. 4, St. Vincent's Hospital, 1864–70.

58. Ibid., Vol. 3, Benada Convent, 1862–64.

59. MacSuibhne, *Paul Cullen*, Vol. 4, p. 50.

60. Annals, Tullow Convent, 1807, B/B.

61. Ibid.

62. Peter Leo Johnson, "The American Odyssey of the Irish Brigidines," *Salesianum*, 32 (1944): 61–67.

63. Annals, Tullow Convent, 1808, B/B.

64. Annals, 1846, P/C.

65. Official Annals, Vol. 4, Tramore Convent, 1866, SOC/M.

66. Annals, 1799, P/C.

67. Sister Mary Catherine Callaghan to Dean John Hamilton, 12 May 1860, File 37/4, folder Nuns, Hamilton Papers, DDA.

68. Official Annals, Vol. 7, Ballaghadereen Convent, 1882–88, SOC/M.

69. Ibid., Vol. 3, Clonmel Convent, 1860.

70. Ibid.

71. Typescript titled "Abstracts of Reports of Inspectors of Reformatory and Industrial Schools—Ireland," 1871–83, File Monaghan, St.L/M.

72. See for example, Official Annals, Vol. 3, Benada Convent, 1863, SOC/M.

73. Ibid.

74. This society was one of many that flourished during the nineteenth century. Sodalities had been begun by the Jesuits in 1563 as a means of increasing religious zeal among European Catholics. With the suppression of the Jesuits in 1773, sodalities in general experienced a period of decay that lasted until the Society was reinstated in 1824. After that, sodalities began to flourish again. But in contrast to the earlier period, when they were organized at the level of the guild, this time they were organized at the level of the parish and especially by the convents of the parish. With the growth of popular Catholic education during the century, sodalities became a youth movement, and for the first time in their history they were formed particularly for young women. This modern development was the consequence of the growth of women's religious communities. For a thorough treatment of the history of sodalities, see Douglas E. Daly, *An Introduction to Sodalities of Our Lady* (St. Louis, 1957).

75. Register of the Sodality of Mary, "Plan of the Sodality of the Children of Mary," U/C.

76. Ibid.

77. Annals of the Children of Mary, Tullow Convent, 28 Feb. 1875, B/B.

78. See, for example, Annals of the Children of Mary, April 1865, B/B.

79. Register of the Sodality of Mary, "Plan of the Sodality of the Children of Mary," U/C.

80. Annals of the Children of Mary, 15 Sept. 1878, Feast of the Annunciation, 1881, B/B.

81. Register of the Sodality of Mary, "Plan of the Sodality," U/C.

82. Official Annals, Vol. 3, Clonmel Convent, 1862–65, SOC/M.

83. Annals of the Children of Mary, 31 Jan. 1872, B/B.

84. Official Annals, Vol. 8, Harold's Cross Convent, 1888–94, SOC/M.

85. Ibid., Vol. 4, Tramore Convent, 1864–70.

86. Ibid., Clarenbridge Convent.

87. Ibid., Benada Convent, 1865.

88. Ibid.

89. Ibid., Vol. 8, Clarenbridge Convent, 1888–94.

90. Ibid.

91. Ibid., Harold's Cross Convent, 1888.

92. Ibid.

93. Annals of the Children of Mary, April, 1865, B/B.

94. Ibid., 1868–79.

95. Register of the Sodality of Mary, U/C.

96. Suellen Hoy, "The Journey Out: The Recruitment and Emigration of Irish Religious Women to the United States, 1812–1914," *Journal of Women's History*, 6–7 (Winter/Spring 1995), pp. 64–98.

97. Official Annals, Vol. 8, Harold's Cross Convent, 1888, SOC/M.

98. Ibid.

99. Annals, "Community," Sister Mary Stanislaus Donohoe, P/GH.

100. Citizen of Dublin to Archbishop Daniel Murray, 27 June 1831, File 31/3, folder Nuns, Murray Papers, DDA.

Chapter 7

1. Annals, P/F: "The edifice was erected and exclusively designed to fulfill the intention and promote the pious wish of the said Miss Angelina Gould who, previous to her solemn profession in the order (which she made in the Presentation convent of Doneraile, the parent house in the Diocese of Cloyne), assigned . . . the residuary part of her property in trust, chiefly for the purpose of propagating and extending the Presentation Order"; Sermon preached by John McCarthy, Bishop of Cloyne at the Funeral Mass of Mother Gould, P/F: "Previous to her profession she had vested in trustees, for the founding of convents in the then united dioceses of Cloyne and Ross, the whole of her immense wealth"; List of Presentation Foundresses until 1841, File Box "Very old documents", Folder "Information about Convents and Nuns," P/C; Annals, 1869, P/Y.

2. Morgan O'Brien to Dean John Hamilton, 5 Aug. 1830, File 35/2, folder Priests, Hamilton Papers, DDA; Mother M. A. Gould to Dean John Hamilton, 21 May 1835, File 35/5, folder Nuns, Hamilton Papers, DDA.

3. Timothy Murphy to Michael Slattery, 15 Apr. 1851, 1851/3, p. 6003, CAA, NLI.

4. Ibid. Emphasis in the original.

5. Ibid. Emphasis in the original.

6. Walsh, *Nano Nagle*, pp. 62–63, 118–19. William Coppinger was an outspoken advocate for the Presentation Order, speaking to charitable institutions in order to gain public support for the work of the sisters, especially in the 1790s when the congregation almost failed. On Bishop Crotty, see Annals, 1838, P/C.

7. Paul Cullen to Michael Slattery, 13 May 1852, 1852/15, p. 6004, CAA, NLI; Annals, P/F.

8. For example, in 1829 several of the prominent mothers of the Dominican convent in Cabra, Co. Dublin, asked to come under episcopal jurisdiction. In that year, Archbishop Daniel Murray gave evidence before a select committee of the House of Lords, and when asked to give the names of all the religious communities of nuns then in the archdiocese of Dublin, he failed to name the Cabra community. The women were dismayed to discover that their monastery, founded more than one hundred years earlier, seemed to be an unknown entity in the diocese. Though long in existence in the capital city, this convent, like others attempting to survive penal-law proscription, had adopted a necessarily obscure profile. Because of this obscurity, as well as the general disorganization of the Irish church at the time, the Cabra community rarely came

to the attention of male church authorities. It was only occasionally visited by the male Dominican superiors who exercised ecclesiastical jurisdiction over it, and the right of the local bishop to visit all convents in his diocese was apparently exercised in Cabra's case only once. By 1829 new and dynamic religious congregations of women were springing up in the diocese. The Cabra community, aware of this new development and weary of struggling after one hundred years of tenuous existence, decided that it was time to do something to change their situation. A particularly influential woman in the community, Mother Mary Columba Maher, persuaded the prioress, Mother Mary Rose Murphy, that the interests of the convent would best be served by transferring the jurisdictional authority vested by custom in the male superiors of the Dominican order to the archbishop of Dublin. The prioress applied for and received from the Pope permission to come under the authority of Dr. Murray, and after this modification the fortunes of the Cabra convent rose decidedly. The order soon became a popular educator of the wealthier classes of Catholic girls, providing progressive and all-to-rare secondary education for many young Catholic women in the nineteenth century. For a complete account of this transition see, *Annals of the Dominican Convent of St. Mary's, Cabra, with Some Account of Its Origin, 1647–1912* (Cabra, Co. Dublin, n.d.).

9. Rules and Constitutions, p. 23, M/B.

10. Ibid., pp. 23–25.

11. Sister M. A. McKeown to Dean John Hamilton, [?], File 37/7, folder undated Nuns, Hamilton Papers, DDA.

12. Mother Teresa Ball to Dean John Hamilton, 16 Dec. 1831, File 31/3, folder Nuns, Murray Papers, DDA. Letters of this type and tone are ubiquitous in the diocesan archives, making up a large percentage (perhaps even the majority) of the surviving correspondence in the DDA.

13. Annals, 1802, copy of a letter dated 10 Feb. 1802, Mother Mary Francis Tobin to Bishop Francis Moylan, P/C.

14. Ibid., 1829. Collins requested that he be buried in the community graveyard with Nano Nagle and the early leaders of the new order. His request was granted; Collins is the only man buried in the cemetery.

15. Sister Murray to Archbishop Daniel Murray, 11 Dec. 1846, File 32/2, folder Ordinary, Murray Papers, DDA.

16. See, for example, Sister M. C. Fahey to Archbishop Daniel Murray, 1 Feb. 1852, File 32/8, folder Ordinary, Murray Papers, DDA.

17. Mother Mary de Chantal Coleman to Mary Aikenhead, 11 Dec. 1847, Correspondence, 1/B/104, SOC/M.

18. Ibid.

19. Chapter Book, 7 Aug. 1807, P/GH.

20. Annals of the Congregation, 1841, SOC/M.

21. Mother Magdalen Rafferty to Dean John Hamilton, 22 June 1849, File 37/2, folder Nuns, Hamilton Papers, DDA.

22. See, for example, the obituaries of the following chaplains, each of whom was employed by their convents for over thirty years: Jeremiah Collins, Annals, 1829, P/C; John O'Connor, Annals, vol. 2, pp. 53–54, SOC/M; Rev. Horgan, Annals, 1890, P/C.

23. Annals, 1890, P/C.

24. Ibid., 1835.

25. Sr. M. A. Murphy to Dean John Hamilton, 20 Feb. 1841, File 36/4, folder Nuns, Hamilton Papers, DDA.

26. Sister Gertrude White to Archbishop Daniel Murray, 29 Oct. 1845, File 36/7, folder Nuns, Murray Papers, DDA.

27. Father Henry S. O'Shea to Dean John Hamilton, 13 Sept. 1847, File 37/1, folder Priests, Hamilton Papers, DDA.

28. Sister Gertrude White to Archbishop Daniel Murray, 29 Oct. 1845, File 36/7, folder Nuns, Hamilton Papers, DDA; Father Henry S. O'Shea to Dean John Hamilton, 13 Sept. 1847, 7 Oct. 1847, 22 Nov. 1847, 3 Dec. 1847, File 37/1, folder Priests, Hamilton Papers, DDA.

29. Sister Gertrude White to Archbishop Daniel Murray, 29 Nov. 1847, File 37/1, folder Nuns, Hamilton Papers, DDA.

30. This remains the custom in Ireland even to the present day. In addition to the advantages that accrued to women religious from a system that allowed them fuller control over their spiritual life, male clergy also benefited from this practice. An Irish priest who was staying at the South Presentation convent in Cork while I was working there suggested that the opportunity of joining in the community life of religious women offered many priests a vital means of combating the loneliness that often accompanied their lives.

31. Annals, Community, Deeds of Great Nuns, Mother Mary Ignatius Taylor, P/GH. Archbishop Walsh, nephew of Mother Taylor, was himself a frequent visitor to the convent.

32. Mother Mary Vincent Whitty to Dean Meyler, 9 May 1851, Correspondence, M/B.

33. Official Annals, Vol. 1, Cork Convent, 1830, SOC/M.

34. Sr. Gertrude White to Archbishop Daniel Murray, [?], File 33/3, folder undated Nuns, Murray Papers, DDA (emphasis in the original).

35. Mary Francis Tobin to Teresa Mullaly, 28 Feb. 1795, Correspondence, P/C.

36. Ibid. (emphasis in the original). Though attempts to challenge hierarchical authority appear to have been considerably more frequent during the prefamine period, consciousness of the limits and abuses of episcopal power was apparent in the postfamine period as well. See, for example, a copy of a letter from the Jesuit advisor of the Sisters of Charity, Henry Jones, who in 1869 wrote to the congregation from Rome, where he was attending the Vatican Council. Jones told the sisters that it was a good thing that there was a Pope. "Take away that and every bishop would be a little Pope and mould and change the orders to suit his taste. If we had only the bishops to deal with in the council, I think it would be all over with us." Official Annals, Vol. 4, 1869, SOC/M.

37. Annals, 1800, P/C.

38. Thomas [?] to Archbishop Paul Cullen, 23 Nov. 1854, File 332/2, folder Priests, Cullen Papers, DDA. (Emphasis in the original.)

39. Mother M. Rorke to Dean John Hamilton, 14 March 1849, 24 March 1849, File 37/2, folder Nuns, Hamilton Papers, DDA. The custom of interpreting silence on the part of male superiors as permission was universally practiced throughout the nineteenth century. The custom was attractive to the male superiors of convents in the early years. Priests and bishops disliked the many routine duties requiring their frequent attention that were part of overseeing a religious community. They could reduce the burden by allowing the convents to act on their own behalf as long as the obligatory letter informing them of their actions was written and permission formally requested. Women themselves liked this way of doing business because they could exploit the system in their favor.

40. Mother Vincent Whitty to Rev. Walter Meyler, 6 May 1851, Correspondence, M/B.

41. Mother Vincent Whitty to Rev. Walter Meyler, 9 May 1851, Correspondence, M/B.

42. Dean Meyler to Rev. Mother, 8 Jan. 1849, 9 Jan. 1849, Correspondence, M/B.

43. This story, as well as the almost continual conflict between Archbishop Murray and the Mercy Order from its foundation, is well documented in a series of letters between the reverend mothers of the convent and Dean Meyler and Archbishop Murray from 23 October 1833 through 15 August 1851, Correspondence, M/B.

44. Annals, 1858, M/A.

45. Returns of the Visitation of the Convents in the Archdiocese of Dublin, 1854, Cullen Papers, DDA.

46. See, for example, Clear, *Nuns*, pp. 55–66.

47. Mother de Chantal Coleman to Mary Aikenhead, 11 Dec. 1847, Correspondence, 1/B/104, SOC/M: "You told me of an application from the S[iste]rs of Mercy to have a head Superior. Will they then be as we are with regard to the Bishops, or how could they do so where they were already established?" "A General Meeting of the Mother Superiors of this Order of our Lady of Mercy for Compiling a Guide," in a manuscript notebook entitled "Chapter Decisions, 1859–1894," M/L: "The death of Mother M. C. McAuley, depriving the young Institute of her guidance and experience before its objects were fully developed, it was deemed advisable to consult on some points of difference that had crept in and adopt only such things as were calculated to preserve the congregation in tact and prevent its gradually changing from its primitive end and design."

48. Sr. M. Aloysius to Revd. Mother, 28 Feb. 1864, Mercy Guide Letters, M/L.

49. Sr. M. Aloysius to Revd. Mother, 28 Feb. 1864, Sr. M. G. White to Revd. Mother, [?], Mercy Guide Letters, M/L. There were a few Mercy sisters who defended the order's decision to run pension schools. They believed that McAuley had sanctioned the practice because of certain statements she made to the Carlow community. She was reported to have told these sisters that "the middle class was the connecting link between high and low and was therefore a most important class in society." But this same sister also liked the schools because "the bishops and other ecclesiastics consider them very serviceable." See Sister Mary Catherine to Sister M. C. McNamara, 24 Feb. 1864, Mercy Guide Letters, M/L.

50. It should be noted, however, that there were some Mercy members who did not object to the "balkanization" of the order. They did not see themselves as members of a women's order with clearly defined goals so much as members of the "church." Consequently, the fact that the sisters could adapt to local needs at the wishes of priests and bishops was to them a decided advantage that encouraged the popularity of their order. According to one sister who took this position, "the fact that our rule has been drawn up with such a wonderful simplicity . . . it is capable of application to every want of the church in every part of the world and under all circumstances. This admirable capability of enlargement and development would, in my opinion, be sadly cramped by any exposition which contract[s] the sphere of our usefulness." See Sister M. Aloysia to Sister M. C. McNamara, 27 Feb. 1864, Mercy Guide Letters, M/L.

51. The Limerick community felt deep pain at the fact that Baggot Street refused to attend and tried very hard to convince them to participate, even suggesting that the meeting hold its plenary session in Dublin. The superior in 1864, Sister Mary of Mercy Norriss, felt perfectly confident that "the essentials are strictly adhered to" in the Baggot

Street community and that they were "perfectly satisfied with our institute as it stands." See Sister Mary of Mercy Norriss to Sister M. C. McNamara, 19 Feb. 1864, Mercy Guide Letters, M/L.

52. Sister M. Gonzague Morris to Sister M. C. McNamara, [?], Mercy Guide Letters, M/L.

53. Sister M. Magdalene to Sister M. C. McNamara, 3 March 1864, Mercy Guide Letters, M/L.

54. Sister M. Aloysius Maughan to Sister M. C. McNamara, [?], Mercy Guide Letters, M/L.

55. Sr. M. Paul to Rev. Mother [M. C. McNamara], [?], Mercy Guide Letters, M/L.

56. Thomas Grant to Revd. Mother [Mercy convent, Bermondsey], 24 February 1864, Mercy Guide Letters, M/L.

57. Sister Mary of Mercy Norriss to Sister M. C. McNamara, 19 Feb. 1864, Mercy Guide Letters, M/L.

58. Mother Joseph Jones, "Notes Relating to the Organization of our Diocesan Congregation," file marked "Amalgamation," M/A.

59. Ibid.

60. *Rule of the Society of Jesus*, given to Mother Joseph Jones by her brother Fr. Daniel Jones, S.J., 1870, M/A; Mother Joseph Jones, "Notes," File Amalgamation, M/A; *Rules and Constitutions*, p. 23.

61. Mother Joseph Jones, "Notes," File Amalgamation, M/A.

62. Ibid.

63. Annals, 1864, M/A.

64. Annals, 1864–70, M/A; Mother Joseph Jones, "Notes," File Amalgamation, M/A. It should also be mentioned that centralization meant that individual convents that were formerly autonomous units would lose some of their autonomy. In the case of the Elphin amalgamation, the sisters were no longer sure that they would live their entire lives in the community with which they professed, for the general superior now had the right to move sisters from one convent to another as the need arose. Furthermore, the money and property of all of the convents was communalized and redistributed by order of the general superior. This practice was not a controversial one in orders originally set up as centralized organizations, for it assured all individual convents of an equal share in the wealth of the congregation. But to independent convents that were subsequently made subordinate to a motherhouse, it represented a very visible and painful loss of autonomy. To the mothers of individual convents, then, as well as to the bishops, centralization after the fact meant a loss of control.

65. Annals, Remarkable Events, 1866, P/GH.

66. See, for example, Mother de Chantal Coleman to Mary Aikenhead, 27 Jan. 1846, Correspondence, 1/B/91, SOC/M.

67. See, for example, the battle between the Holy Faith leaders and a parish priest during the late 1880s, File MF/C/24, nos. 38, 43, 47, 54, and 61, HF/G; see also the struggle between Mother Mary Xavier Finnegan and the bishop of Waterford in the late 1890s, File "Founders' Letters and Early Documents," Notebook of Draft Letters of M. X. Finnegan, St.L/M.

Chapter 8

1. Annals, p. 5, P/C.

2. During the 1880s, Aylward was involved in a heated battle with an interfering

priest who was acting as confessor to a Holy Faith convent in his parish. He had written a letter to the sister in charge of the community in which he insulted Aylward. Aylward responded personally. To charges that the convent was not paying enough dues to the priest, she replied:

> Why did you not tell me quietly, long ago, that they were not sufficient? There is no doubt that the attendance of a priest once a week to comply with the law in regard of the reservation of the Blessed Sacrament is a matter you can charge for. . . . What I say is, name your terms, and if we can't meet them, we must forgo the blessing of having the Blessed Sacrament. I believe our Lord would not wish us to be involved in debt on His account. [About] the claim that you make . . . to interfere with the internal government of the community, this claim is put in such general and, I was going to say, wild words that it does not admit of a definite answer till properly formulated. But if you maintain that you can, at your will, set aside the rules . . . I submit that you cannot. . . . If again, you mean to claim the right of taking the superior's place and making changes in the duties or mode of living of the community, or of setting up new regulations, I submit you cannot, and if you were allowed to try, you would very soon regret it. . . . In conclusion, I say in all sincerity I am sorry for your own sake you ever wrote that letter.

Margaret Aylward died before this fight was concluded, but the bishop eventually came to Dublin to settle the matter with Mother Vickers. The priest did not fare well in this exchange. See Margaret Aylward to [?], 7 May, 1889, File MF/C/24, no. 43; handwritten account of meeting between Mother Vickers and Bishop Abraham Brownrigg, File AV/C/10, no. 71, HF/G.

3. One old mother at the South Presentation convent in Cork, for example, refused to hear a mass said by a bishop who was visiting the convent while I was working there. When she was teased by some of the other sisters at breakfast about her absence, she told us all in no uncertain terms that she would have "nothing to do with bishops" for they were "not the friends of nuns." Another convent mother, a leader of the Sisters of Charity convent at Harold's Cross, Dublin, lamented the fact that there were no longer any "great" women leaders in the orders today. There were certainly many bright and competent women but no truly outstanding ones. Not since the early years, she believed, had there been women in the order of the caliber of Mary Aikenhead, Mother de Chantal Coleman, or Mother Magdalen MacCarthy, women who could (and did) "stand up to the bishops."

BIBLIOGRAPHY

Manuscript Sources

Convent Archives

Brigidine Sisters, Generalate, Blackrock, Co. Dublin
  Annals, Tullow Convent
  Annals of the Children of Mary, Tullow Convent
  Ceremony of Reception, Sodality of the Sacred Heart of Jesus and Mary, Tullow
    Convent
  Documents relating to the Brigidines at Roscrea
    "Some Details relating to the Union of the Brigidine Community of Roscrea,
      with the Society of the Sacred Heart"
    "The Brigidines at Roscrea—Their First Convents"
  Documents relating to the Life of Dr. Daniel Delaney
  Documents relating to the Wogan-Browne Family
    "The Advice and Opinion of Counsellor Scully on the Poor Bishop's Affairs for
      Miss Browne" Correspondence
  Inactive Files, List of Entrants to the Congregation
  Report of the Council of the Children of Mary, Tullow Convent
  Rule of the Sodality of the Children of Mary, Tullow Convent
  A Short Sketch of Mother Teresa MacMahon, 1791–1866
  Souvenir Annals, Convent of the Sacred Heart, Roscrea, 1842–1976

Presentation Sisters, South Presentation Convent, Cork
  Account Book, 1827–1907
  Alms House Notebook
  Alms House Account Book, 1845–48
  Annals of the South Presentation Convent, Cork, 1771–1892
  Documents relating to the Ursuline Convents
    "Ursuline Letters"
    "Ursuline Convent, St. Mary's, Waterford"

"Convents of Presentation Order from Its Foundation in the year 1777 to the year
    1841"
Documents relating to Presentation Foundresses
    Notes relating to Mother M. Magdalen Gould
    Notes relating to Mrs. O'Connell
Account Book, 1827–1912
Correspondence, "Letters"
    Letters of Mother Mary Francis Tobin
    Miscellaneous Correspondence
    "Information about Convents and Nuns"
Documents relating to Mother Mary de Pazzi Leahy
    Biography
    Rules and Customs, MS Written in 1843
    Manuscript Collection of her Writings
    Notebook of Sister Mary de Pazzi Leahy
Documents relating to the Rosmor Estate
    Letters from Collins Family to Mother Leahy
Register of Professions and Deaths
Customs of the Presentation Convent, MS
Account of the Life of Mother de Chantal Wilmerding, MS
Miscellaneous Legal Documents

Presentation Sisters, Fermoy
Annals of the Presentation Convent, Fermoy
Sermon preached by John McCarthy, Bishop of Cloyne, at the Funeral Mass for
    Mother Gould

Presentation Sisters, George's Hill, Dublin
Annals, George's Hill Presentation Convent
Book of Professions
Chapter Book
Documents relating to Sr. Mary Teresa Paul Higgins
    "Composition Written in 1861 concerning Sr. Mary Teresa Paul Higgins, Mis-
    tress of Novices who trained Mother Mary Catherine McAulay"
Register of Girls in the Orphanage, 1849–1934
Register of the Members of the Sodality of the Most Sacred Heart of Jesus, 1809–86
School Annual Accounts, 1919–46
"The Story of George's Hill," MS History of the Foundation

Presentation Sisters, Kilkenny
Account of Foundation at Carlow, 1811
Account of Sr. M. Augustine Hayes, 1822
Account of First Portarlington Foundation
Annual Accounts, 1800–1882
Documents relating to Convent Foundation
    "Account of the Founding of Kilkenny"
    Miscellaneous Notes on Foundation
    Instructions to Sisters Acting as School Mistresses
    Letters and Documents from 1800
    Miscellaneous Correspondence

Register of Decisions of Discreets, 1800–1860
Register of Postulants and Novices
Register of Benefactors for School, 1818–1915

Presentation Sisters, Youghal
Annals of the Presentation Convent, Youghal

Sisters of Charity Generalate, Milltown, Dublin
Annals of the Sisters of Charity, Stanhope Street, 1815 and 1816
Annals of the Congregation of the Religious Sisters of Charity, Founded in Ireland
      in 1815
Official Annals, Vols. 1–8, 1815–94
Alphabetical Catalogue
Account Books
   Books Kept by Mary Aikenhead
   Accounts, 1845–98
   Accounts, 1899–1901
Correspondence
   Letters of Daniel Murray to Mary Aikenhead
   Letter of Mary Aikenhead to Commissioners of Inquiry into the State of the Irish
      Poor, 30 Dec. 1833
   Letters of Mother de Chantal Coleman to Mary Aikenhead
   Letters of Robert St. Leger to Mary Aikenhead
   Letters of Peter Kenny to Mary Aikenhead
Documents relating to Elizabeth Bodenham
   "Original Letter of Mary Aikenhead to Sister Mary Patrick Ennis"
   "The Propositions and Conclusions of Meetings of Discreets, Ursuline Convent,
      Waterford, 22 June 1835"
   Letters of Elizabeth Bodenham to Margaret Aylward (Originals in Archives of the
      Holy Faith Convent, Glasnevin, Dublin)
   Miscellaneous Correspondence
Constitution of the Religious Sisters of Charity
General Customs of the Congregation of the Religious Sisters of Charity
Letters of the Pembroke Estate, Sandymount
Mother Catherine's Diary
Old Rule Book, 1834
Ordinations Notebook
School Government Book, Compiled by Sr. Mary Hennessy
Sisters Professed from 1815 to April 1890

Sisters of the Holy Faith, Glasnevin, Dublin
Account of the Life of Ada Allingham
Correspondence of Margaret Aylward
Correspondence of Ada Allingham
Correspondence of John Stelner
Documents relating to the Trial of Margaret Aylward
   "Trial of Margaret Aylward"
   33d Annual Report of St. Brigid's Orphanage
   Miscellaneous Correspondence
Ladies Association of Charity of St. Vincent de Paul, Annual Reports

Letters of Margaret Aylward to Paul Cardinal Cullen
Letters of Mother Agnes Vickers
Notebook of Sr. M. Francis Allingham, 1864–76
Nurses' Accounts, 1868–74
Register, Sisters of the Holy Faith, 1859–1901
Summary of Constitutions

Sisters of Mercy, Elphin Diocesan Generalate, Athlone
    Annals of St. Peter's Convent, Athlone
    Documents relating to Amalgamation
        "Notes relating to the Organization of Our Diocesan Congregation," Written by
            Mother Joseph Jones
        "Notes re: Amalgamation of Convents in Diocese," Written by Mother Joseph
            Jones
        "Notes on Our Original Organization as Established in January 1871, on the Union
            of All the Convents of Mercy into One Diocesan Congregation," Written by
            Mother Joseph Jones
    Miscellaneous Correspondence
    General Statistics, 1870–1900, St. Patrick's Convent, Sligo
    Miscellaneous Correspondence
    Novitiate Account Book, 1908–38
    Register of Choir Sisters, 1840–1979
    Register of Lay Sisters, 1848–1934
    Sligo Convent Account Book, 1871–77

Sisters of Mercy, Baggot Street, Dublin
    Correspondence
        Letters of Rev. Dr. Michael Blake to Catherine McAuley
        Letters of Mother M. Clare Moore to Sr. M. Clare Augustine Moore
        Letters of Mother Mary Vincent Whitty to Rev. Walter Meyler
        Letters of Rev. Walter Meyler to Mother Mary Vincent Whitty
        Miscellaneous Correspondence
    Documents relating to the Foundation of the Mercy Order
        "Baggot Street Convent"
        "Baggot Street as a Charitable Institution of Secular Ladies," 1827–31
        "Beginning of Baggot St. as a Charitable Society of Secular Ladies"
        "Education Packet"
        "St. Catherine's Convent, Baggot St., Dublin"
    Register of the House of Mercy
    "The Mercy Ideal"
    Summary of Yearly Accounts
    Rules and Constitutions

Sisters of Mercy Diocesan Generalate, Carysfort, Co. Dublin
    Acts of Chapter, 1837 to Present
    Yearly Account
    Documents relating to the Training College
        "Resolution of the Irish Bishops"
        Miscellaneous Correspondence
    Life Stories of Entrants to Baggot Street

Sisters of Mercy, Cork
   Annals

Sisters of Mercy, Limerick
   Annals of the Convent of Mercy, St. Mary's, Limerick, Vols. 1–2
   Chapter Decisions, 1859–94
   Documents relating to the Sick Mission
     "Of the Visitation of the Sick"
     "Names of the Sick Visited by the Sisters from September 1838 to April 1847"
   House of Mercy Register, 1838–58
   Memoir of Sr. M. Vincent Hartnett
   Mercy Guide Letters

Sisters of Our Lady of Charity of Refuge, Drumcondra, Dublin
   Annals of the Monastery of Our Lady of Charity of Refuge, High Park, Vol. 1, 1853–
     1939
   Register of Penitents, St. Mary's Asylum, 1839–1904
   St. Joseph's Reformatory, Book of Discharges of Juvenile Offenders, 1860–1925
   Second Book of Receptions

Sisters of St. Louis Generalate, Monaghan
   Documents relating to Ellen Woodlock
     "Sketch of Mrs. Ellen Woodlock's Life"
   Documents relating to the Industrial School
     Death Registers
     "Industrial School Inmates"
   Documents relating to the Reformatory School
     Abstracts of Reports of Inspectors of Reformatory Schools
     Correspondence
   Chapter Notes of Mother M. X. Finnegan
   Correspondence
     Draft Letters of Mother M. X. Finnegan
     Letters of Ellen Woodlock to Genevieve Beale
     Letters of Mother Genevieve Beale
     Letters of Sister Clare O'Sullivan
     Letters of Mrs. Lloyd to Bishop McNally
     Miscellaneous Correspondence
     Miscellaneous Founders' Letters
   Diary, Sr. Clare O'Sullivan
   Miscellaneous Documents
     "Our Charism, the Irish Dimension"
   Notebooks of Mary McPhillips (Sr. Gonzaga)
   "Sketch [Handwritten] of S. M. Stanislaus Kehoe's Life Written by Herself"
   List of Entrants
   "The Late Reverend Mother Mary Genevieve"

Ursuline Sisters, Blackrock, Co. Cork
   Account of Entrance Money Expended for the Use of the Pensioners, 1784
   Annals of the Ursuline Monastery of Cork, Vols. 1–3

Documents relating to the Schools
  "Lectures on Painting"
  "Catalogue of Books in the Library of the Ursuline Convent, Blackrock," 1879
List of Professions
List of Reverend Mothers and Chaplains, 1771–1943
Register of the Immaculate Heart of Mary, 1840–68
Register of the Sodality of Mary

Diocesan Archives

Dublin Diocesan Archives, Dublin
  Cullen Papers
  Hamilton Papers
  Forde Papers
  Murray Papers

Elphin Diocesan Archives, Sligo
  Documents relating to Diocesan Convents
    Correspondence: "Dr. Clancy and Convents of Nuns"
    Letters from the Mercy Convent, Sligo
    Letters and Accounts of the Ursuline and Mercy Convents
    Miscellaneous Records and Receipts of the Convents of Mercy
    Records of the Franciscan Convent, Grange School

Kerry Diocesan Archives, Killarney
  Coffey Papers
  Higgins Papers
  McCarthy Papers
  Moriarty Papers

Other Archives

National Library of Ireland, Dublin
  Archives of the Catholic Archbishop of Cashel and Emly, on Microfilm
  D'Alton Papers

Printed Sources

Annals of the Dominican Convent of St. Mary's, Cabra, with Some Account of Its Origin, 1647–1912. Dublin, 1912.
One Hundred Years of Progress: Centenary Publication. Loreto Convent, Navan, 1933.
Records and Memories of One Hundred Years, 1817–1917. Presentation Convent, Thurles, 1917.
Rules and Constitutions of the Institute of the Religious Called the Sisters of Mercy. Pittsburgh, 1852.
Rules of the Congregation of the Religious Sisters of Charity. Dublin, 1941.
Selections from the Publications of the Catholic Truth Society of Ireland. Dublin, n.d.
Souvenir of the Golden Jubilee of the Convent of Our Lady of Charity of Refuge, High Park, Drumcondra, Dublin. Dublin, 1903.

Books and Articles

Aelred of Rievaulx. *Spiritual Friendship*, translated by Mary Eugenia Laker. Kalamazoo, Mich., 1977.

Akenson, D. H. *The Irish Education Experiment*. London, 1970.

Arensberg, C. M., and S. T. Kimball. *Family and Community in Ireland*. 2d ed. Cambridge, Mass., 1968.

Atkinson, Sara. *Mary Aikenhead, Her Life, Her Work, and Her Friends: A History of the Foundation of the Congregation of the Irish Sisters of Charity*. Dublin, 1879.

Bolster, Evelyn. *The Sisters of Mercy in the Crimean War*. Cork, 1964.

Bossy, John. "The Counter-Reformation and the People of Catholic Ireland, 1596–1641." *Historical Studies* 8 (1971): 155–69.

Boswell, John. *Christianity, Social Tolerance, and Homosexuality*. Chicago, 1980.

————. Review of Judith Brown, *Immodest Acts*. *New Republic* 194 (1986): 36.

————. "Revolutions, Universals, and Sexual Categories." In Martin Duberman, Martha Vicinus, and George Chauncey Jr., eds. *Hidden from History: Reclaiming the Gay and Lesbian Past*. New York, 1989.

————. *Same-Sex Unions in Premodern Europe*. New York, 1994.

Bourke, Joanna. "'The Best of All Home Rulers': The Economic Power of Women in Ireland, 1880–1914." *Irish Economic and Social History* 18 (1991): 34–47.

————. "Dairymaids and Housewives: The Dairy Industry in Ireland, 1890–1914." *Agricultural History Review* 30 (1990): 149–64.

————. "The Domestic Labor Market in Rural Ireland, 1890–1914." *Journal of Interdisciplinary History* 31 (1991): 479–99.

————. *Husbandry to Housewifery: Women, Economic Change and Housewifery in Ireland 1890–1914*. New York, 1993.

————. "Women and Poultry in Ireland, 1891–1914." *Irish Historical Studies* 25 (1986–87): 293–310.

Branca, Patricia. *Silent Sisterhood: Middle-Class Women in the Victorian Home*. London, 1975.

Brown, Judith C. *Immodest Acts: The Life of a Lesbian Nun in Renaissance Italy*. New York, 1986.

Burke, Helen. *The People and the Poor Law in 19th-Century Ireland*. Littlehampton, England, 1987.

Bynum, Caroline Walker. *Holy Feast and Holy Fast: The Religious Significance of Food to Medieval Women*. Berkeley, 1987.

Canning, Bernard J. *Bishops of Ireland*. Kilmacolm, Scotland, 1987.

Carbery, Mary. *The Farm by Lough Gur: The Story of Mary Fogarty*. 1937. Reprint, Cork, 1973.

Carroll, Michael P. "Rethinking Popular Catholicism in Pre-Famine Ireland." *Journal for the Scientific Study of Religion* 34 (1995): 354–65.

Clear, Caitriona. "The Limits of Female Autonomy: Nuns in Nineteenth-Century Ireland." In Maria Luddy and Cliona Murphy, eds. *Women Surviving: Studies in Irish Women's History in the Nineteenth and Twentieth Centuries*. Swords, Co. Dublin, 1990.

————. "Nuns in Ireland, 1850–1900: Female Religious in the Economy and Society." M.A. Thesis, University College, Galway, 1984.

————. *Nuns in Nineteenth-Century Ireland*. Dublin, 1987.

Cobbe, Frances Power. "What Shall We Do with Our Old Maids?" *Fraser's Magazine* 66 (1862): 594–610.

Concannon, Mrs. Thomas (Helena). *Daughters of Banba*. Dublin, 1922.

————. *Irish Nuns in Penal Days*. London, 1931.

————. *The Poor Clares in Ireland*. Dublin, 1929.

Condren, Mary. *The Serpent and the Goddess: Women, Religion, and Power in Celtic Ireland*. New York, 1989.

Connell, K. H. *Irish Peasant Society: Four Historical Essays*. Oxford, 1968.

————. "Peasant Marriage in Ireland: Its Structure and Development since the Famine." *Economic History Review* 14 (1961–62): 502–23.

Connolly, S. J. *Priests and People in Pre-Famine Ireland, 1780–1845*. Dublin, 1982.

————. *Religion and Society in Nineteenth-Century Ireland*. Dundalk, 1985.

"Convent Boarding-Schools for Young Ladies." *Fraser's Magazine* 9 (1874): 778–86.

Corish, Patrick. *The Catholic Community in the Seventeenth and Eighteenth Centuries*. Dublin, 1981.

————. *The Irish Catholic Experience: A Historical Survey*. Dublin, 1985.

Cullen, Louis M. "Catholic Social Classes under the Penal Laws." In Thomas P. Power and Kevin Whelan, eds. *Endurance and Emergence: Catholics in Ireland in the Eighteenth Century*. Dublin, 1990.

————. *The Emergence of Modern Ireland, 1600–1900*. New York, 1981.

————, ed. *The Formation of the Irish Economy*. Cork, 1969.

Cullen, Mary, ed. *Girls Don't Do Honours: Irish Women in Education in the 19th and 20th Centuries*. Dublin, 1987.

Cullen, Mary, and Maria Luddy, eds. *Women, Power and Consciousness in Nineteenth-Century Ireland*. Dublin, 1995.

Curb, Rosemary, and Nancy Manahan, eds. *Lesbian Nuns: Breaking Silence*. Tallahassee, 1985.

Cusack, M. F. *The Nun of Kenmare: An Autobiography*. London, 1889.

————. *The Patriot's History of Ireland*. Kenmare, Co. Kerry, 1869.

————. *Three Visits to Knock, with the Medical Certificates of Cures and Authentic Accounts of Different Apparitions*. New York, n.d.

Daly, Douglas E. *An Introduction to Sodalities of Our Lady*. St. Louis, 1957.

Daly, Mary. *The Church and the Second Sex*. London, 1968.

Daly, Mary E. "Women in the Irish Workforce from Pre-Industrial to Modern Times." *Saothar* 7 (1981): 74–82.

Degnan, Bertrand. *Mercy unto Thousands*. Dublin, 1958.

Devine, T. M., and David Dickson, eds. *Ireland and Scotland, 1600–1850: Parallels and Contrasts in Economic and Social Development*. Edinburgh, 1983.

Diner, Hasia. *Erin's Daughters in America: Irish Immigrant Women in the Nineteenth Century*. Baltimore, 1983.

Donnelly, James S., Jr. "Patterns, Magical Healing, and the Decline of Traditional Popular Religion in Ireland, 1700–1850." Unpublished lecture delivered at McGill University, Montreal, November 10, 1988.

Donoghue, Emma. *Passions between Women: British Lesbian Culture 1668–1801*. New York, 1996.

Donovan, Mary Ann. *Sisterhood as Power: The Past and Passion of Ecclesial Women*. New York, 1989.

Doyle, M. Aloysius. *Memories of the Crimea*. London, 1897.

Ewens, Mary. *The Role of the Nun in Nineteenth-Century America*. New York, 1978.

Faderman, Lillian. *Surpassing the Love of Men: Romantic Friendship and Love between Women from the Renaissance to the Present*. New York, 1981.

Fahey, Anthony. "Female Asceticism in the Catholic Church: A Case-Study of Nuns in Ireland in the Nineteenth Century." Ph.D. Dissertation, University of Illinois at Urbana, 1981.

————. "Nuns in the Catholic Church in Ireland in the Nineteenth Century." In Mary Cullen, ed. *Girls Don't Do Honours: Irish Women in Education in the 19th and 20th Centuries.* Dublin, 1987.

Fahy, M. de Lourdes. *Education in the Diocese of Kilmacduagh in the Nineteenth Century.* Gort, Co. Galway, 1973.

Familiar Instructions of Reverend Mother McAuley. St. Louis, 1927.

Ferguson, Anne. "Patriarchy, Sexual Identity, and the Sexual Revolution." *Signs: Journal of Women in Culture and Society* (Autumn 1981): 158–66.

ffrench Eager, Irene. *Margaret Anna Cusack.* Dublin, 1979.

Finlay, T. A. "Foxford and Its Factory." *New Ireland Review* 34 (Oct. 1910): 103–12.

Fiorenza, Elizabeth Schussler, and M. Collins, eds. *Concilium: Women, Invisible in Church and Theology.* Edinburgh, 1985.

Foster, R. F. *Modern Ireland, 1600–1972.* London, 1988.

Gately, Mary Josephine. *The Sisters of Mercy: Historical Sketches, 1831–1931.* New York, 1931.

Gibbons, Margaret. *Glimpses of Catholic Ireland in the Eighteenth Century.* Dublin, 1932.

————. *Life of Margaret Aylward.* Dublin, 1928.

Gildea, Denis. *Mother Mary Arsenius of Foxford.* London, 1936.

Ginzberg, Lori D. *Women and the Work of Benevolence: Morality, Politics, and Class in the Nineteenth-Century United States.* New Haven, 1990.

Gleanings from the Brigidine Annals. Naas, 1945.

Glynn, J. "Irish Convent Industries." *New Ireland Review* 1 (1894): 236–44.

Greg, W. R. *Literary and Social Judgments.* London, 1869.

Griffin, Terence C. "Lawrence Gillooly, Bishop of Elphin, 1856–1895, and Educational Issues in the Diocese of Elphin." M.A. Thesis, University College, Galway, 1984.

Holcombe, Lee. *Victorian Ladies at Work.* London, 1973.

Holmes, Janice, and Diane Urquhart, eds. *Coming into the Light: The Work, Politics and Religion of Women in Ulster, 1840–1940.* Belfast, 1994.

Hoy, Suellen. "The Journey Out: The Recruitment and Emigration of Irish Religious Women to the United States, 1812–1914." *Journal of Women's History* 6–7 (1995): 64–98.

Hutch, William. *Nano Nagle: Her Life, Her Labours, and Their Fruits.* Dublin, 1875.

Inglis, Tom. *Moral Monopoly: The Catholic Church in Modern Irish Society.* Dublin, 1987.

Jeffreys, Sheila. *The Spinster and Her Enemies: Feminism and Sexuality, 1800–1930.* London, 1985.

Johnson, Peter Leo. "The American Odyssey of the Irish Brigidines." *Salesianum* 32 (1944): 61–67.

Joyful Mother of Children: Mother Frances Mary Teresa Ball. Dublin, 1961.

Keenan, Desmond. *The Catholic Church in Nineteenth-Century Ireland: A Sociological Study.* Dublin, 1983.

Kennedy, Liam. "The Roman Catholic Church and Economic Growth in Nineteenth-Century Ireland." *Economic and Social Review* 10 (1978): 45–60.

Kennedy, Robert E., Jr. *The Irish: Emigration, Marriage, and Fertility.* Berkeley, 1973.

Kerr, Donal A. *Peel, Priests, and Politics: Sir Robert Peel's Administration and the Roman Catholic Church in Ireland, 1841–46.* Oxford, 1982.

Kingston, John. "The Carmelite Nuns in Dublin, 1644–1829." *Reportorium Novum* 3 (1964): 358–59.

Larkin, Emmet. "The Devotional Revolution in Ireland, 1850–1875." *American Historical Review* 77 (1972): 625–52.

———. "Economic Growth, Capital Investment, and the Roman Catholic Church in Nineteenth-Century Ireland." *American Historical Review* 72 (1967): 852–83.

———. *The Roman Catholic Church and the Creation of the Modern Irish State, 1878–1886.* Dublin, 1975.

Lee, Joseph. *The Modernisation of Irish Society, 1848–1918.* Dublin, 1973.

———. Women and the Church since the Famine." In Margaret MacCurtain and Donncha O. Corrain, eds. *Women in Irish Society: The Historical Dimension.* Dublin, 1978.

Lerner, Gerda. *The Creation of Patriarchy.* New York, 1986.

Levin, Harry, ed. *The Portable James Joyce.* 1947; rev. ed., New York, 1985.

Luddy, Maria. "Prostitution and Rescue Work in Nineteenth-Century Ireland." In Maria Luddy and Cliona Murphy, eds. *Women Surviving: Studies in Irish Women's History in the Nineteenth and Twentieth Centuries.* Swords, Co. Dublin, 1990.

———. *Women and Philanthropy in Nineteenth-Century Ireland.* Cambridge, England, 1995.

Lyons, F. S. L. *Ireland since the Famine.* London, 1973.

MacCurtain, Margaret. "Late in the Field: Catholic Sisters in Twentieth-Century Ireland and the New Religious History." *Journal of Women's History* 6–7 (1995): 49–63.

———. "Towards An Appraisal of the Religious Image of Women." *Crane Bag* 4 (1980): 26–30.

MacCurtain, Margaret, and Donnacha Corrain, eds. *Women in Irish Society: The Historical Dimension.* Dublin, 1978.

MacCurtain, Margaret, and Mary O'Dowd, eds. *Women in Early Modern Ireland.* Edinburgh, 1991.

MacDonald, Katherine. "Women Religious and Bishops: Some Experiences." *Religious Life Review* 100 (1983): 15–23.

MacSuibhne, Peadar. *Paul Cullen and His Contemporaries.* 5 vols. Naas, 1961–77.

"The Magdalens of High Park." *Irish Rosary.* 1 (1897): 176–84.

Maguire, Mrs. Conor. *Father Henry Young (1786–1869), Priest of the Diocese of Dublin.* Dublin, 1928.

Mary Pauline. *God Wills It: The Centenary Story of the Sisters of St. Louis.* Dublin, 1959.

Meagher, William. *Notices of the Life and Character of His Grace Most Rev. Daniel Murray, Late Archbishop of Dublin.* Dublin, 1853.

A Member of the Congregation of the Irish Sisters of Charity. *The Life and Work of Mary Aikenhead, Foundress of the Congregation of Irish Sisters of Charity, 1787–1858.* London, 1925.

A Member of the Order of Mercy. *Leaves from the Annals of the Sisters of Mercy.* New York, 1881.

The Mercy Congregation. *Maxims and Counsels of Mother Catherine McAuley.* N.p., n.d.

Miller, David. *Church, State, and Nation in Ireland, 1898–1921.* Dublin, 1973.

———. "Irish Catholicism and the Great Famine." *Journal of Social History* 9 (1975): 81–98.

Mooney, Desmond. "Popular Religion and Clerical Influence in Pre-Famine Meath." In R. V. Comerford, Mary Cullen, Jacqueline R. Hill, and Colm Lennon, eds. *Religion, Conflict, and Coexistence in Ireland: Essays Presented to Monsignor Patrick J. Corish.* Dublin, 1990.

Murphy, Dominic. *Sketches of Irish Nunneries.* Dublin, 1865.

Murphy, John Nicholas. *Terra Incognita, or the Convents of the United Kingdom.* London, 1873.

Neumann, Mary Ignatia, *The Letters of Catherine McAuley, 1827–41*. Baltimore, 1969.

Newsinger, John. "The Catholic Church in Nineteenth-Century Ireland." *European History Quarterly* 25 (1995): 247–67.

Nolan, Janet. *Ourselves Alone: Women's Emigration from Ireland, 1885–1920*. Lexington, Kentucky, 1989.

O'Brien, Kate. *The Ante-Room*. London, 1934.

———. "Aunt Mary in the Parlour." *University Review* 3 (1963): 3–9.

———. *The Flower of Mary*. London, 1953.

———. *The Land of Spices*. London, 1941.

———. *Presentation Parlour*. London, 1963.

O'Brien, Sylvester. *Poor Clare Ter-Centenary Record, 1629–1929*. Galway, 1929.

O'Carroll, Ide. *Models for Movers: Irish Women's Emigration to America*. Dublin, 1990.

O'Connell, Marie. "The Genesis of Convent Foundations and Their Institutions in Ulster, 1840–1920." In Janice Holmes and Diane Urquhart, eds. *Coming into the Light: The Work, Politics and Religion of Women in Ulster, 1840–1940*. Belfast, 1994.

O'Connor, Pat. *Friendships Between Women: A Critical Review*. London, 1992.

O'Donoghue, Mary Xaverius. *Mother Vincent Whitty: Woman and Educator in a Masculine Society*. Melbourne, 1972.

An Old Convent Girl. "A Word for the Convent Boarding Schools." *Fraser's Magazine* 10 (1874): 473–83.

O Muiri, Reamonn. *Irish Church History Today*. Monaghan, 1991.

O Tuathaigh, Gearoid. *Ireland before the Famine, 1798–1848*. Dublin, 1972.

Power, Eileen. *Medieval English Nunneries, c. 1275 to 1535*. Cambridge, England, 1922.

Power, T. P., and Kevin Whelan, eds. *Endurance and Emergence: Catholics in Ireland in the Eighteenth Century*. Blackrock, Co. Dublin, 1990.

Prochaska, F. K. *Women and Philanthropy in Nineteenth-Century England*. Oxford, 1980.

Prunty, Jacinta. "Margaret Louisa Aylward." In Mary Cullen and Maria Luddy, eds. *Women, Power and Consciousness in Nineteenth-Century Ireland*. Dublin, 1995.

Rapley, Elizabeth. *The Dévotes: Women and Church in Seventeenth-Century France*. Montreal, 1990.

Raymond, Janice G. *A Passion for Friends: Toward a Philosophy of Female Affection*. Boston, 1986.

Reuther, Rosemary Radford, ed. *Religion and Sexism in the Jewish and Christian Traditions*. New York, 1974.

Rev. Mother Frances Mary Teresa Ball, Foundress of the Irish Branch of Institute B.V.M. Known as Loreto Nuns. N.p., n.d.

Rich, Adrienne. "Compulsory Heterosexuality and Lesbian Existence." *Signs: Journal of Women in Culture and Society*, 5 (1980): 631–60.

Robins, Joseph. *The Lost Children: A Study of Charity Children in Ireland, 1700–1900*. Dublin, 1980.

Rushe, Desmond. *Edmund Rice: The Man and His Times*. Dublin, 1981.

Sahli, Nancy. "Smashing: Women's Relationships before the Fall." *Chrysalis* (1979): 17–27.

Savage, Burke R. *A Valiant Dublin Woman: The Story of George's Hill*. Dublin, 1940.

Sayers, Peig. *Peig*. 1974. Reprint, Dublin, 1983.

Schwartz, Joel. *The Sexual Politics of Jean-Jacques Rousseau*. Princeton, N.J., 1984.

Scott, Joan W. "Gender: A Useful Category of Historical Analysis." *American Historical Review* 91 (1986): 1053–75.

———. "Women and War: A Focus for Rewriting History." *Women's Studies Quarterly* 12 (Summer 1984): 2–6.

Sherlock, W. *Some Account of St. Brigid, and of the See of Kildare with Its Bishops, and of the Cathedral, Now Restored*. Dublin, 1896.

Smith, Ailbhe, ed. *Irish Women's Studies Reader*. Dublin, 1993.

Smith, Bonnie. *Ladies of the Leisure Class: The Bourgeoises of Northern France in the Nineteenth Century*. Princeton, N.J., 1981.

Smith-Rosenberg, Carroll. "The Female World of Love and Ritual: Relations between Women in Nineteenth-Century America." *Signs* 1 (1975): 1–29.

Southern, Richard W. *Western Society and the Church in the Middle Ages*. New York, 1970.

Vane, Charles, ed. *Memoirs and Correspondence of Viscount Castlereagh*. 4 vols. London, 1848–49.

Vicinus, Martha. *Independent Women: Work and Community for Single Women, 1850–1920*. Chicago, 1985.

————, ed. *Suffer and Be Still: Women in the Victorian Age*. Bloomington, Indiana, 1972.

Wall, Maureen. *The Penal Laws*. Dundalk, 1961.

————. "The Rise of a Catholic Middle Class in Eighteenth-Century Ireland." *Irish Historical Studies* 11 (1958–59): 91–115.

Walsh, T. J. *Nano Nagle and the Presentation Sisters*. 1959. Reprint. Monasterevan, Co. Kildare, 1980.

Weeks, Jeffrey. *Sexuality and Its Discontents*. London, 1985.

Whelan, Kevin. "The Catholic Church in County Tipperary, 1700–1900." In William Nolan and Thomas G. McGrath, eds. *Tipperary: History and Society*. Dublin, 1985.

————. "The Catholic Community in Eighteenth-Century County Wexford." In Thomas P. Power and Kevin Whelan, eds. *Endurance and Emergence: Catholics in Ireland in the Eighteenth Century*. Dublin, 1990.

————. "The Regional Impact of Irish Catholicism, 1700–1850." In W. J. Smyth and Kevin Whelan, eds. *Common Ground*. Cork, 1988.

Whyte, J. H. *Church and State in Modern Ireland*. Dublin, 1971.

INDEX